T0183428

Lecture Notes in Computer Science   12739

More information about this subseries at http://www.springer.com/series/7409

Ruben Verborgh · Anastasia Dimou ·
Aidan Hogan · Claudia d'Amato ·
Ilaria Tiddi · Arne Bröring ·
Simon Mayer · Femke Ongenae ·
Riccardo Tommasini · Mehwish Alam (Eds.)

The Semantic Web: ESWC 2021 Satellite Events

Virtual Event, June 6–10, 2021
Revised Selected Papers

 Springer

Editors
Ruben Verborgh ⓘ
IMEC
Ghent University
Ghent, Belgium

Aidan Hogan ⓘ
University of Chile
Santiago, Chile

Ilaria Tiddi ⓘ
Faculty of Computer Science
Vrije Universiteit Amsterdam
Amsterdam, The Netherlands

Simon Mayer ⓘ
University of St. Gallen
St. Gallen, Switzerland

Riccardo Tommasini ⓘ
Institute of Computer Science
University of Tartu
Tartu, Estonia

Anastasia Dimou ⓘ
Faculty of Engineering and Architecture
Ghent University
Ghent, Belgium

Claudia d'Amato ⓘ
Università degli Studi di Bari
Bari, Italy

Arne Bröring ⓘ
Corporate Technology
Siemens Aktiengesellschaft
München, Germany

Femke Ongenae ⓘ
Ghent University
Ghent, Belgium

Mehwish Alam ⓘ
Information Infrastructure
FIZ Karlsruhe - Leibniz Institute
for Information Infrastructure
Karlsruhe, Germany

ISSN 0302-9743   ISSN 1611-3349 (electronic)
Lecture Notes in Computer Science
ISBN 978-3-030-80417-6   ISBN 978-3-030-80418-3 (eBook)
https://doi.org/10.1007/978-3-030-80418-3

LNCS Sublibrary: SL3 – Information Systems and Applications, incl. Internet/Web, and HCI

This Springer imprint is published by the registered company Springer Nature Switzerland AG
The registered company address is: Gewerbestrasse 11, 6330 Cham, Switzerland

Preface

This book bundles together the contributions to the Posters and Demos, Industry, PhD, and Workshops and Tutorials tracks of ESWC 2021. Below, the chairs will bring the highlights of their tracks.

This year the Posters and Demos Track attracted 45 submissions, of which 27 (60%) were accepted. Each submission received 3–4 detailed reviews, which were provided by a Program Committee of 55 international experts. This year saw some changes with respect to previous editions. Submissions and reviews were handled for the first time through the OpenReview system, following the precedent set by the Research, In-Use, and Resources Tracks. Due to the COVID-19 pandemic, and the move towards an online ESWC (for the second year running), the Posters and Demos track was held virtually, on gather.town, where webpages replaced traditional posters and one-minute videos provided authors an opportunity to attract interested attendees to their virtual stand.

The PhD symposium received 10 submissions, out of which 6 were accepted, 2 rejected, and 2 conditionally accepted and, after a shepherding process, finally accepted. Each submission received 3 reviews from a Program Committee of 30 international experts. Each PhD student was assigned a mentor to interact with for preparing the final camera-ready version and the paper presentation. Furthermore, all students that submitted a paper to the PhD symposium had the chance to participate, on a voluntary basis, in a review process exercise consisting of reviewing one of the submitted papers and comparing their reviews to those provided by the experts for the same paper. The goal was to understand the review process following the learning by doing approach. All students but one decided to join this activity. Being an exercise, the reviews provided by students were not considered for the paper evaluations. In addition, authors of accepted papers had the chance to join, on a voluntary basis, the posters and demos session to present their work to a (possibly) broader audience than the one of the PhD symposium itself. The accepted papers covered a broad range of topics such as visual intelligent agents and multi-agent systems, improvement of decision making, exploitation of Knowledge Graphs and ontologies in different domains, and event identifications.

The Industry Track of ESWC 2021 solicited success stories as well as reports on failure analysis and the adoption of semantic technologies in real-world industrial environments, along with contributions on current challenges in the industry that might be tackled with semantic technologies. We received a total of 7 submissions, out of which 3 ($\sim$40%) were accepted for extension and presentation as part of this track after reviews were provided by 11 experts from across industry and academia. The accepted articles focused on the automatic construction of knowledge graphs (KGs) from technical support pages and the usage of these KGs to drive applications, the implementation of a semantic information model for supporting the integration of heterogeneous data sources in an industrial production line, and the conceptualization of a taxonomy management software platform for managing enterprise content in a video games company.

During ESWC 2021, the following six workshops took place: i) the Second International Workshop on Deep Learning meets Ontologies and Natural Language Processing (DeepOntoNLP 2021), ii) the Second International Workshop on Semantic Digital Twins (SeDiT 2021), iii) the Second International Workshop on Knowledge Graph Construction (KGC 2021), iv) the 6th International Workshop on eXplainable SENTIment Mining and EmotioN deTection (X-SENTIMENT 2021), v) the 4th International Workshop on Geospatial Linked Data (GeoLD 2021), and vi) the Domain Ontologies for Research Data Management in Industry Commons of Materials and Manufacturing Workshop (DORIC-MM 2021). Additionally, we also had three tutorials that covered the following topics: i) "Modular Ontology Engineering with CoModIDE", ii) "Constructing Question Answering Systems over Knowledge Graphs", and iii) "SPARQL Endpoints and Web API". We thank all the workshop chairs and the tutorial presenters for their efforts to organize and run their respective events.

May 2021

Ruben Verborgh
Anastasia Dimou
Aidan Hogan
Claudia d'Amato
Ilaria Tiddi
Arne Bröring
Simon Mayer
Femke Ongenae
Riccardo Tommasini
Mehwish Alam

The original version of the book was revised: The name of Simon Mayer has been updated. The correction to the book is available at https://doi.org/10.1007/978-3-030-80418-3_39

Organization

General Chair

Ruben Verborgh — Ghent University, Belgium

Program Chairs

Katja Hose — Aalborg University, Denmark
Heiko Paulheim — University of Mannheim, Germany

In-Use Chairs

Oscar Corcho — Universidad Politécnica de Madrid, Spain
Petar Ristoski — IBM Research, USA

Resources Chairs

Pierre-Antoine Champin — Université Claude Bernard Lyon 1, France
Maria Maleshkova — University of Bonn, Germany

Digital Conference Chairs

Violeta Ilik — Adelphi University Libraries, USA
Christian Hauschke — Leibniz Information Center for Science and Technology, University Library (TIB), Germany

Workshops and Tutorials Chairs

Femke Ongenae — Ghent University, Belgium
Riccardo Tommasini — University of Tartu, Estonia

Posters and Demos Track Chairs

Anastasia Dimou — Ghent University, Belgium
Aidan Hogan — Universidad de Chile and IMFD, Chile

PhD Symposium Chairs

Ilaria Tiddi — Vrije Universiteit Amsterdam, the Netherlands
Claudia d'Amato — University of Bari, Italy

Industry Track Chairs

Simon Mayer   University of St. Gallen, Switzerland
Arne Bröring   Siemens AG, Germany

Sponsoring Chairs

Daniele Dell'Aglio   Aalborg University, Denmark
Christian Dirschl   Wolters Kluwer Deutschland GmbH, Germany

Project Networking Chair

Alexandra Garatzogianni   Leibniz Information Center for Science and
                           Technology, University Library (TIB), Germany

Web and Publicity Chair

Cogan Shimizu   Kansas State University, USA

Semantic Technologies Chair

François Scharffe   Columbia University, USA

Proceedings Chair

Mehwish Alam   FIZ-Kalrsruhe, Leibniz Institute for Information
                           Infrastructure and Karlsruhe Institute
                           of Technology, Germany

Posters and Demos Program Committee

Albert Meroño-Peñuela   King's College London, UK
Andriy Nikolov   The Open University, UK
Anisa Rula   University of Brescia, Italy
Artem Revenko   Semantic Web Company, Austria
Ben De Meester   Ghent University, Belgium
Bojan Bozic   Technological University Dublin, Ireland
Carlos Bobed Lisbona   Universidad de Zaragoza, Spain
Carlos Buil-Aranda   Universidad Técnica Federico Santa María, Chile
Catherine Faron   Université Côte d'Azur, France
Catia Pesquita   Universidade de Lisboa, Portugal
Céline Alec   Université de Caen-Normandie, France
David Chaves-Fraga   Universidad Politécnica de Madrid, Spain
Davide Buscaldi   École Polytechnique, France
Edelweis Rohrer   Universidad de la República, Uruguay
Eero Hyvönen   Helsinki University of Technology, Finland

Evgeny Kharlamov	University of Oslo, Norway
Fatiha Sais	Paris-Saclay University, France
Flavius Frasincar	Erasmus University Rotterdam, the Netherlands
Franck Michel	University Côte d'Azur, CNRS, and Inria, France
Gong Cheng	Nanjing University, China
Harald Sack	FIZ Karlsruhe - Leibniz Institute for Information Infrastructure and Karlsruhe Institute of Technology, Germany
Henry Rosales-Méndez	Universidad de Chile, Chile
Herminio García-González	University of Oviedo, Spain
Hideaki Takeda	National Institute of Informatics, Japan
Jodi Schneider	University of Illinois Urbana-Champaign, USA
Jose Emilio Labra Gayo	University of Oviedo, Spain
Jose Manuel Gomez-Perez	expert.ai, Spain
Josiane Xavier Parreira	Siemens AG, Austria
Julián Andrés Rojas	Ghent University, Belgium
Julien Corman	Free University of Bozen-Bolzano, Italy
Karl Hammar	Jönköping University, Sweden
Kouji Kozaki	Osaka Electro-Communication University, Japan
Maria M. Hedblom	Universität Bremen, Germany
Marilena Daquino	University of Bologna, Italy
Matteo Palmonari	University of Milan-Bicocca, Italy
Mayank Kejriwal	USC/ISI, USA
Mehwish Alam	FIZ Karlsruhe - Leibniz Institute for Information Infrastructure and Karlsruhe Institute of Technology, Germany
Michael Cochez	VU Amsterdam, the Netherlands
Pasquale Lisena	EURECOM, France
Pierpaolo Basile	University of Bari, Italy
Pieter Colpaert	Ghent University, Belgium
Renzo Angles	Universidad de Talca, Chile
Sabrina Kirrane	Vienna University of Economics and Business, Austria
Sebastián Ferrada	Linköping University, Sweden
Stefan Schlobach	VU University Amsterdam, the Netherlands
Sven Lieber	Ghent University, Belgium
Tobias Käfer	Karlsruhe Institute of Technology, Germany
Tomáš Kliegr	Prague University of Economics and Business, Czech Republic
Umutcan Simsek	Universität Innsbruck, Austria
Vassil Momtchev	Ontotext, Bulgaria
Victor Charpenay	École des Mines de Saint-Étienne, France
Vinh Nguyen	U.S. National Library of Medicine, USA
Wei Hu	Nanjing University, China, China
Weizhuo Li	Nanjing University of Posts and Telecommunications, China
Yoan Chabot	Orange Labs, France

PhD Symposium Mentors

Enrico Daga	The Open University, UK
Mathieu D'Aquin	National University of Ireland Galway, Ireland
Javier D. Fernández	F. Hoffmann-La Roche AG
Fabien Gandon	Inria, France
Jose Manuel Gomez-Perez	expert.ai, Spain
Aidan Hogan	DCC, Universidad de Chile, Chile
Steffen Staab	Universität Stuttgart, Germany, and University of Southampton, UK
Maria Esther Vidal	TIB Leibniz Information Center for Science and Technology, Germany

PhD Symposium Program Committee

Enrico Daga	The Open University, UK
Javier D. Fernández	F. Hoffmann-La Roche AG, Switzerland
Maria Esther Vidal	TIB Leibniz Information Center for Science and Technology, Germany
Mehwish Alam	FIZ Karlsruhe - Leibniz Institute for Information Infrastructure, AIFB Institute, and KIT, Germany
Valeria Fionda	University of Calabria, Italy
Christoph Lange	Fraunhofer Institute for Applied Information Technology FIT and RWTH Aachen University, Germany
Riccardo Tommasini	University of Tartu, Estonia
Stefan Schlobach	Vrije Universiteit Amsterdam, the Netherlands
Giuseppe Rizzo	LINKS Foundation, Italy
Anna Lisa Gentile	IBM Research, USA
Frank Van Harmelen	Vrije Universiteit Amsterdam, the Netherlands
John Domingue	The Open University, UK
Michael Cochez	Vrije Universiteit Amsterdam, the Netherlands
Mathieu D'Aquin	National University of Ireland Galway, Ireland
Jose Manuel Gomez-Perez	expert.ai, Spain
Paul Groth	University of Amsterdam, the Netherlands
Luca Costabello	Accenture Labs, Ireland
Aidan Hogan	DCCU, Universidad de Chile, Chile
Vojtěch Svátek	Prague University of Economics and Business, Czech Republic
Anastasia Dimou	Ghent University, Belgium
Steffen Staab	Universität Stuttgart, Germany, and University of Southampton, UK
Albert Meroño-Peñuela	King's College London, UK
Alasdair Gray	Heriot-Watt University, UK
Daniele Dell'Aglio	Aalborg University, Denmark
Abraham Bernstein	University of Zurich, Switzerland

Gerardo Simari	Universidad Nacional del Sur and CONICET, Argentina
Enrico Motta	The Open University, UK
Fabien Gandon	Inria, France
Harith Alani	The Open University, UK
Gianluca Demartini	The University of Queensland, Australia
Christophe Guéret	Accenture Labs, Ireland

Industry Track Program Committee

Aneta Koleva	Siemens Corporate Technology, Germany
Anna Himmelhuber	Siemens Corporate Technology, Germany
Antoine Zimmermann	Ecole des Mines de Saint-Etienne, France
Aparna Saisree Thuluva	Siemens Corporate Technology, Germany
Josiane Xavier Parreira	Siemens Corporate Technology, Germany
Kimberly Garcia	University of St. Gallen, Switzerland
Konrad Diwold	Pro2Future AG and Graz University of Technology, Austria
Maria Husmann	Siemens Corporate Technology, Switzerland
Nelia Lasierra	Roche, Switzerland
Victor Charpenay	École des Mines de Saint-Étienne, France
Yushan Liu	Siemens Corporate Technology, Germany

Sponsors

Platinum

Silver

Bronze

metaphacts

Supporter

Contents

PhD Symposium Track Papers

Industry Track Papers

Poster and Demo Track Papers

BiodivOnto: Towards a Core Ontology for Biodiversity

Nora Abdelmageed[1,2,3](✉) ⓘ, Alsayed Algergawy[1] ⓘ, Sheeba Samuel[1,3] ⓘ,
and Birgitta König-Ries[1,3] ⓘ

[1] Heinz Nixdorf Chair for Distributed Information Systems,
Friedrich Schiller University Jena, Jena, Germany
{nora.abdelmageed,alsayed.algergawy,sheeba.saamuel,
birgitta.koenig-ries}@uni-jena.de
[2] Computer Vision Group, Friedrich Schiller University Jena, Jena, Germany
[3] Michael Stifel Center Jena, Friedrich Schiller University Jena, Jena, Germany

Abstract. Biodiversity is the variety of life on earth which covers the
evolutionary, ecological, and cultural processes that sustain life. Therefore, it is important to understand where biodiversity is, how it is changing over space and time, the driving factors of these changes and the
resulting consequences on the diversity of life. To do so, it is necessary
to describe and integrate the conditions and measures of biodiversity to
fully capture the domain. In this paper, we present the design of a core
ontology for biodiversity aiming to establish a link between the foundational and domain-specific ontologies. The proposed ontology is designed
using the fusion/merge strategy by reusing existing ontologies and it is
guided by data from several resources in the biodiversity domain.

Keywords: Biodiversity · Knowledge representation · Core ontology

1   Introduction

The recent IPBES global assessment[1] foresees a dramatic decline in biodiversity
and caused by this a dramatic decline in important ecosystem functions. To preserve biodiversity, research to understand its underlying mechanisms is needed
which requires integrated data [6]. An increasing amount of heterogeneous data
is generated and publicly shared in biodiversity research. There are also a lot of
efforts to semantically describe biodiversity datasets and research outputs. Multiple ontologies, like ENVO[2] and IOBC[3], model specific parts of the domain.
However, in order to support integrative biodiversity research, there is a growing need to bridge between the more refined biodiversity concepts and general
concepts provided by the foundational ontologies.

---

[1] https://ipbes.net/global-assessment.
[2] https://bioportal.bioontology.org/ontologies/ENVO.
[3] https://bioportal.bioontology.org/ontologies/IOBC.

© Springer Nature Switzerland AG 2021
R. Verborgh et al. (Eds.): ESWC 2021 Satellite Events, LNCS 12739, pp. 3–8, 2021.
https://doi.org/10.1007/978-3-030-80418-3_1

Core ontologies provide a precise definition of structural knowledge in a specific field that connects different application domains [3,4,10]. They are located in the layer between upper-level (fundamental) and domain-specific ontologies, providing the definition of the core concepts from a specific field. They aim at linking general concepts of a top-level ontology to more domain-specific concepts from a sub-field. Looking at the biodiversity domain, one can observe that existing ontologies tend to model parts of the domain while ignoring related parts. Furthermore, most of them connect directly to one of the existing foundational ontologies, such as BFO[4] and GFO[5]. This results in a number of challenges, e.g., the same concept can be represented in a different level of abstraction and use in different ontologies.

In this paper, we propose the design of a core ontology for the biodiversity domain using a semi-automatic approach to overcome these problems. We make use of the fusion/merge strategy [9] during the design of the core ontology, where the new ontology is developed by assembling and reusing one or more ontologies. Our design is guided by data from several databases in the biodiversity field. In particular, we develop a four-stage pipeline involving biodiversity experts and computer scientists at different phases. A set of heterogeneous biodiversity data sources is collected and analyzed. We make use of the existing ontologies from Bioportal[6] and AgroPortal[7] for extracting keywords from the collected data repository. This set of extracted terms is then filtered and revised to construct the final list of keywords. Using automated approaches of clustering and the help of biodiversity experts, we generate the list of core concepts. The links between the core concepts are discussed and determined by the domain experts.

2   Methodology

In this section, we describe the main steps of the proposed pipeline.

Data Acquisition: The aim of this step is to get sufficient data sources from which we can extract relevant terms. To this end, we have developed a crawling method, as shown in Fig. 1, considering structured and unstructured data resources. To extract relevant unstructured data, first a relaxed version of the QEMP corpus [7] is used and a number of keywords, such as *'abundance'*, *'benthic'*, *'biomass'*, *'carbon'*, *'climate change'*, *'decomposition'*, *'earthworms'*, *'ecosystem'* have been selected. The selected set of keywords is used later as input to the Semedico search engine [1] to get relevant publications from PubMed. Among them, 100 abstracts have chosen, as shown in Fig. 1 reflecting the biodiversity domain by applying an iterative manual process for revision and cleaning for the crawled data. To take tabular data into consideration, we have used two

---

[4] https://bioportal.bioontology.org/ontologies/BFO.
[5] https://bioportal.bioontology.org/ontologies/GFO.
[6] https://bioportal.bioontology.org/.
[7] http://agroportal.lirmm.fr.

well known data portals with very different characteristics (*BEFChina*[8] and *data.world*[9]). The result of this phase is a data repository[10] which contains 100 abstracts, more than 50 tables, some datasets are given by multiple tables and, 50 metadata files.

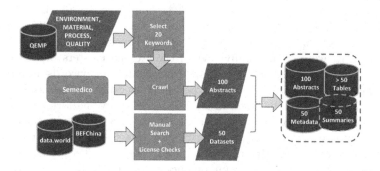

Fig. 1. Crawling phase

Term Extraction: Once we have the data repository, the next step is to extract domain-specific terms. To this end, we manually annotated the collected data following the annotation scheme in [7] making use of the same ontologies and adding more important ontologies knowledge bases, like *IOBC*, *SWEET*[11], *ECO-CORE*[12], *ECSO*[13], *CBO*[14], *BCO*[15] and the *Biodiversity A-Z* dictionary[16] to cover wider ranges of terms. During the extraction process, several challenges have been addressed. Our main challenge is the handling of compound words. For example, *photosynthetic O2 production* is expanded into the following keyword list: ["photosynthetic", "O2", "O2 production", "photosynthetic O2 production"]. Finally, the extracted list of terms has been enriched using other existing resources: 1) annotated keywords in QEMP corpus, 2) keywords from AquaDiva[17] project, and 3) soil related keywords [11].

Keywords Filtration: To get a final list of relevant terms, we applied an automatic filtration step, where we normalized keywords to be case insensitive and in a singular form. Furthermore, we manually revised the final list of keywords to exclude spelling mistakes. At the end of this step, we have 1107 unique keywords, which is 1.8× of QEMP corpus in size and covers a broader range of Biodiversity.

---

[8] https://china.befdata.biow.uni-leipzig.de/.
[9] https://data.world/.
[10] https://github.com/fusion-jena/BiodivOnto/tree/main/data.
[11] https://bioportal.bioontology.org/ontologies/SWEET.
[12] https://bioportal.bioontology.org/ontologies/ECOCORE.
[13] https://bioportal.bioontology.org/ontologies/ECSO.
[14] https://bioportal.bioontology.org/ontologies/CBO.
[15] https://bioportal.bioontology.org/ontologies/BCO.
[16] https://www.biodiversitya-z.org/.
[17] http://www.aquadiva.uni-jena.de/.

Concepts and Relations Determination: Given the huge output list from the previous step, we have automatically calculated the intersection among our work, QEMP and AquaDiva lists. This yields a narrowed list of keywords which we define as *Seeds* as they are the most important keywords and are common among various projects dealing with Biodiversity. We have then applied a distance-based clustering technique with the objective to assign each of the remaining words to the closest seed. Seeds and words are represented by 300D word embedding using word2vec [5]. Our selected metric is the cosine similarity. Afterwards, we have manually revised the created clusters multiple times. For each revision iteration, we check how the remaining keywords are grouped, discuss the results with Biodiversity experts, and modify the selected seeds by tending to more general concepts. In the last iteration, we performed the Word-Net [8] similarity among the remaining seeds, clusters centriods, such that, if the similarity is 0.0, very unique seed, we pick this seed as a core concept. In case of having some similarity with other seeds, we have checked BioPortal for those seeds and have picked the common ancestor for them. In the previous step, we have used PATO[18], and SWEET ontologies for looking to a common ancestor. We have discussed our final list of seeds or core concepts with Biodiversity experts. Finally, we discussed the possible relations that could co-occur among our core concepts. Figure 2 represents our core categories and their core links (relations) as been validated by domain experts. Each category has a set of terms as a result of the clustering algorithm. To implement the fusion/merge strategy, we make use of the ontology modularization and selection tool (*JOYCE*) [2] to extract relevant modules from each category. Table 1 shows the results of this process. The next step is to combine (merge) the set of modules in each category to get a core ontology representing the category. All the resources related to the design of the core ontology as well as the current preliminary results are publicly available[19].

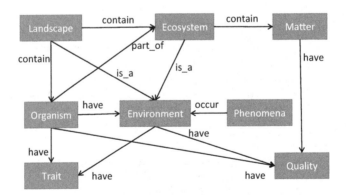

Fig. 2. Core concepts and their relations.

---

[18] https://bioportal.bioontology.org/ontologies/PATO.
[19] https://github.com/fusion-jena/BiodivOnto.

Table 1. Core concepts in existing ontologies with examples.

Category	Ontology modules	Terms sample inside category
Environment	ENVO, ECOCORE, ECSO, PATO	Groundwater, garden
Organism	ENVO ECOCORE, ECSO, BCO	Mammal, insect
Phenomena	ENVO, PATO, BCO	Decomposition, colonization
Quality	ENVO, PATO, CBO, ECSO	Volume, age
Landscape	ENVO	Grassland, forest
Trait	BCO	Texture, structure
Ecosystem	ENVO, ECOCORE, ECSO, PATO	Biome, habitat
Matter	ENVO, ECSO	Carbon, H2O

Acknowledgments. The authors thank the Carl Zeiss Foundation for the financial support of the project "A Virtual Werkstatt for Digitization in the Sciences (K3, P5)" within the scope of the program line "Breakthroughs: Exploring Intelligent Systems" for "Digitization - explore the basics, use applications". Alsayed Algergawy' work has been funded by the *Deutsche Forschungsgemeinschaft (DFG)* as part of CRC 1076 AQUADIVA. Our sincere thanks to Tina Heger (Berlin-Brandenburg Institute of Advanced Biodiversity Research (BBIB)) as the domain expert.

References

1. Faessler, E., Hahn, U.: Semedico: a comprehensive semantic search engine for the life sciences. In: Proceedings of ACL 2017, System Demonstrations, July 2017
2. Faessler, E., Klan, F., Algergawy, A., König-Ries, B., Hahn, U.: Selecting and tailoring ontologies with JOYCE. In: Ciancarini, P., et al. (eds.) EKAW 2016. LNCS (LNAI), vol. 10180, pp. 114–118. Springer, Cham (2017). https://doi.org/10.1007/978-3-319-58694-6_12
3. Fathalla, S., Vahdati, S., Auer, S., Lange, C.: SemSur: a core ontology for the semantic representation of research findings. In: SEMANTICS (2018)
4. Garcia, L.F., et al.: The GeoCore ontology: a core ontology for general use in geology. Comput. Geosci. **135**, 104387 (2020)
5. Goldberg, Y., Levy, O.: word2vec explained: deriving Mikolov et al'.s negative-sampling word-embedding method. arXiv preprint arXiv:1402.3722 (2014)
6. Gadelha Jr., L.M.R., et al.: A survey of biodiversity informatics: concepts, practices, and challenges. Wiley Interdiscip. Rev. Data Min. Knowl. Discov. **11**(1), e1394 (2021)
7. Löffler, F., Abdelmageed, N., Babalou, S., Kaur, P., König-Ries, B.: Tag me if you can! Semantic annotation of biodiversity metadata with the QEMP corpus and the BiodivTagger. In: Proceedings of The 12th Language Resources and Evaluation Conference, pp. 4557–4564 (2020)
8. Pedersen, T., Patwardhan, S., Michelizzi, J., et al.: WordNet: similarity-measuring the relatedness of concepts. AAAI **4**, 25–29 (2004)
9. Pinto, H.S., Martins, J.P.: Ontologies: how can they be built? Knowl. Inf. Syst. **6**(4), 441–464 (2004)

10. Scherp, A., Saathoff, C., Franz, T., Staab, S.: Designing core ontologies. Appl. Ontol. **6**(3), 177–221 (2011)
11. Udovenko, V., Algergawy, A.: Entity extraction in the ecological domain-a practical guide. BTW 2019-Workshopband (2019)

scikit-learn Pipelines Meet Knowledge Graphs

The Python kgextension Package

Tabea-Clara Bucher, Xuehui Jiang, Ole Meyer, Stephan Waitz,
Sven Hertling(iD), and Heiko Paulheim(✉)(iD)

Data and Web Science Group, University of Mannheim, Mannheim, Germany
{tbucher,xujiang,olmeyer,swaitz}@mail.uni-mannheim.de
{sven,heiko}@informatik.uni-mannheim.de

Abstract. Python is currently the most used platform for data science
and machine learning. At the same time, public knowledge graphs have
been identified as a valuable source of background knowledge in many
data science tasks. In this paper, we introduce the kgextension package for Python, which allows for using knowledge graph in data science
pipelines built in Python. The demo shows how data from public knowledge graphs such as DBpedia and Wikidata can be used in data mining pipelines based on the popular Python package scikit-learn. We
demonstrate the package's utility by showing that the prediction accuracy on a popular Kaggle task can be significantly increased by using
background knowledge from DBpedia.

Keywords: Python · scikit-learn · Knowledge graph · Background
knowledge · Data mining

1 Introduction

According to a recent poll, Python is the most used platform for data science
and machine learning.[1] At the same time, public knowledge graphs have been
acknowledged as a valuable source for background knowledge in such tasks [14].
While packages such as rdflib[2] are quite popular for processing knowledge
graphs, they do not build a bridge between graph processing and widely used
data mining packages, such as scikit-learn[3].

In this paper, we present the kgextension package for Python,[4] which builds
exactly that bridge. It builds on the ideas of previous implementations for
Weka [7] and *RapidMiner* [10]. The package provides functionalities for linking a dataset to public knowledge graphs, as well as for extracting features from

---

[1] https://www.kdnuggets.com/2019/05/poll-top-data-science-machine-learning-
platforms.html.
[2] https://github.com/RDFLib/rdflib.
[3] https://scikit-learn.org/.
[4] https://github.com/om-hb/kgextension.

© Springer Nature Switzerland AG 2021
R. Verborgh et al. (Eds.): ESWC 2021 Satellite Events, LNCS 12739, pp. 9–14, 2021.
https://doi.org/10.1007/978-3-030-80418-3_2

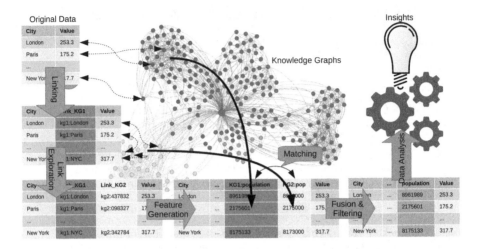

Fig. 1. Data analysis pipeline using background knowledge from knowledge graphs

those graphs. It comes with preconfigured connections to DBpedia and Wikidata, but can also be used with custom SPARQL endpoints and local RDF dumps.

2   Package Functionalities

A data analytics pipeline using background knowledge from knowledge graphs typically comprises different steps, as shown in Fig. 1. The final step is performing the actual data analysis, for which built-in methods of `scikit-learn` or other data mining packages are used. The remaining steps are supported by `kgextension`.

2.1   Linking and Link Exploration

The first step is to identify entities from the dataset to analyze in a knowledge graph. For example, on a dataset of cities, this step would be in identifying the corresponding cities in a knowledge graph. To that end, different entity linkers are available, which implement techniques such as user-defined URI patterns[5], lookup via SPARQL queries, or wrappers for specific services such as DBpedia Lookup[6]. Once links to one knowledge graph are established, links to other datasets (e.g., `owl:sameAs`) may be explored for generating additional links.

2.2   Feature Generation

In the next step, features are extracted from the linked entities in the knowledge graph. The package implements a number of techniques, ranging from the creation of individual features for datatype properties (e.g., the city population),

---

[5] Such as http://dbpedia.org/resource/*ENTITY*.

[6] https://lookup.dbpedia.org/.

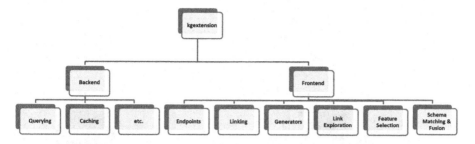

Fig. 2. Package structure

binary features for types (e.g., binary features for types such as `capital city`, `european city`, etc.), and different flavours of aggregation of properties [11] (e.g., using TF-IDF based measures). Moreover, custom SPARQL queries can be used for constructing specific features.

2.3   Feature Filtering

While `scikit-learn` provides a lot of generic techniques for feature filtering[7], the `kgextension` package also implements a number of specific methods from the literature, which consider the ontology underlying the knowledge graph for guiding the feature selection process. These methods do not only use internal measures such as information gain, but also take, e.g., the hierarchy in the ontologies into account for identifying the most distinctive features [5,6,12,19].

2.4   Matching and Fusion

When extracting features from more than one knowledge graph, there might be duplicate attributes (e.g., population values extracted from Wikidata and DBpedia). The `kgextension` includes a set of methods for identifying similar attributes (e.g., based on string similarity of the attribute names, or on value overlap), and includes a number of heuristics for fusing the values of joined attributes (e.g., voting, averaging, etc.).

2.5   Other Functionalities

As shown in Fig. 2, the `kgextension` package also comprises a number of useful backend functionalities, e.g., for efficient access to endpoints and caching. They facilitate an efficient execution of the overall pipeline.

---

[7] https://scikit-learn.org/stable/modules/feature_selection.html.

```
# Link dataset to DBpedia
from kgextension.linking_sklearn import DbpediaLookupLinker
linker = DbpediaLookupLinker(column='Author')
df_enhanced = linker.fit_transform(df_raw.drop(columns='Genre'))

# Extract features from DBpedia
from kgextension.generator_sklearn import SpecificRelationGenerator
generator = SpecificRelationGenerator(columns=['new_link'], direct_relation='http://purl.org/dc/terms/subject')
df_enhanced = generator.fit_transform(df_enhanced)
```

(a) Code example

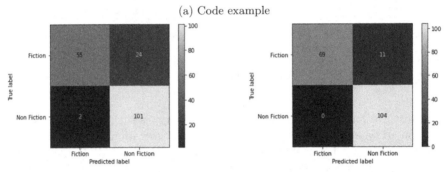

(b) Confusion matrix without added features

(c) Confusion matrix with features added from DBpedia

Fig. 3. Adding features from DBpedia significantly improves the results

3   Demonstration Contents

We demonstrate an end to end use case (i.e., from a dataset to a prediction), which is also available online as a Jupyter notebook[8]. In this use case, we use a prediction task from Kaggle[9] and show how to extend the dataset with information from different public knowledge graphs using the different functionalities of the package. The prediction target is to classify books in fiction and non-fiction books. We show that by using a few simple Python commands, the performance increases significantly from an accuracy of 0.86 to an accuracy of 0.94, and the number of wrongly classified examples reduced to more than half, as shown in Fig. 3. Since the notebook is interactive, different variants can be explored together with attendees of the demo.

4   Future Developments

The kgextension package itself is developed in a modular fashion, which allows for integrating new functionalities. Thus, for the future, we are planning to integrate, e.g., novel methods for linking [2]. Since knowledge graph embeddings have been proven useful for many data science tasks [1,13,15], we also plan to integrate libraries for creating knowledge graph embedding vectors [16], as

---

[8] https://github.com/om-hb/kgextension/blob/master/examples/book_genre_predi ction.ipynb.

[9] https://www.kaggle.com/sootersaalu/amazon-top-50-bestselling-books-2009-2019.

well as adapters for repositories for pretrained knowledge graph embeddings [9]. Moreover, on the knowledge graph access side, we plan to integrate efficient generators for Triple Pattern Fragment endpoints [17] and HDT files [3].

Moreover, the framework provide an interesting test bed for designing comparative studies of different public knowledge graphs [4] on various downstream tasks [8], a field which has not been much considered yet [18].

References

1. Cochez, M., Ristoski, P., Ponzetto, S.P., Paulheim, H.: Global RDF vector space embeddings. In: d'Amato, C., et al. (eds.) ISWC 2017. LNCS, vol. 10587, pp. 190–207. Springer, Cham (2017). https://doi.org/10.1007/978-3-319-68288-4_12
2. Jiménez-Ruiz, E., et al. (ed.): Semantic Web Challenge on Tabular Data to Knowledge Graph Matching (2020)
3. Fernández, J.D., et al.: Binary RDF representation for publication and exchange (HDT). Web Semantics **19**, 22–41 (2013)
4. Heist, N., Hertling, S., Ringler, D., Paulheim, H.: Knowledge graphs on the web-an overview (2020)
5. Jeong, Y., Myaeng, S.H.: Feature selection using a semantic hierarchy for event recognition and type classification. In: IJCNLP, pp. 136–144 (2013)
6. Lu, S., et al.: Domain ontology-based feature reduction for high dimensional drug data and its application to 30-day heart failure readmission prediction. In: COLLABORATECOM, pp. 478–484 (2013)
7. Paulheim, H., Fürnkranz, J.: Unsupervised generation of data mining features from linked open data. In: WIMS, pp. 1–12 (2012)
8. Pellegrino, M.A., Cochez, M., Garofalo, M., Ristoski, P.: A configurable evaluation framework for node embedding techniques. In: Hitzler, P., et al. (eds.) ESWC 2019. LNCS, vol. 11762, pp. 156–160. Springer, Cham (2019). https://doi.org/10.1007/978-3-030-32327-1_31
9. Portisch, J., Hladik, M., Paulheim, H.: KGvec2go-knowledge graph embeddings as a service. In: LREC, pp. 5641–5647 (2020)
10. Ristoski, P., Bizer, C., Paulheim, H.: Mining the web of linked data with RapidMiner. J. Web Semant. **35**, 142–151 (2015)
11. Ristoski, P., Paulheim, H.: A comparison of propositionalization strategies for creating features from linked open data. Linked Data Knowl. Discov. **6** (2014)
12. Ristoski, P., Paulheim, H.: Feature selection in hierarchical feature spaces. In: Discovery Science, pp. 288–300 (2014)
13. Ristoski, P., Paulheim, H.: RDF2Vec: RDF graph embeddings for data mining. In: Groth, P., et al. (eds.) ISWC 2016. LNCS, vol. 9981, pp. 498–514. Springer, Cham (2016). https://doi.org/10.1007/978-3-319-46523-4_30
14. Ristoski, P., Paulheim, H.: Semantic web in data mining and knowledge discovery: a comprehensive survey. Web Semant. **36**, 1–22 (2016)
15. Ristoski, P., Rosati, J., Di Noia, T., De Leone, R., Paulheim, H.: RDF2Vec: RDF graph embeddings and their applications. Semantic Web **10**(4), 721–752 (2019)
16. Vandewiele, G., et al.: pyRDF2Vec: Python Implementation and Extension of RDF2Vec. IDLab (2020). https://github.com/IBCNServices/pyRDF2Vec
17. Verborgh, R., et al.: Triple Pattern Fragments: a low-cost knowledge graph interface for the Web. Web Semantics 37–38, 184–206 (2016)

18. Voit, M., Paulheim, H.: Bias in knowledge graphs - an empirical study with movie recommendation and different language editions of DBpedia. In: LDK (2021)
19. Wang, B.B., et al.: A comparative study for domain ontology guided feature extraction. In: ACSC, pp. 69–78 (2003)

SLURP: An Interactive SPARQL Query Planner

Jannik Dresselhaus, Ilya Filippov, Johannes Gengenbach, Lars Heling[✉][iD], and Tobias Käfer[iD]

Institute AIFB, Karlsruhe Institute of Technology, Karlsruhe, Germany
{jannik.dresselhaus,ilya.filippov,johannes.gengenbach}@student.kit.edu,
{lars.heling,tobias.kaefer}@kit.edu

Abstract. Triple Pattern Fragments (TPFs) allow for querying large RDF graphs with high availability by offering triple pattern-based access to the graphs. The limited expressivity of TPFs leads to higher client-side querying and communication costs with potentially many intermediate results that need to be transferred. Thus, the challenge of devising efficient query plans when evaluating SPARQL queries lies in minimizing these costs. Different heuristics and cost-based query planning approaches have been proposed to obtain such efficient query plans. However, we also require means to visualize, manually modify, and execute alternative query plans, to better understand the differences between existing planning approaches and their potential limitations. To this end, we propose SLURP (https://people.aifb.kit.edu/zg2916/slurp/), an interactive SPARQL query planner that assists RDF data consumers to visualize, modify, and compare the performance of different query execution plans over TPFs.

1 Introduction

Motivation. Since the inception of the Linked Data Fragment (LDF) framework [6] to describe Web interfaces for publishing and querying Linked Data, a variety of LDF interfaces have been proposed. These interfaces differ in their emphasis on server load, availability, and expressivity. This development also drove research in client-side query processing because less expressive LDF interfaces, such as Triple Pattern Fragment (TPF) servers, require the clients to devise efficient query plans to execute SPARQL queries. These TPF clients [1,3,5,6] rely on simple statistics to obtain efficient query plans that minimize the runtime and the number of requests during execution. To this end, the clients implement different query planning methods ranging from heuristics [1,5,6] to cost-model-based [3] approaches. However, it is difficult to understand the differences between these approaches by just comparing their execution performance on benchmark queries. Moreover, researchers might want to investigate alternative, custom query plans, which are potentially more efficient than the plans obtained by the well-known query planning approaches. For instance, for specific

R. Verborgh et al. (Eds.): ESWC 2021 Satellite Events, LNCS 12739, pp. 15–20, 2021.
https://doi.org/10.1007/978-3-030-80418-3_3

types of queries or RDF datasets with uncommon data distribution, the existing approaches might not find the optimal query plans, which can lead to excessive runtimes and a larger number of requests submitted to the server.

In this demo, we present SLURP[1] to address these shortcomings. SLURP is a Web application for interactive SPARQL query planning that allows to visualize, modify, execute, and analyze the performance of execution plans for basic graph patterns over a given Triple Pattern Fragment (TPF) server. The tool is designed to help users to understand and compare different query planning approaches as well as to allow expert users to modify and optimize query plans to their needs. Moreover, SLURP can be used to support teaching students about query planning and query optimization.

Related Work. In the area of relational databases, approaches to visualize query execution plans have been proposed [2] and many databases support the EXPLAIN keyword to provide information on the execution plan. However, few approaches have focused on the visualization, modification, and analysis of SPARQL query execution plans. Jakobsen et al. [4] propose the Performance Inspector and Plan Explorer (PIPE). PIPE enables the comparison of query plans devised by different federated SPARQL query engines with respect to their planning time, execution time, and the number of answers. Moreover, PIPE allows for visualizing and comparing the execution plans obtained by these engines. Similar to PIPE, SLURP enables the visualization and execution of query plans for different query planning approaches. In contrast to PIPE, SLURP does not focus on federated query processing over multiple SPARQL endpoints but on client-side query processing over single TPF servers. Furthermore, SLURP also allows users to modify execution plans and analyze their execution performance regarding runtime, requests performed, and answers produced.

2   System Architecture

An overview of the SLURP architecture is provided in Fig. 1. The architecture can be separated in the Web application frontend and an API provided by the backend. The source code for our demonstration is available online on GitHub[2].

Frontend. The frontend consist of a Main Page, an Editor page, and a Result Page. The Main Page provides an overview of the recently executed query plans. On the Editor page, users can specify a new query and the TPF server to execute the query over. As of now, queries with basic graph patterns are supported. SLURP allows the user to choose a query plan optimizer to obtain an initial query plan for the query. This enables users to (i) get an initial starting point when modifying the query plan, and (ii) compare query plans devised by different query planning approaches. For this demonstration, SLURP provides a basic *left-linear* query planner that uses the triple patterns' count metadata for join ordering.

---

[1] https://people.aifb.kit.edu/zg2916/slurp/.

[2] https://github.com/Lars-H/slurp.

Moreover, SLURP also supports the query planner from nLDE[3] and the planner from CROP[4] with parameters settings used in [3]. For the initial query plan, the users can inspect the cardinalities of the individual triple patterns as well as the join cardinalities estimated by the query planning approach. The Editor Page provides an interactive execution plan editor that allows users to modify the initial plan or build a new plan in a drag-and-drop fashion. The leaves of the execution plan correspond to triple patterns evaluated over the selected TPF server and the inner nodes represent join operators. Users can build query plans with an arbitrary join order and place nested loop join (NLJ) or symmetric hash join (SHJ) operators in the execution plan. Upon modification, the plan can be executed and the user is redirected to the Result Page. On this page, which is automatically refreshed during query execution, the user can analyze the execution plan's performance with respect to its execution time, requests performed, intermediate result (i.e., join cardinalities), and answers produced.

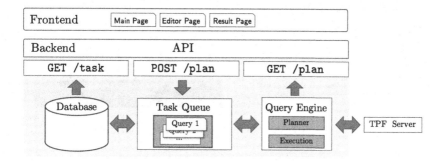

Fig. 1. Overview of the SLURP system architecture.

Backend. The backend consists of three components that the frontend interacts with via an API. The query planer is used by the frontend to obtain the query plan for a given query, TPF server, and planning approach (GET/plan). The task queue manages the execution plans to be executed by the engine in a first-in-first-out queue (POST/plan). For this demonstration, a single execution plan is executed at once and we set a timeout to 60 s. In a local deployment of the tool, these parameters can be adjusted accordingly. The database stores the queries, execution plans, and statistics of their execution (GET/task).

Given a SPARQL query, a TPF server URL, and the name of an optimizer, the query planning component in the backend obtains an initial query plan which is serialized as a JSON object and provided to the frontend. The planning component currently implements the nLDE optimizer, the CROP optimizer, and a left-linear optimizer. Further optimizers may be implemented in the planning component and exposed to the frontend. When a user submits a query plan to

---

[3] https://github.com/maribelacosta/nlde.
[4] https://github.com/Lars-H/crop.

be executed, the frontend serializes the plan as a JSON object and the SLURP backend creates the corresponding physical query plan. We use the network of Linked Data Eddies (nLDE) [1] as the engine to execute physical query plans.

Interoperability and Reuse. The source code of SLURP is publicly available on GitHub (See Footnote 2) and licensed under the open source MIT License. SLURP is developed in a containerized fashion using docker and docker-compose to facilitate installation and deployment. With the SLURP API, any application can interact with the query planner (`GET/plan`) and the query execution engine (`POST/plan`). The query plans are represented in a binary tree with the triple patterns as the tree's leaves and join operators as its inner nodes. The query plans are serialized in JSON. In future work, we want to investigate a more generic and flexible query plan representation and serialization to support the integration of additional query planning approaches and query execution engines.

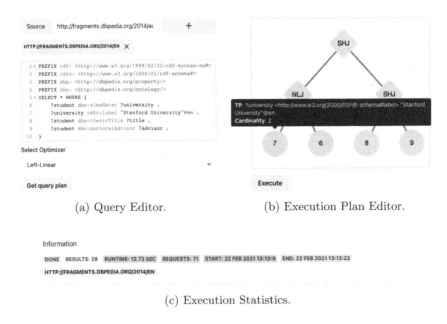

(a) Query Editor.   (b) Execution Plan Editor.

(c) Execution Statistics.

Fig. 2. SLURP: Query editor, plan visualization, and execution statistics.

3   Demonstration

In the demonstration at the conference, SLURP (https://people.aifb.kit.edu/ zg2916/slurp/) will be used to showcase different query planning approaches and how the modification of query execution plans affects their execution performance. The attendees will use SLURP to formulate SPARQL queries in the query editor over a public Triple Pattern Fragment (TPF) server (Fig. 2a). Thereafter, they will obtain an initial execution plan using one of the query plan optimizers.

The attendees will be able to inspect and modify the plan in the execution plan editor (Fig. 2b): (1) changing the join order by switching triple patterns, (2) selecting nested loop or hash join operators, or (3) building a query plan from scratch by dragging and dropping sub-plans. Upon modification, the attendees will be able to execute the query plan and analyze its performance concerning its execution time, the number of performed requests, and the answers produced (Fig. 2c). In summary, the attendees will learn about client-side query planning over TPF servers and the challenges in devising query plans that minimize the execution time and requests.

4   Conclusion

In this paper, we presented our demonstration of SLURP, an interactive SPARQL query planner that allows users to visualize, modify, execute, and analyze the performance of SPARQL query execution plans over Triple Pattern Fragment (TPF) servers. SLURP enables the users to compare alternative query plans obtained by different planning methods for client-side query processing. Furthermore, the users are able to modify or build query execution plans from scratch. Finally, with the query execution engine in the backend, these query plans can be executed and their performance can be compared according to the execution time, the number of requests performed, and query answers produced. In future work, we want to extend SLURP to support more features of SPARQL (e.g., filter, union, and optional expressions), additional LDF interfaces, and further query plan execution engines. Moreover, we further want to improve the tool's usability as well as facilitate the creation and comparison of alternative execution plans for the same query.

Acknowledgement. This work was supported by the grant QUOCA (FKZ 01IS17042) from the German Federal Ministry of Education and Research (BMBF).

References

1. Acosta, M., Vidal, M.-E.: Networks of linked data eddies: an adaptive web query processing engine for RDF data. In: Arenas, M., et al. (eds.) ISWC 2015. LNCS, vol. 9366, pp. 111–127. Springer, Cham (2015). https://doi.org/10.1007/978-3-319-25007-6_7
2. Gawade, M., Kersten, M.L.: Stethoscope: a platform for interactive visual analysis of query execution plans. Proc. VLDB Endow. **5**(12), 1926–1929 (2012)
3. Heling, L., Acosta, M.: Cost-and robustness-based query optimization for linked data fragments. In: Pan, J.Z., et al. (eds.) ISWC 2020. LNCS, vol. 12506, pp. 238–257. Springer, Cham (2020). https://doi.org/10.1007/978-3-030-62419-4_14
4. Jakobsen, A.L., Montoya, G., Hose, K.: How diverse are federated query execution plans really? In: Hitzler, P., et al. (eds.) ESWC 2019. LNCS, vol. 11762, pp. 105–110. Springer, Cham (2019). https://doi.org/10.1007/978-3-030-32327-1_21

5. Taelman, R., Van Herwegen, J., Vander Sande, M., Verborgh, R.: Comunica: a modular SPARQL query engine for the web. In: Vrandečić, D., et al. (eds.) ISWC 2018. LNCS, vol. 11137, pp. 239–255. Springer, Cham (2018). https://doi.org/10.1007/978-3-030-00668-6_15
6. Verborgh, R., et al.: Triple pattern fragments: a low-cost knowledge graph interface for the web. J. Web Semant. **37–38**, 184–206 (2016)

Towards Easy Vocabulary Drafts
with Neologism 2.0

Johannes Lipp[1,3]([⊠])(ⅅ), Lars Gleim[1]([⊠])(ⅅ), Michael Cochez[2](ⅅ), Iraklis Dimitriadis[3](ⅅ),
Hussain Ali[3](ⅅ), Daniel Hoppe Alvarez[3], Christoph Lange[1,3](ⅅ), and Stefan Decker[1,3](ⅅ)

[1] Chair of Information Systems, RWTH Aachen University, Aachen, Germany
{lipp,gleim,lange,decker}@dbis.rwth-aachen.de
[2] Department of Computer Science, Vrije Universiteit Amsterdam,
Amsterdam, The Netherlands
[3] Fraunhofer Institute for Applied Information Technology FIT,
Sankt Augustin, Germany
{johannes.lipp,iraklis.dimitriadis,hussain.ali,daniel.alvarez,
christoph.lange,stefan.decker}@fit.fraunhofer.de

Abstract. Shared vocabularies and ontologies are essential for many applications. Although standards and recommendations already cover many areas, adaptations are usually necessary to represent concrete use-cases properly. Domain experts are unfamiliar with ontology engineering, which creates special requirements for needed tool support. Simple sketch applications are usually too imprecise, while comprehensive ontology editors are often too complicated for non-experts. We present Neologism 2.0 – an open-source tool for quick vocabulary creation through domain experts. Its guided vocabulary creation and its collaborative graph editor enable the quick creation of proper vocabularies, even for non-experts, and dramatically reduces the time and effort to draft vocabularies collaboratively. An RDF export allows quick bootstrapping of any other Semantic Web tool.

Keywords: Vocabulary creation · Ontology creation · Vocabulary drafts · Knowledge graph · Semantic Web

1 Introduction

The benefits of good ontologies and vocabularies are undisputed in the Semantic Web community and the need for semantics is driven by recent trends such as Industry 4.0. General domains received much attention and yielded many recommendations and standards (e.g., SKOS, DCAT, and FOAF). Niche areas, in contrast, often face the problem that no suitable vocabularies exist. At the same time, creating an ontology is a complex, time-consuming task and rarely something domain experts are used to doing – this also holds for lightweight ontologies, which we call "vocabularies". Reducing both effort and ontology expert involvement is crucial, particularly for small-scale application contexts [2]. We identify the key requirements *ease of use* [11], *development speed, compatibility with RDF, vocabulary reuse, ease of publication,* and *collaboration*. This paper presents a remake of *Neologism* [1], which was used to define and

© Springer Nature Switzerland AG 2021
R. Verborgh et al. (Eds.): ESWC 2021 Satellite Events, LNCS 12739, pp. 21–26, 2021.
https://doi.org/10.1007/978-3-030-80418-3_4

publish vocabularies on the US Government Open Data portal[1]. It is available open-source (MIT) at https://github.com/Semantic-Society/Neologism, where we also provide a live demonstration website, a video, and further development towards a fully-featured extension of the original solution. Neologism 2.0 guides users in drafting vocabularies in a graph editor and is, intentionally, not a feature-complete ontology editing tool such as Protégé [13]. It creates vocabulary drafts for bootstrapping other Semantic Web applications.

2   Related Work

There are several tools for vocabulary creation, but none that meets all our requirements and fills the gap of creating decent but simple vocabularies easily. The NeOn Toolkit [7] is a Java-based open-source ontology editor that was maintained by the NeOn Foundation until 2011. The AceWiki [10] project enables collaborative ontology management through ACE sentences, a subset of English directly translatable to first-order logic and even more expressive than OWL. SADL [3] enables the definition of semantic models and rules using an English-like DSL, which can be translated to OWL with an Eclipse plugin. Mobi [9] is a free and collaborative knowledge graph platform to publish and discover data models, which is built on RDF and OWL. The fully-featured ontology editor Protégé [13] also provides a web version [16]. The commercial tool TopBraid Composer [15] provides comprehensive support in ontology creation and editing. Another commercial tool called Grafo [4] provides both visual knowledge graph design in a collaborative manner and RDF import/export. ExcelRDF [8] allows RDF vocabulary creation from Excel spreadsheets. CoModIDE [14] combines modular ontology engineering with graphical modeling and is available as a Protégé plugin. Ontology visualization can be done via WebVOWL [12], an interactive web application that supports editing as well [17], or via Protégé plugins that leverage the graph drawing tool Graphviz [5].

A major focus in our related work research is comparing Neologism 2.0 and Neologism 1.0 [1], which both are easy-to-use web-based systems that simplify the process of creating and publishing RDF vocabularies, and use a limited subset of RDFS and OWL. Neologism 2.0 focuses more on a simplified UI to support non-experts by even skipping complex elements like *class disjointness* or *inverse properties*, add autocompleting fields wherever possible (e.g., identifiers). The focus on editing in Neologism 2.0 differs from that on publishing in Neologism 1.0: We provide a graphical editor compared to a viewer. As reliable tools such as Widoco [6] exist that create documentations and visualizations of ontologies, there is no need any more to redundantly implement such features in version 2.0. Besides publishing, Neologism 1.0 used Vapour for validating content negotiation correctness. Consistency checking is out of scope for both versions. Neologism 2.0 intentionally aims at simplifying the creation process for domain users and therefore refrains from overwhelming the user with warnings they might not understand. The quickly created drafts are later repaired and evolved by Semantic Web experts.

In general, the aforementioned tools either lack simplicity or do not meet all our requirements. Fully-featured ontology editors such as Protégé are ideal for ontology

---

[1] See: https://joinup.ec.europa.eu/node/45149.

experts but overwhelming for users with little to no knowledge about ontologies. As in the comparison with Neologism 1.0, we argue in general that a graphical editor provides strong benefits over text-based editors, particularly for naïve users. Tools like WebVOWL do support graph-based editing, but miss features such as real-time collaboration or publishing ontologies. Additionally, managing and maintaining ontologies in Neologism 2.0 is kept very simple, so that creators can manage access rights to the ontology quite easy and can publish ontologies by themselves. Neologism 2.0 does not focus on only one feature, but combines multiple features, while simplifying them to assist rapid vocabulary creation. We see Neologism 2.0 as proposal to fill the gap between simple sketches and fully-fletched ontology editors, and aim for a strong integration with state-of-the-art tools.

Fig. 1. The vocabulary drafting process embedded into a typical user workflow.

3   Embedding Neologism 2.0 in Common Workflows

Most existing solutions have an extensive feature set and are too complex for domain experts who are unfamiliar with the Semantic Web. Neologism 2.0 particularly addresses the requirement of being easy to use in the first iterations of vocabulary creation in specific domains: It provides simple primitives for quick and dirty prototyping of first vocabulary drafts while encouraging best practices and the reuse of existing concepts from configurable sources. Each vocabulary draft is assigned a unique shareable URL that enables easy publishing and collaboration. Figure 1 depicts a suggested workflow that uses Neologism 2.0 for creating early vocabulary drafts and imports its RDF export into Protégé for subsequent refinements by Semantic Web experts, which can finally yield fully-featured ontologies.

4   Vocabulary Drafting with Neologism 2.0

Figure 2 depicts the high-level architecture of Neologism 2.0, which consists of the three main components frontend, backend, and recommender. The web frontend is written in TypeScript and uses Angular 9.0, and offers authentication and authorization. A simple dashboard allows managing, creating, editing, sharing, searching, and exporting vocabularies. Data persistence is managed by the Meteor backend, which serves

REST endpoints for edit operations on classes and properties. As a major feature, Neologism 2.0 immediately synchronizes changes among all clients and the server to enable real-time collaboration, which avoids confusion among users caused by asynchronous edits.

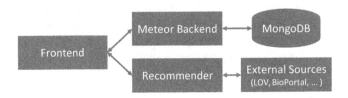

Fig. 2. Neologism 2.0's frontend communicates with a backend to persist information, and might interact with a recommender to improve the quality of drafted vocabularies.

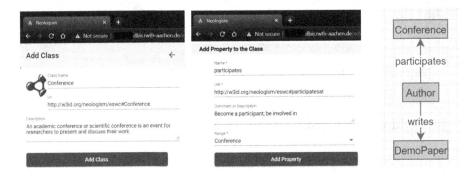

Fig. 3. Users add new classes via name and description (left), or add properties by choosing a range and entering name and description to a popup (center). The graph editor (right) is interactive. All URIs are generated automatically to ease access.

Users create vocabularies in Neologism 2.0's graphical editor; see the screenshots in Fig. 3. Only name and description are needed to create new classes, while the URI is autocompleted from a generated ontology base URI and the class name. The same holds for properties, which additionally require a range definition. User input from the web frontend later adds to the ontology export as follows. We use `rdf:type` to define `rdfs:Class`, `owl:Class`, and `owl:ObjectProperty`. The names and descriptions of classes and properties in the graph editor are serialized as `rdfs:label/comment`, respectively. We finally use `rdfs:domain` and `rdfs:range` to express each property's nodes in the generated export RDFS/OWL file in turtle format.

The graph editor depicts the current state and allows interactions on both classes and properties, including editing and deletion. It supports real-time collaboration by continuously synchronizing its state. The work-in-progress recommender suggests existing terms from configurable sources, depending on the deployment. It can also act as a proxy to recommendation systems such as LOV or BioPortal.

Limitations. Motivated by a focus on simplicity for quick ontology drafting, Neologism 2.0 intentionally omits support for more complex OWL semantics, such as cardinality restrictions etc., thus restricting its applicability as a general purpose ontology editor compared to related work. However, this restriction by design is in line with the drafting process depicted in Fig. 1. Furthermore, Neologism 2.0 does not currently support importing existing RDF vocabularies for further drafting.

5   Future Work

The open-source vocabulary prototyping tool Neologism 2.0 fits well in Semantic Web workflows where domain experts create first drafts, which are later revised in more comprehensive tools by Semantic Web experts. The current state covers all key requirements except for the following *ease of publication* and *vocabulary reuse*. Ongoing research will tackle the former by adding the features of the initial Neologism tool, and the latter by enhancing the recommender's consideration of the context of ontologies to improve the quality of designs and thus facilitate subsequent ontology development. Finally, a user study in different Semantic Web projects from the production and mobility sectors will evaluate both usability and integration in real-world use-cases. Our open-source GitHub repository allows collaboration and discussions with the community to close the gap between simple sketches and comprehensive ontology editors and finally improve collaboration between experts from the domain and the Semantic Web.

Acknowledgment. Funded by the Deutsche Forschungsgemeinschaft (DFG, German Research Foundation) under Germany's Excellence Strategy – EXC – 2023 Internet of Production – 390621612.

References

1. Basca, C., Corlosquet, S., Cyganiak, R., Fernández, S., Schandl, T.: Neologism: easy vocabulary publishing. In: Scripting and Development for the Semantic Web (SFSW) (2009)
2. Blomqvist, E., Sandkuhl, K.: Patterns in ontology engineering: classification of ontology patterns. In: ICEIS (3) (2005)
3. Crapo, A., Moitra, A.: Toward a unified English-like representation of semantic models, data, and graph patterns for subject matter experts. Int. J. Semant. Comput. **7**(03), 215–236 (2013)
4. data.world Inc: Grafo Toolkit (2020). https://gra.fo/
5. Ellson, J., Gansner, E., Koutsofios, L., North, S.C., Woodhull, G.: Graphviz—open source graph drawing tools. In: Mutzel, P., Jünger, M., Leipert, S. (eds.) GD 2001. LNCS, vol. 2265, pp. 483–484. Springer, Heidelberg (2002). https://doi.org/10.1007/3-540-45848-4_57
6. Garijo, D.: WIDOCO: a wizard for documenting ontologies. In: d'Amato, C., et al. (eds.) ISWC 2017. LNCS, vol. 10588, pp. 94–102. Springer, Cham (2017). https://doi.org/10.1007/978-3-319-68204-4_9
7. Haase, P., et al.: The NeOn ontology engineering toolkit. In: WWW (2008)
8. Hammar, K.: Linked data creation with ExcelRDF. In: Harth, A., et al. (eds.) ESWC 2020. LNCS, vol. 12124, pp. 104–109. Springer, Cham (2020). https://doi.org/10.1007/978-3-030-62327-2_18

9. iNovex: Mobi: Distributed Knowledge Graph Platform (2017). https://mobi.inovexcorp.com/
10. Kuhn, T.: Acewiki: collaborative ontology management in controlled natural language. arXiv preprint arXiv:0807.4623 (2008)
11. Lipp, J., Gleim, L., Decker, S.: Towards reusability in the semantic web: decoupling naming, validation, and reasoning. In: WOP at the 19th International Semantic Web Conference (2020)
12. Lohmann, S., Negru, S., Haag, F., Ertl, T.: Linked data creation with ExcelRDF. SW **7**, 399–419 (2016)
13. Noy, N.F., Sintek, M., Decker, S., Crubézy, M., Fergerson, R.W., Musen, M.A.: Creating semantic web contents With Protege-2000. IEEE Intell. Syst. **16**(2), 60–71 (2001)
14. Shimizu, C., Hammar, K.: CoModIDE - the comprehensive modular ontology engineering IDE. In: ISWC 2019 Satellite Tracks co-located with 18th International Semantic Web Conference (ISWC 2019), vol. 2456, pp. 249–252. CEUR-WS (2019)
15. TopQuadrant: TopBraid Composer (2020). topquadrant.com/products/topbraid-composer/
16. Tudorache, T., Nyulas, C., Noy, N.F., Musen, M.A.: WebProtégé: a collaborative ontology editor and knowledge acquisition tool for the web. Semant. Web **4**(1), 89–99 (2013)
17. Wiens, V., Lohmann, S., Auer, S.: WebVOWL editor: device-independent visual ontology modeling. In: International Semantic Web Conference (P&D/Industry/BlueSky) (2018)

Dataset Generation Patterns for Evaluating Knowledge Graph Construction

Markus Schröder[1,2](✉), Christian Jilek[1,2], and Andreas Dengel[1,2]

[1] Smart Data and Knowledge Services Department, DFKI GmbH,
Kaiserslautern, Germany
{markus.schroeder,christian.jilek,andreas.dengel}@dfki.de
[2] Computer Science Department, TU Kaiserslautern, Kaiserslautern, Germany

Abstract. Confidentiality hinders the publication of authentic, labeled datasets of personal and enterprise data, although they could be useful for evaluating knowledge graph construction approaches in industrial scenarios. Therefore, our plan is to synthetically generate such data in a way that it appears as authentic as possible. Based on our assumption that knowledge workers have certain habits when they produce or manage data, generation patterns could be discovered which can be utilized by data generators to imitate real datasets. In this paper, we initially derived 11 distinct patterns found in real spreadsheets from industry and demonstrate a suitable generator called Data Sprout that is able to reproduce them. We describe how the generator produces spreadsheets in general and what altering effects the implemented patterns have.

Keywords: Pattern language · Generator · Synthetic data

1 Introduction and Motivation

Personal and enterprise data is usually produced and managed by knowledge workers during their work. One of our research efforts[1] is concerned with the construction of enterprise knowledge graphs from such datasets. Although, in the past we worked with various data assets, we were not allowed to publish them (together with labeled data) because of usual confidentiality reasons in personal and enterprise data. Even if this was possible under certain circumstances, there is still a high effort to label such data with intended knowledge graphs to conduct meaningful evaluations. For example, labeling could mean to define what RDF statements can be expected for which data records. Therefore, our plan is to synthetically generate labeled datasets in such a way that they appear as authentic as possible.

When knowledge workers work with data, we observe that they show certain behaviors. We assume that whenever data is entered or modified, a user tends

---

[1] https://comem.ai/SensAI

© Springer Nature Switzerland AG 2021
R. Verborgh et al. (Eds.): ESWC 2021 Satellite Events, LNCS 12739, pp. 27–32, 2021.
https://doi.org/10.1007/978-3-030-80418-3_5

to do it in a way the person is used to. This also includes habits or workarounds which may result in rather messy datasets, especially, if data management strategies are neglected. A particular way in which something is done or organized is usually called a *pattern*. By exploring enterprise data and interviewing its users, such reoccurring patterns may be collected and cataloged.

This emerging pattern language could then be utilized by data generators that reproduce these patterns to imitate real datasets. Such synthetically generated data, if authentic enough, would appear like knowledge workers had produced them in the first place. By mixing patterns in various ways, generators are able to produce arbitrary large and complex data assets – even with pattern combinations which have not been observed before. That is why the construction of knowledge graphs from such data can easily become a non-trivial task: since patterns and especially their combinations will typically introduce ambiguities, a simple pattern recognition procedure may not be sufficient enough.

Our envisioned generators take two inputs: the generation patterns and a given knowledge graph. Since generators know what statements resulted in what data, the provenance information can be used to measure the performance of construction approaches on that data. Researchers are also able to generate synthetic datasets that matches just those patterns present in their non-publishable real-world ones. Computational results are expected to be on the same level for both the real and the synthetic datasets (due to identical complexity as expressed by the underlying patterns), thus making the synthetic-based results valid.

Generation patterns are usually dependent on a given domain (such as chemistry, biology, healthcare) and a given data format in focus. In this paper, we would like to present our idea using the example of spreadsheets.

2   A Pattern Language and Generator for Spreadsheets

Pattern Language. Spreadsheets are widely used, especially in the industrial sector. They can model complex workbooks containing multiple sheets with meta data rich cells (content and appearance). The structure of our envisioned patterns are heavily inspired by Alexander's patterns in the architectural domain [1], however with the difference that our patterns describe for some given circumstances (situations, issues, facts) concrete possibilities about how to model them using spreadsheets. We manually found for now 11 distinct patterns which form a pattern language for spreadsheets[2]. Nine patterns, which have been implemented in the generator, are listed in Table 1 with their titles and descriptions. Regarding the website, such a pattern typically comes with a title and a context hinting to a specific issue. This circumstance is described in more detail followed by a solution how to store the containing facts in a spreadsheet (second column in Table 1). After that, an example illustrates with an image how the pattern could be applied. Some patterns provide links to related ones and they are grouped in categories.

---

[2] http://www.dfki.uni-kl.de/~mschroeder/pattern-language-spreadsheets.

Table 1. Generation patterns which are implemented in our generator.

Title	Description
Numeric Information as Text	There is numeric information, therefore, it can be also represented as text
Acronyms or Symbols	An entity refers to a value, therefore, to save time a rather short acronym or symbol string is used to refer to it
Multiple Surface Forms	Entities can be mentioned in various ways, therefore, different cells contain distinct surface forms of equal entities
Property Value as Color	Some entities have different values for the same property, therefore, different colors encoding property values are chosen to color ranges
Partial Formatting Indicates Relations	Multiple entities in one cell have different relationships with another entity, therefore, partial formatting is used to indicate their relations
Outdated is Formatted	Information is not valid anymore, but must not be removed completely, therefore, outdated information is formatted
Multiple Entities in one Cell	Multiple entities have to be referred to, therefore, entities are listed in the same cell
Intra-Cell Additional Information	Additional information is related to already recorded information in a cell, therefore, the additional one is recorded in the same cell
Multiple Types in a Table	Some entities of different types share same properties, therefore, they are recorded in the same table

These initial patterns were obtained in an industry project where a power supply company provided five sheets that were managed over years by changing authors. The sheets consist of meta-data about documents and their revisions. After several open interviews with two authors, lasting about four hours in total, almost all of the approx. 90 columns in the spreadsheets were intensively discussed. In these conversations we learned from the domain experts why they modeled and designed spreadsheets in certain ways. To check if these patterns occur also in other domains, 3692 spreadsheets from the U.S. Government's open data platform[3] (data.gov) were downloaded. We manually inspected 200 of them and found these patterns as well, although their number is much lower in comparison.

Generator. On the basis of the proposed pattern language, a data generator called "Data Sprout" was implemented[4]. An online demo[5] lets users generate diverse Microsoft Excel spreadsheets with desired generation patterns from a

---

[3] https://www.data.gov.
[4] https://github.com/mschroeder-github/datasprout.
[5] http://www.dfki.uni-kl.de/~mschroeder/demo/datasprout.

given RDF graph. Parts of the graph will be differently represented in sheets, depending what generation patterns are activated. Patterns introduce noise in data by uniformly or randomly picking different options for each cell, sheet or workbook. In the following, we will describe how Data Sprout produces spreadsheets in general and what altering effects the implemented patterns have (mentioned in italic, see also Table 1).

Layout. Broadly, the graph's terminology (i.e. classes and properties) determines how sheets are structured while assertions are used to populate cells with data. In Data Sprout's default configuration, each RDF class corresponds to a sheet, whereas each class property (i.e. properties having a domain of that class) corresponds to a column in the sheet. Class instances (i.e. resources which are type of that class) are listed per row, meaning that at respective property columns their objects (resources or literals) are mentioned in cells. The *Multiple Entities in one Cell* pattern allows that multiple objects are listed in a single cell which is useful since RDF graphs are usually multi-edged graphs (i.e. one property has multiple objects). Some generation patterns change the default behavior for structuring tables: *Multiple Types in a Table* makes sure that some randomly picked sheets correspond to two classes. This way, we naturally find instances of different types in one table. *Intra-Cell Additional Information* ensures that some randomly selected columns are related to two or three properties. This means that a single cell can contain multiple RDF nodes (resources and/or literals) from different properties.

Modelling. Storing a literal value in a cell can be done in more than one way. By instruction manuals spreadsheets may state an intended way of how to record information, for example, that dates should be stored as numeric values. However, the pattern *Numeric Information as Text* also allows that some literals will be stored using a textual representation instead. In case of resources, the generator has to decide how to mention them in cells, usually by using their labels. Instead of naming them consistently, the pattern *Multiple Surface Forms* ensures that different labeling variations are considered. For instance, in case of persons "there can be a high variation which of their names are used, how their names are ordered and if their names are abbreviated" [4]. Additionally, the generation pattern *Acronyms or Symbols* also ensures the use of short acronym labels and that symbols may represent Boolean literals (e.g. "✓" stands for *true*).

Formatting. Instead of a cell's content, its formatting can also convey meaning. Background and foreground color (more precisely: a cell's font color) can be used to encode certain property values, as described in *Property Value as Color*. To carry out this pattern, our generator searches for appropriate property-value-pairs and randomly assigns colors to them. Because colors alone now provide enough information, the corresponding property columns are removed from the sheet. Additionally, spreadsheets allow to format individual parts in texts by using rich text. In case of the *Outdated is Formatted* pattern, our generator ensures that once preselected properties are involved that refer to outdated information, mentioned resources will be crossed out. As soon as multiple objects come from different properties and their relations are not distinguishable anymore, the pattern *Partial Formatting Indicates Relations* can be applied. In this case, our generator randomly allocates colors or styles (like bold, italic or underlined) to properties in order to make the property recognizable again.

Since the generator completes every cell in a sheet, it knows the corresponding statements which were involved during the generation. This provenance information describes the intended statements that should be rediscovered when analyzing a cell's content. Such ground truth labels are essential for evaluating approaches that construct knowledge graphs from this data.

3   Related Work

In former work [2, Section 3.7] we discussed in more detail the problem of missing publicly available Personal Information Model (PIM) dataset and that pseudo desktop collections do not meet our needs. The most related datasets seem to be test cases for KG construction tools, like the ones provided for RDF Mapping Language (RML) approaches[6]. However, such test sets are far too small and simple, since they are made with a testing purpose in mind. That is why data generation might be a reasonable option. However, after investigating several generator approaches (for a recent survey see [3]), we did not find a suitable one that would produce similar datasets we typically deal with in practice.

4   Conclusion and Outlook

For evaluating knowledge graph construction results, we propose the idea to synthetically generate appropriate datasets. Based on our observation that knowledge workers show certain behaviors when creating data, an initial catalog of generation patterns in the domain of spreadsheets was derived. A demonstrator was presented that generates from a given knowledge graph diverse sheets by reproducing such patterns.

In the future, we will extend our pattern language with more patterns and describe their creation process in a dedicated paper. In this context, we will also investigate how authentic the generated data appears to users. Moreover, we would like to show that evaluations yield similar results, regardless whether real or synthetic data was used.

Acknowledgements. This work was funded by the BMBF project SensAI (grant no. 01IW20007).

---

[6] https://github.com/RMLio/rml-test-cases.

References

1. Alexander, C., Ishikawa, S., Silverstein, M., Jacobson, M., Fiksdahl-King, I., Angel, S.: A Pattern Language - Towns, Buildings, Construction. Oxford University Press, Oxford (1977)
2. Jilek, C., et al.: Managed forgetting to support information management and knowledge work. Künstliche Intell. **33**(1), 45–55 (2019)
3. Popic, S., Pavkovic, B., Velikic, I., Teslic, N.: Data generators: a short survey of techniques and use cases with focus on testing. In: 9th IEEE International Conference on Consumer Electronics, ICCE, Berlin, Germany, pp. 189–194. IEEE (2019)
4. Schröder, M., Jilek, C., Schulze, M., Dengel, A.: The person index challenge: extraction of persons from messy, short texts. In: Proceedings of the 9th International Conference on Agents and Artificial Intelligence, ICAART 2021, pp. 531–537, January 2021

National Library of Latvia Subject Headings as Linked Open Data

Mārīte Apenīte⬤ and Uldis Bojārs⁽✉⁾⬤

National Library of Latvia, Mūkusalas iela 3, Riga 1423, Latvia
{marite.apenite,uldis.bojars}@lnb.lv

Abstract. This paper presents the linked data representation of the National Library of Latvia (NLL) authority data consisting of topical, geographic name and form/genre thesauri. It is an important step from a data silo (MARC 21 data) to linked open datasets, represented using SKOS, that can be reused both within and outside the library domain. The datasets are converted to SKOS using mc2skos and are published as linked data using the Skosmos application for publishing SKOS datasets. The paper describes the datasets, including information about their external links. The NLL topical terms dataset, in particular, contains many external links – 85% of its concepts have links to the Library of Congress subject headings dataset that is available as linked open data. The published datasets can be applied to interconnecting Latvia's cultural heritage information by describing museum and archive items with URIs from these datasets.

Keywords: Authority control · Linked data · SKOS · National Library of Latvia Subject Headings (NLLSH)

1 Introduction

Library authority files are controlled vocabularies that provide standard names and identifiers for different types of headings[1] such as personal names, corporate bodies, geographic names, topical headings, and form or genre terms that library catalogs may need to refer to in a unified way. Authority control plays an important role in library information systems. Authority data ensures: 1) common use of terms, including synonyms, quasi-synonyms, and homonyms; 2) compatibility of metadata with other international controlled vocabularies.

The National Library of Latvia Subject Headings (NLLSH) have been developed and maintained since 2000 as a fundamental and universal vocabulary that forms the basis of the National Thesaurus of Latvia. NLLSH contains topical headings, geographic names, and form/genre terms. Most of topical headings are adopted from the Library

---

[1] Heading is the name of a person, corporate body, or geographic location; the title proper of a work; or an authorized content descriptor (subject heading), placed at the head of a catalog entry or listed in an index. In library cataloging, genre/form terms are also used. http://library.wcsu.edu/people/reitz/ODLIS/odlis%20new.html

© Springer Nature Switzerland AG 2021
R. Verborgh et al. (Eds.): ESWC 2021 Satellite Events, LNCS 12739, pp. 33–37, 2021.
https://doi.org/10.1007/978-3-030-80418-3_6

of Congress Subject Headings (LCSH)[2] [4] according to Latvian language and terminology. The form/genre terms are adopted from the Faceted Application of Subject Terminology (FAST)[3] and Library of Congress Genre/Form terms (LCGFT)[4]. NLLSH has a thesaurus-like structure – it contains thesaurus relationships between terms: Broader Term (BT), Narrower Term (NT), Related Term (RT), and Used for (UF).

NLLSH authority records ensure a qualitative use of terms in the NLL electronic catalog and special collections, including digital collections. NLLSH authority data are also used by scientific, special, and public libraries in Latvia. NLLSH authority records are created according to international standards and are usable both nationally and internationally. They provide unified subject access and retrieval of various information resources in Latvian, English and other languages.

The development of information technologies, the diversity and digitization of library information resources, and the introduction of linked data are also introducing changes to authority data at NLL. This paper presents the linked data representation of the National Library of Latvia authority data consisting of topical heading, geographic name, and form/genre thesauri.

2 NLLSH Linked Data

In 2019, NLL began to enrich NLLSH authority records with external links to other linked data sources. The NLL topical terms dataset, in particular, contains many external links – 85% of its concepts have links to the LCSH dataset that is available as linked open data. The geographic name dataset contains external links to the Place Names Database of Latvia[5] (11% of concepts), Wikidata (5.3%) and Virtual International Authority File dataset (VIAF, 3.5% of concepts) [2]. The form/genre dataset contains external links to the FAST Linked Data dataset (21% of concepts), the Czech National Authority Database (11.7%) and the Library of Congress Genre/Form dataset (8%).

Examples of NLLSH authority records that are too specific and can not be found in LCSH or Wikidata are "Teņa diena" (Tenis' day, related to Latvian traditions and folklore) and "Composite amber threads" (specific to research publications).

The path from MARC 21 authority records to NLL authority linked data consists of three steps:

1) Enriching MARC 21 records;
2) Converting MARC records to SKOS concepts;
3) Publishing SKOS datasets as linked open data.

2.1 Enriching MARC 21 Data

The original dataset (in MARC 21 format) contains thesaurus relationships between its terms but these links use authority records' primary labels as keys. As a result, these links

---

[2] https://id.loc.gov/authorities/subjects.html

[3] http://fast.oclc.org/searchfast/

[4] https://id.loc.gov/authorities/genreForms.html

[5] http://vietvardi.lgia.gov.lv/

would be lost in the conversion process described in the next step, which expects records to be linked using authority record numbers. To preserve these links, we enriched MARC 21 records by adding unique record identifiers – record system numbers (MARC field 001) – whenever the record contained links to other records in the dataset. The original authority records created before 2020 do not contain information about the language of concept labels (preferred and alternative labels) which is an obstacle to the correct display of these labels in Skosmos. In order to resolve this shortcoming, we assigned language code "lv" (Latvian) to all preferred labels. This fixes the issue but may not always correctly match the labels' language. It remains future work to automatically determine label language.

2.2   Converting MARC 21 Data to SKOS

The datasets are converted to SKOS using the mc2skos application[6] that takes MARC/XML data as input and produces SKOS concepts in Turtle syntax. In order to interlink the resulting datasets mc2skos calls Skosify to infer skos:narrower and skos:related links[7]. Concepts are given URIs based on scheme parameters in mc2skos configuration using the following URI prefixes:

- Topical terms: http://dati.lnb.lv/onto/subject/
- Geographic names: http://dati.lnb.lv/onto/geo/
- Form/genre terms: http://dati.lnb.lv/onto/genre/

The resulting datasets contain 44'407 concepts for topical terms, 9'671 concepts for geographic names and 1'662 concepts for forms/genres.

Links from NLLSH to other datasets are represented using skos:closeMatch following the example of LCSH which represents most of its external links using this property. We decided not to use skos:exactMatch because the concepts in different datasets may change in time and as a result might not be exact matches any more.

2.3   Publishing SKOS Datasets

The datasets[8] are published using Skosmos – a web-based tool for browsing and publishing SKOS data [5]. According to Skosmos installation instructions[9] RDF data is loaded into a Fuseki RDF store and the resulting Skosmos concept pages are published on the web. Skosmos offers both a human-friendly view as an HTML page, machine-readable RDF data via its API and access to linked data using HTTP content negotiation[10]. We created a custom Skosmos plugin that enriches HTML pages with links to the original ALEPH library information system authority records.

---

[6] https://github.com/scriptotek/mc2skos/
[7] https://skosify.readthedocs.io/en/latest/
[8] http://dati.lnb.lv/onto/lv/
[9] https://github.com/NatLibFi/Skosmos/wiki/InstallTutorial
[10] https://github.com/NatLibFi/Skosmos/wiki/ServingLinkedData

Skosmos also shows information about concepts' external links and automatically retrieves labels of the linked concepts published as linked data (e.g. Library of Congress Subject Headings). Figure 1 displays an example of a Skosmos concept page with a link to LCSH linked data.

PREFERRED TERM	**Ontoloģijas (informācijas izguve) (lv)**
BROADER CONCEPT	Datu struktūras (datorzinātne) (lv)
ENTRY TERMS	*Ontologies (Information retrieval)*
NOTE	Source: Ilustrētā svešvārdu vārdnīca, 2005:
IDENTIFIER	LNC10-000123185 => ALEPH authority record
IN OTHER LANGUAGES	*Ontologies (Information retrieval)* **Ontoloģijas (informācijas izguve)** Latvian
URI	http://dati.lnb.lv/onto/subject/LNC10-000123185
Download this concept:	RDF/XML TURTLE JSON-LD Created 10/29/08, last modified 9/30/15
CLOSELY MATCHING CONCEPTS	Ontologies (Information retrieval) Library of Congress Subject Headings

Fig. 1. NLLSH linked data page about the concept "Ontologies" (https://dati.lnb.lv/onto/nllsh/en/page/LNC10-000123185).

Now that NLLSH has been published as linked data, it can be interlinked with the existing library linked open datasets. We plan to make use of the fact that NLLSH has links to LCSH and that LCSH is already linked to other library datasets – it has outgoing links to a number of linked data sources including Wikidata [1], FAST Linked Data[11] and the General Finnish Ontology YSO [3].

In the future, the published NLL datasets could be applied to interconnecting Latvia's cultural heritage information by describing museum and archive items with URIs from these datasets. Thus, the NLL ontology service could provide new possibilities for interoperability and data reuse for other Latvia's memory institutions and for memory institutions worldwide.

3   Conclusion

NLLSH authority data that forms the basis of the National Thesaurus of Latvia has been transformed into SKOS and published as linked data. The NLL linked authority data consists of 3 datasets: topical terms, geographic names, and form/genre terms. These linked authority datasets can be used for interlinking cultural heritage information, for example, by referring to their concepts not just from library information systems but also from other memory institutions such as archive and museum data. While preparing datasets for publishing as linked data, NLLSH data was enriched with linked record

---

[11] http://experimental.worldcat.org/fast/

identifiers and language codes. We plan to provide regular updates to NLLSH linked data and to publish a related dataset – Latvia's National Bibliography – as linked data. Future work includes exploring options for automated addition of language codes, adding links to various cultural heritage information systems, and linking to other external linked data sets.

Acknowledgments. This work was supported by the Latvian Council of Science project no. lzp-2019/1-0365 "Latvian Memory Institution Data in the Digital Space: Connecting Cultural Heritage".

References

1. Erxleben, F., Günther, M., Krötzsch, M., Mendez, J., Vrandečić, D.: Introducing wikidata to the linked data web. In: Mika, P., et al. (eds.) ISWC 2014. LNCS, vol. 8796, pp. 50–65. Springer, Cham (2014). https://doi.org/10.1007/978-3-319-11964-9_4
2. Hickey, T.B., Toves, J.: Managing ambiguity in VIAF. D-Lib Mag. **20**(7/8) (2014). https://doi.org/10.1045/july2014-hickey
3. Niininen, S., Nykyri, S., Suominen, O.: The future of metadata: open, linked, and multilingual – the YSO case. J. Doc. **73**(3), 451–465 (2017). https://doi.org/10.1108/JD-06-2016-0084
4. Summers, E., Isaac, A., Redding, C., Krech, D.: LCSH, SKOS and linked data. In: Proceedings of the International Conference on Dublin Core and Metadata Applications (DC 2008), Berlin, Germany, pp. 25–33 (2008)
5. Suominen, O., et al.: Publishing SKOS vocabularies with Skosmos. Manuscript submitted for review, June 2015. http://skosmos.org/publishing-skos-vocabularies-with-skosmos.pdf

Automatic Skill Generation for Knowledge Graph Question Answering

Maria Angela Pellegrino[✉], Mario Santoro, Vittorio Scarano,
and Carmine Spagnuolo

Dipartimento di Informatica, Università degli Studi di Salerno, Fisciano, Italy
{mapellegrino,vitsca,cspagnuolo}@unisa.it, m.santoro75@studenti.unisa.it

Abstract. Knowledge Graphs are a critical source for Question Answering, but their potential may be threatened due to the complexity of their query languages, such as SPARQL. On the opposite side, Virtual Assistants have witnessed an extraordinary interest as they enable users to pose questions in natural language. Many companies and researchers have combined Knowledge Graphs and Virtual Assistants, but no one has provided end-users with a generic methodology to generate extensions for automatically querying knowledge graphs. Thus, we propose a community shared software framework to create custom extensions to query knowledge graphs by virtual assistants, unlocking the potentialities of the Semantic Web technologies by bringing knowledge graphs in the "*pocket*" of everyone, accessible from smartphones or smart speakers.

Keywords: Question Answering · Knowledge Graphs · Virtual Assistant · Software framework

1 Introduction and Motivation

Knowledge Graphs (KGs), i.e., graph-structured knowledge bases, are fast becoming a key instrument in disseminating and exploiting knowledge, but their potential might be threatened by the complexity of their query languages, such as SPARQL, too challenging for lay users [2,16].

Natural Language (NL) interfaces can mitigate these issues, enabling more intuitive data access and unlocking the potentialities of KGs to the majority of end-users [10] by losing in expressiveness while gaining in usability. NL interfaces may provide lay users with question-answering (QA) features where users can adopt their terminology and receive a concise answer. Researchers argue that multi-modal communication with virtual characters is a promising direction in accessing knowledge [4]. Thus, many companies and researchers have combined KGs and Virtual Assistants (VAs) [1,5,8,9,12], but no one has provided end-users with a generic methodology to automatically generate extensions to query KGs.

To fill this gap, we propose a community shared software framework (a.k.a. generator) that enables lay users to create ready-to-use custom extensions for

© Springer Nature Switzerland AG 2021
R. Verborgh et al. (Eds.): ESWC 2021 Satellite Events, LNCS 12739, pp. 38–43, 2021.
https://doi.org/10.1007/978-3-030-80418-3_7

performing question-answering over knowledge graphs (KGQA) for any cloud provider. Our proposal may unlock the Semantic Web technologies potentialities by bringing KGs in the *"pocket"* of everyone, accessible from smartphones or smart speakers. It is the first attempt, to the best of our knowledge, to empower lay users in actively creating VA extensions by requiring little/no technical skills in query languages and VA extension development.

2 Related Work

KGQA is a research field widely explored in the last years [6,7] and DBpedia gains a particular interest in being accessed by friendly user interfaces [13,14,17].

KGQA requires matching an input question to a subgraph. The simplest case requires matching a single KG triple, and it is also called simple QA [3]. In contrast to it, the task of complex QA requires matching more than one triple in the KG [15]. We present an approach general enough to deal with both simple and more complex queries. At the moment, we mainly cover patterns related to single triples enhanced by class refinement, numeric filters, and sorting options.

Focusing on KGQA in VA, it is natively offered in well-established personal assistants, like Google Assistant and Alexa, which provides users with content from generic KGs (Google Search and Microsoft Bing, respectively). Moreover, the Semantic Web community invested in increasing VA capabilities by providing QA over open KGs (e.g., Haase et al. [8] proposed an Alexa skill to query Wikidata by a generic approach) or in domain-specific applications (e.g., Krishnan et al. [11] explored the NASA System Engineering domain while Machidon et al. [12] and Anelli et al. [1] focus on the Cultural Heritage (CH) domain). While these approaches are demonstrated on custom but specific KGs, we propose a generic approach and we openly publish VA extensions for general-purpose KGs (e.g., DBpedia and Wikidata) and CH KGs (use cases are available on GitHub[1]).

3 Virtual Assistant Extensions Generator

The proposed generator automatically creates VA extensions performing KGQA by requiring little/no technical skills in programming and query languages. It provides users with the opportunity to customize and generate ready-to-use VA extensions. The implemented process is graphically represented in Fig. 1.

The generator takes as input a configuration file that defines the SPARQL endpoint of interest, the VA extension language (`en` and `it` are supported at the moment), the invocation name (i.e., the skill wake-up word), and the list of desired intents. The implemented intents are tailored towards SPARQL constructs, and they cover `SELECT` and `ASK` queries, `class specification`, numeric `filters`, `order by` to get the superlative and path traversal. We model each supported SPARQL query template as an intent. Each intent is modelled by a set of utterances and can be completed by slot values. A custom slot represents each

---

[1] https://github.com/mariaangelapellegrino/virtual_assistant_generator.

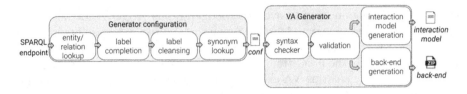

Fig. 1. Process implemented in the proposed generator to create a Virtual Assistant extension to perform question-answering over knowledge graphs.

slot, and it requires the specification of a (complete or partial) set of values that it can assume. Therefore, users can specify entity and relation dictionaries to customize the set of values, and the mapping between entity and relation labels and their URIs. The generator checks the syntactical correctness of the configuration file during the `syntax checker` phase; validates the semantic correctness of the configuration during the `validation`; during the `interaction model generation`, it creates the `interaction_model.json` which contains configured intents, its utterances and the slot values as defined in the configuration file, while during the `back-end generation` phase, it produces the `back-end` (as a ZIP file) containing the back-end logic implementation. If any error occurs, the generator immediately stops and returns a message reporting the occurred error. If the configuration is properly provided, the generator returns a folder entitled as the skill wake-up word containing the `interaction model` as a JSON file and the `back-end` Node.js code as a ZIP file. The generated skill is ready to be used, i.e., it can automatically be uploaded on Amazon developer[2] and Amazon AWS (see footnote 2), respectively. It corresponds to manually created skills, but our proposal may reduce required technical competencies and development time.

According to users' skills, they can provide the generator with a custom configuration file. Otherwise, they can exploit the `generator configuration` component that takes as input the SPARQL endpoint of interest, automatically retrieves both classes and relations labels and their URIs, and returns the configuration file that can be directly used to initialize the VA generator.

Each phase is kept separate by satisfying the modularity requirement, and it is implemented as an abstract module to enable extension opportunities easily. The actual version ($v1.0$), freely available on GitHub (see footnote 1) is provided with a command-line interface and supports the Amazon Alexa provider.

As a future direction, we aim to enhance our generator by providing it with a (simple) graphical user interface and improve the intent identification, by using a Named Entity Recognition and Relation Extraction mechanism, and performing a disambiguation approach during the linking phase.

---

[2] Links for Alexa skill deployment: developer.amazon.com and aws.amazon.com.

4   Virtual Assistant Extension Usage

In a VA-based process (see Fig. 2), users pose a question in NL by pronouncing or typing it via a VA app or dedicated device (e.g., Alexa app/device).

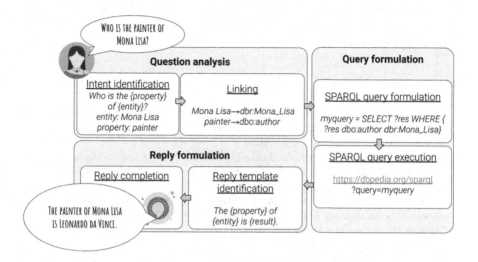

Fig. 2. Process to use VA extension for KGQA.

VAs are provided with an NL processing component to analyse questions. Thus, they perform intent identification to recognize the intent that matches the user query and solve the intent slots. Then, the back-end has to perform the (entity and relation) linking task, i.e., determine the URIs corresponding to the used labels. It can be accomplished by consulting a lookup dictionary or by calling an API service. Once completed the *question analysis* step, we can move to the *query formulation* phase. The back-end has to recognize the SPARQL pattern that fulfills the user request, formulate SPARQL query, and then run it over the SPARQL endpoint. Once results are returned, the VA extension can perform the *reply formulation* step, i.e., the reply template is identified and completed by actual results. Finally, the reply is returned to the user.

5   Demonstration

As a demonstration example[3], we show that users can automatically create an Alexa skill for querying well-known KGs, such as DBpedia. Thus, we see how to exploit the `generator configuration` and the `VA generator` components, we discuss the required steps to upload the skill on Alexa service providers, and we demonstrate the skill in practice by posing questions on Alexa Developer

---

[3] Demo link: http://automatic_skill_generation_for_KGQA-DEMO-ESWC2021.mp4.

Console. The demo can reply to questions like *Who is the creator of goofy? How tall is Michael Jordan? Can you define Madama Butterfly?* to retrieve the object value of a KG triple; *How many programming languages are there?* as a special case of class refinement; *Which movie has producer equals to Hal Roach?* to retrieve the subject of KG triples; *Which library has established before 1400?* representing of a numeric filter; *Which is the river with maximum length?* modeling superlatives; *Can you check if Goofy has Walt Disney as creator?* representing an ask query.

References

1. Anelli, V.W., Noia, T.D., Sciascio, E.D., Ragone, A.: Anna: a virtual assistant to interact with puglia digital library. In: Proceedings of the 27th Italian Symposium on Advanced Database Systems (2019)
2. Bellini, P., Nesi, P., Venturi, A.: Linked open graph: browsing multiple SPARQL entry points to build your own LOD views. J. Vis. Lang. Comput. **25**(6), 703–716 (2014)
3. Bordes, A., Usunier, N., Chopra, S., Weston, J.: Large-scale simple question answering with memory networks. CoRR abs/1506.02075 (2015)
4. Cimiano, P., Kopp, S.: Accessing the web of data through embodied virtual characters. Semantic Web **1**, 83–88 (2010)
5. Cuomo, S., Colecchia, G., Cola, V., Chirico, U.: A virtual assistant in cultural heritage scenarios. Concurr. Comput. Pract. Experience **33**, e5331 (2019)
6. De Donato, R., Garofalo, M., Malandrino, D., Pellegrino, M.A., Petta, A., Scarano, V.: QueDI: from knowledge graph querying to data visualization. In: Blomqvist, E., et al. (eds.) SEMANTICS 2020. LNCS, vol. 12378, pp. 70–86. Springer, Cham (2020). https://doi.org/10.1007/978-3-030-59833-4_5
7. Diefenbach, D., Giménez-García, J., Both, A., Singh, K., Maret, P.: QAnswer KG: designing a portable question answering system over RDF data. In: Harth, A., et al. (eds.) ESWC 2020. LNCS, vol. 12123, pp. 429–445. Springer, Cham (2020). https://doi.org/10.1007/978-3-030-49461-2_25
8. Haase, P., Nikolov, A., Trame, J., Kozlov, A., Herzig, D.M.: Alexa, ask Wikidata! Voice interaction with knowledge graphs using Amazon Alexa. In: ISWC (2017)
9. Jalaliniya, S., Pederson, T.: Designing wearable personal assistants for surgeons: an egocentric approach. IEEE Pervasive Comput. **14**(3), 22–31 (2015)
10. Kaufmann, E., Bernstein, A.: How useful are natural language interfaces to the semantic web for casual end-users? In: Aberer, K., et al. (eds.) ASWC/ISWC - 2007. LNCS, vol. 4825, pp. 281–294. Springer, Heidelberg (2007). https://doi.org/10.1007/978-3-540-76298-0_21
11. Krishnan, J., Coronado, P., Reed, T.: SEVA: a systems engineer's virtual assistant. In: AAAI Spring Symposium: Combining Machine Learning with Knowledge Engineering (2019)
12. Machidon, O.M., Tavčar, A., Gams, M., Duguleanã, M.: Culturalerica: a conversational agent improving the exploration of European cultural heritage. J. Cult. Herit. **41**, 152–165 (2020)
13. Mynarz, J., Zeman, V.: DB-quiz: a DBpedia-backed knowledge game. In: Proceedings of the 12th International Conference on Semantic Systems, pp. 121–124 (2016)

14. Singh, K., Lytra, I., Radhakrishna, A.S., Shekarpour, S., Vidal, M.E., Lehmann, J.: No one is perfect: analysing the performance of question answering components over the DBpedia knowledge graph. J. Web Semant. **65**, 100594 (2020)

15. Trivedi, P., Maheshwari, G., Dubey, M., Lehmann, J.: LC-QuAD: a corpus for complex question answering over knowledge graphs. In: d'Amato, C., et al. (eds.) ISWC 2017. LNCS, vol. 10588, pp. 210–218. Springer, Cham (2017). https://doi.org/10.1007/978-3-319-68204-4_22

16. Vargas, H., Buil-Aranda, C., Hogan, A., López, C.: RDF explorer: a visual SPARQL query builder. In: Ghidini, C., et al. (eds.) ISWC 2019. LNCS, vol. 11778, pp. 647–663. Springer, Cham (2019). https://doi.org/10.1007/978-3-030-30793-6_37

17. Vega-Gorgojo, G.: Clover quiz: a trivia game powered by DBpedia. Semantic Web **10**(4), 779–793 (2019)

Converting UML-Based Ontology Conceptualizations to OWL with Chowlk

Serge Chávez-Feria$^{(\boxtimes)}$ ⓘ, Raúl García-Castro ⓘ, and María Poveda-Villalón ⓘ

Ontology Engineering Group, Universidad Politécnica de Madrid, Madrid, Spain
serge.chavez.feria@upm.es, {rgarcia,mpoveda}@fi.upm.es

Abstract. During the ontology conceptualization activity, developers usually generate preliminary models of the ontology in the form of diagrams. Such models drive the ontology implementation activity, where the models are encoded using an implementation language, typically by means of ontology editors. The goal of this demo is to take advantage of the developed ontology conceptualizations in order to accelerate the ontology implementation activity. For doing so we present Chowlk, a converter to transform digital UML-based ontology diagrams into OWL. This system aims at supporting users in the generation of the first versions of ontologies by reusing the ontology conceptualization output.

Keywords: Ontology engineering · Ontology conceptualization · Ontology implementation

1 Introduction

One important step in ontology development is the conceptualization one, during which the ontology development team defines a set of concepts and properties to represent the knowledge of an specific domain. Often, this conceptualization is materialized in a diagram that displays the ontology elements and their connections. From this model, the ontology implementation is carried out normally using an ontology editor, encoding the model in OWL. In this process the diagram is in most of the cases only used as a guideline to manually implement the ontology. To address this issue, some tools have been proposed to allow the graphical creation or modification of ontologies [2–5].

The present work aims at leveraging the above-mentioned diagrams in order to allow for a smoother transition from the conceptualization activity to the actual implementation, that is transforming XML diagrams following a UML-based ontology visual notation into OWL. For doing so, rather than building a graphical ontology editor, the process builds on top of a well-adopted system such as diagrams.net which allows collaborative and synchronous edition of the conceptualization models.

This work has been supported by the BIMERR project funded from the European Union's Horizon 2020 research and innovation programme under grant agreement no. 820621.

R. Verborgh et al. (Eds.): ESWC 2021 Satellite Events, LNCS 12739, pp. 44–48, 2021.
https://doi.org/10.1007/978-3-030-80418-3_8

2   Chowlk Features

Chowlk is a web application that takes as input an ontology conceptualization created with diagrams.net and generates the OWL implementation. The service is available online[1] (See Fig. 1) and the source code is shared in a GitHub repository[2] under the Apache 2.0 license.

The conceptualization should follow the Chowlk visual notation[3] which is also provided as a diagrams.net library[4] to allow users to easily reuse the correct shapes to avoid problems during the transformation and save to time during the conceptualization.

The converter is able to identify concepts, object properties, datatype properties, and restrictions between those elements. Also, the converter identifies ontology metadata, namespaces and the prefixes being used in the model, due to specific blocks dedicated to this type of information. Labels to each ontology element are added during the detection process. Once the XML diagram is loaded into the system, Chowlk starts searching for all the ontology elements in the conceptualization ignoring shapes not included in the specification. After the detection and creation of the corresponding associations between the ontological elements, Chowlk proceeds to write the implementation using the OWL language. Finally, the ontology is provided in two downloadable formats: Turtle and RDF/XML (see Fig. 2).

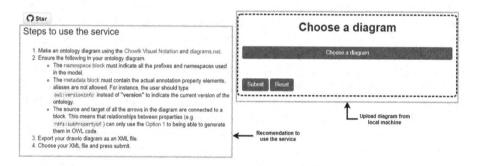

Fig. 1. Screenshot excerpt of Chowlk home page

---

[1] https://chowlk.linkeddata.es.
[2] https://github.com/oeg-upm/Chowlk.
[3] https://chowlk.linkeddata.es/chowlk_spec.
[4] https://github.com/oeg-upm/chowlk_spec/blob/master/chowlk-drawio-library.xml.

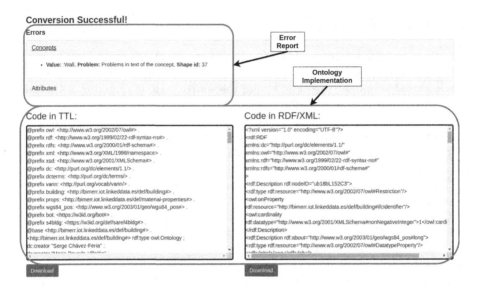

Fig. 2. Screenshot of the web GUI showing the output serializations.

3   Architecture

The architecture of the Chowlk converter is shown in Fig. 3. It has been developed as a single page web application where the user can upload its ontology conceptualization and the converter returns the corresponding OWL ontology. The conceptualization diagram should be provided as an XML file including only the parts of the diagram intended to be translated. Once the conceptualization is parsed, using standard XML Python libraries, the converter proceeds with the detection of the ontology elements inside the diagram. The detection module analyzes the fields inside the XML structure of each shape in order to make the appropriate mapping with the OWL elements. The information inside the XML should follow the Chowlk visual notation that provides the specification with respect to the type and style of the shapes to be used. Shapes that do not follow the visual notation are discarded during the transformation process and passed to the writing module as an error report.

The association module performs the connection between the ontology elements identified by the detection module. For each concept, the module iterates over the object properties and datatype properties in the conceptualization and identifies which ones are connected physically in the diagram. Afterwards, OWL restrictions are detected between the concepts and the properties associated previously by identifying keywords such as "some" or "all" in the properties text. If no restriction is specified then the association is discarded even if the elements are connected. The reasoning behind this is that in the diagram a modeller can make recommendations about which properties are expected to be used for a concept but if it is not formalized, by means of a class restriction (universal, existential or cardinality), it has no effect on the OWL implementation further than the declaration of the class and the property.

Finally, the writing module receives the information associated from the previous module and performs the serialization of the model into two different formats (Turtle and RDF/OWL) which are presented to the user through the web interface. The output interface also displays the possible errors that the diagram could contain, indicating not only the problematic shapes but also the possible cause of the problem.

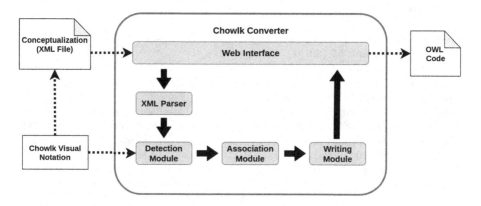

Fig. 3. Chowlk architecture.

4   Demonstration

During the demonstration,[5] some examples will be developed to show the participants how to use Chowlk. First, the conceptualization will be developed using diagrams.net following the Chowlk visual notation. The shapes for the construction of the model will be provided as a diagrams.net library that can be loaded into the diagramming tool. The final conceptualization will be exported an uploaded into the Chowlk web app that will generate the corresponding OWL implementation. The GUI will return the ontology in two formats: RDF/XML and Turtle. As a final step, the ontology will be uploaded into Protégé to demonstrate the syntax correctness of the exported implementation.

5   Conclusions and Future Work

This paper presents the Chowlk converter that facilitates the ontology development process by leveraging the ontology conceptualization diagrams to transform them into OWL. The system is currently being used within the authors research group[6] and also by researchers from other institutions[7]. Next steps involve the

---

[5] A demo video of Chowlk is available at https://youtu.be/1oF0qDhParA.

[6] See the BIMERR European project https://bimerr.iot.linkeddata.es/ or contributions to the W3C WoT-discovery task https://tinyurl.com/w653me9f.

[7] http://mired.uspceu.es/microrrelatos/.

announcement and promotion of the system to get feedback from users. Additionally, we plan to develop a REST API so that Chowlk can be easily integrated within third-party software such as OnToology [1]. It is also planned to develop a plugin for diagrams.net in order to embed the ontology generation feature into the diagramming tool. Besides, we plan to integrate the prefix.cc[8] service to suggest an URI for prefixes not declared. Including support for including additional metadata, such as comments and labels, is also being explored.

References

1. Alobaid, A., et al.: Automating ontology engineering support activities with OnToology. J. Web Semant. **57** (2019)
2. Barzdins, J., Barzdins, G., Cerans, K., Liepins, R., Sprogis, A.: UML style graphical notation and editor for OWL 2. Perspect. Bus. Inform. Res. **64**, 102–114 (2010). https://doi.org/10.1007/978-3-642-16101-8_9
3. Dudás, M., Lohmann, S., Svátek, V., Pavlov, D.: Ontology visualization methods and tools: a survey of the state of the art. Knowl. Eng. Rev. **33**, e10:1–e10:39 (2018)
4. Weiten, M.: Ontostudio as a ontology engineering environment. Semant. Knowl. Manage. 51–60 (2009). https://doi.org/10.1007/978-3-540-88845-1_5
5. Wiens, V., Lohmann, S., Auer, S.: Webvowl editor: device-independent visual ontology modeling. In: International Semantic Web Conference 2180 (2018)

---

[8] http://prefix.cc/.

Monetising Resources on a SoLiD Pod Using Blockchain Transactions

Hendrik Becker⬤, Hung Vu⬤, Anett Katzenbach⬤, Christoph H.-J. Braun⬤,
and Tobias Käfer$^{(\boxtimes)}$⬤

Institute AIFB, Karlsruhe Institute of Technology (KIT), Karlsruhe, Germany
{ukuiq,ublxf,ususm,uvdsl}@student.kit.edu, tobias.kaefer@kit.edu

Abstract. Our demo showcases a system that allows users to provide access to web resources in exchange for payments via the blockchain. The system enables users to create offers for their resources or buy access rights for resources belonging to other users. Access rights can be granted only for a limited amount of time. We built our system as SoLiD Pods and Apps: We developed two server modules for SoLiD Pods that automatically (1) grant access for valid payments via the blockchain and (2) remove expired access rights. On top, we developed a SoLiD App that allows to offer resources, browse and request offered resources, and make payments via the blockchain.

Video http://people.aifb.kit.edu/co1683/2021/eswc-demo-solibra/#v
Code https://github.com/bright-fox/SolidBlockchain

1 Introduction

In today's web, companies keep user data in centralised platforms, outside of the control of the user. Users are thus unable to control, use and profit from their own data. Multiple recent projects want to tackle this issue: First, Jack Dorsey, the CEO of Twitter, a microblogging platform, recently announced Twitter's effort of re-decentralisation based on decentralised data and open standards for the benefit of all Twitter users[1]▲In addition, he mentions blockchain technology as one potential building block, especially regarding monetisation.

Second, Tim Berners-Lee's on-going endeavour to re-decentralise the web manifests in the Social Linked Data project (SoLiD). The SoLiD specification[2] provides the basis for decoupling data and applications, while ensuring data privacy through user-defined access control. Users store their data in personal online data storages (Pods) and define access control on their resources as they wish.

Also in the decentralised spirit, blockchain technologies, as pioneered by Bitcoin [5], allow for peer-to-peer transactions of money. In the context of those

---

[1] https://twitter.com/jack/status/1204766078468911106.
[2] https://solid.github.io/specification/.

© Springer Nature Switzerland AG 2021
R. Verborgh et al. (Eds.): ESWC 2021 Satellite Events, LNCS 12739, pp. 49–53, 2021.
https://doi.org/10.1007/978-3-030-80418-3_9

decentralised technologies, we built a proof-of-concept that is set in a decentralised web scenario and allows for trading access to web resources via the blockchain.

Our approach is not limited to a specific use-case or specific types of resources: As long as a resource can be stored on a SoLiD Pod, users can monetise it. Users decide, if and under which conditions they are willing to share their resources by specifying a price and a duration for which access will be granted.

In this demo, we showcase:

- A general approach to enable users to monetise digital resources stored on SoLiD Pods using blockchain transactions.
- An implementation[3] that automates access control management based on payment and time.

We built our demonstration as SoLiD Apps that communicate with SoLiD Pods and the Ethereum network, a blockchain implementation. The server part of our implementation builds on SoLiD's semantic access control (ACL) rules to automatically update resource access based on payments and elapsed time. Resource access is granted upon incoming payments and revoked when access rights expire. We use Resource Description Framework (RDF) to model resource offers, purchases and user notifications.

This paper is structured as follows: First, we give a short overview on related work. Next, we present the system's architecture and cover briefly data modeling. Then, we showcase a walkthrough for the demonstrator. Finally, we conclude.

2   Related Work

We work in the intersection of SoLiD, blockchain, and monetisation on the web. Seminal writings in each area include an early description about the SoLiD project [4], foundational articles about Bitcoin [5] and Ethereum [2] as two blockchain implementations that allow for peer-to-peer transactions, and the recent Patreon platform[4] for selling and buying digital artistic work on the web.

The intersection is laden with visions, and less with solutions: [8] presents the vision of an app for musicians to sell their songs to others. The app should use SoLiD for data management, and a blockchain facilitate payments. Our demo is an implementation of a more general version of this idea. [3] presents the vision of a data marketplace to fund the maintenance of the infrastructure for decentrally provided Linked Data. Our demo is not about a marketplace as central intermediary but instead about using blockchain for decentralised payment. We found descriptions of solutions only where the solution is in the intersection blockchain+SoLiD, without the monetisation aspect. Consider for instance [6] who examine different approaches in SoLiD-based applications using blockchains and focus on the combination of the two technologies to make data

---

[3] A link to the code can be found on page 1.

[4] https://www.patreon.com/.

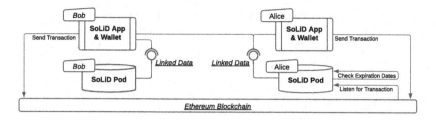

Fig. 1. The system architecture. One SoLiD Pod and wallet per user.

verifiable through transparency without losing data sovereignty. Similarly, [1] uses Linked Data and the blockchain for verification of data along a supply chain.

Our approach uses Web Access Control (WAC), the current default technology from SoLiD, as basis to provide simple access control. There are more sophisticated approaches, which, e.g., also allow for usage control, such as the Open Digital Rights Language (ODRL)[5]. In previous work, ODRL has been proposed as basis for a Policy-Driven Linked Data Market, where Linked Data can be offered and requested, and agreements can be described and enforced [7].

3   System Architecture

Figure 1 illustrates the components of this demo. The demo set-up consists in a SoLiD App with two UIs for buyer and seller of a resource. Those UIs both consume SoLiD Pods and have access to the Ethereum blockchain to send transactions. The SoLiD Pod of the buyer maintains the WebID and wallet address of the buyer and a list of pending purchasing requests. The SoLiD Pod of the seller maintains the WebID and wallet address of the seller, the resources offered next to their descriptions and ACLs. This Pod has specialised modules to (1) access the blockchain to listen for transactions and (2) modify the ACLs according to time and the transactions.

4   Data Modeling

We model the data in RDF using terms from a range of vocabularies: We use (1) schema.org[6] to model offers and pending resource purchases including price and corresponding currency; (2) OWL Time[7] to describe the duration of the access to resources; (3) Linked Data Notifications[8] (LDN) for notifications about incoming payments; (4) EthOn[9] to describe (a) blockchain transactions such that

---

[5] https://www.w3.org/TR/odrl-model/.
[6] https://schema.org/.
[7] https://www.w3.org/TR/owl-time/.
[8] https://www.w3.org/TR/ldn/.
[9] https://ethon.consensys.net/.

a resource owner can verify the validity of the purchase request, and (b) to link the address of the cryptocurrency wallet to the user's SoLiD profile; (5) WAC[10] to define ACL rules including read, write, and append rights for specific agents or agent groups, which we augment with OWL Time for durations.

5   Walkthrough for the Demonstrator

Our demo shows how our system can be used by Alice who offers a resource, and by Bob who buys time-restricted access to it, cf. the video linked on Page 1.

Resource and offer creation. Using the UI, Alice uploads a resource to be sold to her SoLiD Pod and defines the resource's price and access duration. The corresponding offer with the defined conditions is automatically created on her SoLid Pod. For now, only Alice has access rights for this resource.

Offer retrieval. Bob uses his UI to browse all available offers for resources from Alice on her SoLiD Pod. The UI filters out resources, for which Bob has a pending request or which Bob has already bought.

Resource purchase. Bob selects an offer and sends a transaction to Alice's wallet via the blockchain with the specified price. The transaction also contains the offered resource's URI, Bob's WebID, the price and duration. This enables Alice to verify Bob's blockchain transaction for the purchase. The UI automatically sends an LDN to Alice to inform her of the purchase and stores a pending resource purchase in Bob's SoLiD Pod for record keeping.

Access grant. Alice's Pod runs a server module, which continuously monitors the LDNs in her inbox for access requests for her offers. The LDNs are compared to the information of offers in the Pod and transactions on the blockchain. If the information from the offer, the transaction and the LDN matches, the access rights of Bob are added to the ACL of the resource. Approving of access requests can also be done by Alice manually through the access control panel of the user interface.

Access rights housekeeping. Alice's Pod runs another server module that continuously checks for and removes expired access rights.

6   Conclusion

In this demo, we presented a general approach to enable monetisation of web resources stored on SoLiD Pods using blockchain transactions. Our implementation automatically grants access rights upon incoming payments and revokes expired access rights. Of course, SoLiD Pod extensions like our ACL-updating server module need to be trusted by the trading parties. In particular, the party running the Pod software needs to be trusted, who would be responsible for deploying the module. In a completely decentralised web setting, this trust is not trivial to establish. Just as there is no certification process to go through

---

[10] https://www.w3.org/wiki/WebAccessControl.

before a web server implementation may be connected to the internet, there is no certification process for SoLiD Pod software. Even if the code had been certified, it needs to be made sure that the code eventually executed is the same as the certified code. Code signing has been proposed to deal with such issues. In the physical world, governments require organisations in the financial business (e.g. banks) to go through a vetting process before they are allowed to offer the services and take part in the federated financial services system. Similarly, in the virtual world, if your web server uses some (centralised/federated) payment service (e.g. MasterCard) on the web, you need to show to the respective financial service provider that you adhere to security and privacy guidelines. Also, if you commercially trade on the web in Europe you need to follow the national implementation of the EU directive 2000/31/EG about e-commerce, which for instance in some countries requires you to state your name and address such that, e.g. customers can lay charges against you, and this possibility introduces some trust. For a SoLiD Pod hosting provider this could mean that users need to go through a know-your-customer process before users may use the services.

References

1. Braun, C., Käfer, T.: Verifying the integrity of hyperlinked information using linked data and smart contracts. In: Acosta, M., Cudré-Mauroux, P., Maleshkova, M., Pellegrini, T., Sack, H., Sure-Vetter, Y. (eds.) SEMANTiCS 2019. LNCS, vol. 11702, pp. 376–390. Springer, Cham (2019). https://doi.org/10.1007/978-3-030-33220-4_28
2. Buterin, V.: Ethereum white paper (2013). https://ethereum.org/en/whitepaper/
3. Grubenmann, T., Dell'Aglio, D., Bernstein, A., Moor, D., Seuken, S.: Decentralizing the semantic web: who will pay to realize it? In: Proceedings of the Workshop on Decentralizing the Semantic Web (DeSemWeb) at the 16th International Semantic Web Conference (ISWC) (2017)
4. Mansour, E., et al.: A demonstration of the solid platform for social web applications. In: Proceedings of Posters and Demos at the 25th International Conference on World Wide Web (WWW) (2016)
5. Nakamoto, S.: Bitcoin: A Peer-to-Peer Electronic Cash System (2008). https://bitcoin.org/bitcoin.pdf
6. Ramachandran, M., Chowdhury, N., Third, A., Domingue, J., Quick, K., Bachler, M.: Towards complete decentralised verification of data with confidentiality: different ways to connect solid pods and blockchain. In: Proceedings of the Decentralised Web Workshop at the 29th Web Conference (WWW) (2020)
7. Steyskal, S., Kirrane, S.: If you can't enforce it, contract it: enforceability in Policy-Driven (Linked) Data Markets. In: Proceedings of Posters and Demos at the 11th International Conference on Semantic Systems (SEMANTiCS) (2015)
8. Story, H.: The Hyper-Music App (2018). https://medium.com/@bblfish/the-hyper-music-app-aed2be2390a7

Towards Scientific Data Synthesis Using Deep Learning and Semantic Web

Alsayed Algergawy$^{(\boxtimes)}$ ⓘ, Hamdi Hamed ⓘ, and Birgitta König-Ries ⓘ

Heinz-Nixdorf Chair for Distributed Information Systems,
Institute for Computer Science, University of Jena, Jena, Germany
{alsayed.algergawy,hamdi.hamed,birgitta.koenig-ries}@uni-jena.de

Abstract. One of the added values of long running and large scale collaborative projects is the ability to answer complex research questions based on the comprehensive set of data provided by their central repositories. In practice, however, finding data in such a repository to answer a specific question often proves to be a demanding task even for project scientists. In this paper, we aim to ease this task, thereby enabling cross-cutting analyses. To achieve that we introduce a new data analysis and summarization approach combining semantic web and machine learning approaches. In particular, the proposed approach makes use of the capability of machine learning to categorize a given dataset into a domain topic and to extract hidden links between its data attributes and data attributes from other datasets. The proposed approach has been developed in the frame of CRC AquaDiva (http://www.aquadiva.uni-jena.de/) and has been applied to its datasets.

1 Introduction

The Collaborative Research Center (CRC) AquaDiva is a large collaborative project spanning a variety of domains including biology, geology, chemistry, and computer science with the common goal to better understand the Earth's critical zone. Datasets collected within AquaDiva, like those of many other cross-institutional, cross-domain research projects, are complex and difficult to reuse since they are highly diverse and heterogeneous [2,10]. This limits the dataset accessibility to the few people who were either involved in creating the datasets or have spent a significant amount of time aiming to understand them. This is even true for scientists working in other parts of the same project. They, too, will need time to figure out the major theme of unfamiliar datasets. We believe that dataset analysis and summarization can be used as an elegant way to provide a concise overview of an entire dataset. This makes it possible to explore in depth datasets of potential interest, only [7–9].

Most previous work on data summarization focuses on text summarization [4], while few works only are pivoted to summarizing tabular data [7,9]. Most of them focus on schema summarization, which provides an overview of a schema with a set of representative attributes [8]. Even though there are a

© Springer Nature Switzerland AG 2021
R. Verborgh et al. (Eds.): ESWC 2021 Satellite Events, LNCS 12739, pp. 54–59, 2021.
https://doi.org/10.1007/978-3-030-80418-3_10

number of approaches creating a summarization of instances of a table instead of schema elements [6,7], they ignore the context of the dataset, i.e., they deal with the dataset independent from other datasets in the same data repository. This makes it difficult to find related datasets. In contrast, we aim to summarize and link datasets thereby enabling cross-cutting analyses. To this end, we develop an approach that semantically classifies data attributes of scientific datasets (tabular data) based on a combination of semantic web and deep learning. This classification contributes to summarizing individual datasets, but also to linking them to others. We view this as an important building block for a larger data summarization system. We believe that figuring out the subject of a dataset is an important and basic step in data summarization. To this end, the proposed approach categorizes a given dataset into a domain topic. With this topic, we then extract hidden links between different datasets in the repository. The proposed approach has two main phases: 1) *off-line* to train and build a classification model using a supervised deep learning using convolution layers and 2) *on-line* making use of the pre-trained model to classify datasets into the learned categories. With this, we (i) allocate the dataset into a set of dataset topics called *domain signatures*, and (ii) locate hidden links between the dataset and other datasets in the same data repository. To demonstrate the applicability of the approach, we analyzed and synthesized datasets from the AquaDiva Data Portal[1].

2   Proposed Approach

Over the last few years, convolutional networks have been successfully used for numerous classification tasks. It thus seemed natural to explore whether they could be useful in our dataset classification task, too. We faced two main challenges: First, we needed to decide which information contained in a dataset was most likely to contribute to the classification. The second was how to encode this information in such a way that on the one hand it would be suitable input to a CNN and on the other hand could be done with reasonable effort.

To address the first challenge, let us take a closer look at datasets: A dataset is defined as a tuple of primary data and metadata organized for a specific purpose. Each tuple in the primary data is a collection of data cells containing data values (called *data points*) [1]. The metadata contains information about, e.g., the data owner, data curators, the methodology used to produce primary data, etc. The primary data represents the actual data organized according to a specific structure, called *data structure*. Each data structure consists of a set of data attributes, each data attribute has a name, datatype, (optional) unit, description, as well as a semantic annotation based on a domain ontology. In the context of dataset analysis and summarization, this annotation is an important basis. Consider as an example, two datasets DS_1 and DS_2 stored in the AquaDiva data repository. Almost all data attributes of available datasets in that repository are annotated using the

---

[1] https://addp.uni-jena.de/.

AquaDiva ontology ($ADOn$) as the domain specific ontology. The first dataset DS_1 contains `weather and soil monitoring` data. It has a data structure with 50 data attributes including *"soil temperature"* annotated with the concepts soil (http://purl.obolibrary.org/obo/ENVO_00001998) and characteristic temperature (http://purl.obolibrary.org/obo/PATO_0000146). The second dataset DS_2 provides information about `soil moisture` in the Hainich forest. DS_2 has a data structure with 13 data attributes. The *"mean_theta_forestbottom"* data attribute is also annotated with the concept soil and the characteristic soil moisture (http://www.aquadiva.uni-jena.de/ad-ontology/ad-ontology.0.0/ad-ontology-characteristics.owl#SoilMoisture). Analysing the dataset annotation, a possible relationship of the two datasets DS_1 and DS_2 can be determined. Based on these considerations, we argue that data attributes are the most important parts of the dataset and the data preparation process will take place around them. Furthermore, metadata provides an important source for understanding and interpreting datasets. Therefore, constructing a new structure via data preparation is mainly based on data attributes and metadata. We gathered all information related to data attributes, where for each data attribute we consider *name, datatype, unit, data points* attached to the data attribute as well as its *semantic annotation*. Furthermore, we use the dataset title contained in the metadata as textual representation of the dataset.

With respect to the second challenge, we took the following approach: Convolutional networks are fundamentally geared towards image data, (i.e., matrices with size $n \times m$) and perform feature extraction and classification via hidden layers [5]. We therefore decided to experiment with a very straightforward encoding. We basically take "photos" of relevant parts of the dataset containing the information described above. More precisely, an image is generated for each data attribute. Figure 1 illustrates the *"Air temperature_mean"* data attributes from the *"Weather and soil data monitoring"* along with its annotation, data type (decimal), unit (Celsius), and 30 data points.

Together, this results in the approach shown in Fig. 2, with the *model building (training)* and *model deployment (operating)* phases. In the following, we describe the main steps of each phase.

Data Preparation. The main objective of this component is to prepare the large number of heterogeneous datasets for analysis. It is needed both during the model building (*training phase*) and the model deployment (*operating phase*) to convert each dataset into a structure suitable for the next component, *image generation*. To this end, we propose a new structure that combines the selected features described above from the dataset into a single container.

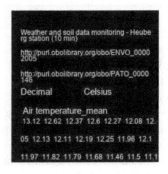

Fig. 1. Image content

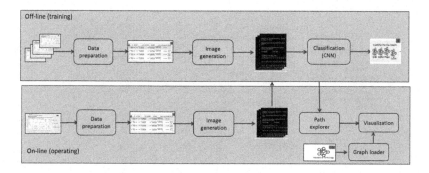

Fig. 2. Framework architecture

Image Generation. This components transforms the created structure in a series of images as described above.

Classification. In this step, we aim to cluster dataset data attributes according to the domain signatures (collected and defined by domain experts) that the dataset relates to. It applies a set of convolutional layers over the input images representing dataset characteristics over the mentioned dimensions, to extract the hidden features from the textual representations of the 5 dimensions. The classification outputs the top 5 classifications results, corresponding to the top 5 domain signatures the dataset relates to in the data repository. In the current implementation, we use the ResNet18 convolutional neural network [3] to build the classification model, as it achieved the best results in our trials.

Model-Deployment (Operating) Phase. Once we have build the classification model, the system is ready to analyze new datasets, as shown in Fig. 2. A first step is to prepare the input dataset through the *data preparation* component and to generate the corresponding set of images via the *image generation* component. These images are used as input to the pre-trained model to get the correct scientific domain signature. The outcome of the classification model along with the domain specific ontology are used to generate the domain signature of the given dataset and also to link its data attributes to corresponding data attributes from other datasets in the same data repository. The results are then visualized using the *visualization* component, as shown in Fig. 2. A screen shot of the result is illustrated in Fig. 3. The result of this analysis illustrates that the main topic of this dataset is "site and water quality". The figure also shows that the dataset is linked to a number of other datasets, e.g. datasets 92, 128 and 214 via the concept "groundwater" as shown in Fig. 3.

We build and test the proposed approach using datasets of the AquaDiva data portal[2]. We used 114 datasets representing different domain topics, such as weather monitoring, groundwater hydrochemistry, gene abundance, or soil

---

[2] Due to the data policy of the CRC, we can not publish these datasets.

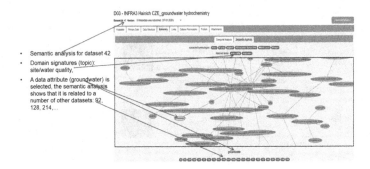

Fig. 3. Semantic linking visualization

physical parameters. 70% of these were used for training and 30% for evaluation. The total number of data attributes is 1300; the number of data points within a dataset ranges from 300 (5 data attributes × 60 tuples) to 12,000,000. Example results were presented to domain experts from CRC AquaDiva. They confirmed the correctness and usefulness of this classification. Based on these promising first results, we aim to extend and further evaluate the approach in future work.

All resources related to the proposed approach as well as the preliminary results are accessible at https://github.com/fusion-jena/JeDaSS.

Acknowledgments. This work has been funded by the *Deutsche Forschungsgemeinschaft* (CRC AquaDiva, Project 218627073).

References

1. Chamanara, J., Owonibi, M., Algergawy, A., Gerlach, R.: An extensible conceptual model for tabular scientific datasets. In: The Fifth International Conference on Advances in Information Mining and Management (2015)
2. Fillinger, S., de la Garza, L., Peltzer, A., Kohlbacher, O., Nahnsen, S.: Challenges of big data integration in the life sciences. Anal. Bioanalytical Chem. **411**(26), 6791–6800 (2019). https://doi.org/10.1007/s00216-019-02074-9
3. He, K., Zhang, X., Ren, S., Sun, J.: Deep residual learning for image recognition (2015)
4. El-Kassas, W.S., Salama, C.R., Rafe, A.A., Mohamed, H.K.: Automatic text summarization: a comprehensive survey. Expert Syst. Appl. **165**, 107567 (2021)
5. Sharma, A., Vans, E., Shigemizu, D., Boroevich, K.A., Tsunoda, T.: Deepinsight: a methodology to transform a non-image data to an image for convolution neural network architecture. Sci. Rep. **9**(1), 1–7 (2019)
6. Vollmer, M., Golab, L., Böhm, K., Srivastava, D.: Informative summarization of numeric data. In: Proceedings of the 31st SSDM, pp. 97–108 (2019)
7. Xi, Y., Wang, N., Hao, S., Yang, W., Li, L.: PocketView: a concise and informative data summarizer. In: 36th ICDE, pp. 1742–1745 (2020)
8. Yu, C., Jagadish, H.: Schema summarization. In: Proceedings of the 32nd International Conference on Very Large Databases, pp. 319–330 (2006)

9. Zhang, S., Dai, Z., Balog, K., Callan, J.: Summarizing and exploring tabular data in conversational search. arXiv preprint arXiv:2005.11490 (2020)
10. Zilioli, M., Lanucara, S., Oggioni, A., Fugazza, C., Carrara, P.: Fostering data sharing in multidisciplinary research communities: a case study in the geospatial domain. Data Sci. J. **18**(1), 42 (2019)

RaiseWikibase: Fast Inserts into the BERD Instance

Renat Shigapov$^{(\boxtimes)}$ ⓘ, Jörg Mechnich ⓘ, and Irene Schumm ⓘ

Mannheim University Library, University of Mannheim, Mannheim, Germany
{renat.shigapov,joerg.mechnich,irene.schumm}@bib.uni-mannheim.de

Abstract. We create a knowledge graph of German companies in order to facilitate research with Business, Economic and Related Data (BERD), both modern and historical. For the implementation we chose Wikibase, but the wrappers of the Wikibase API turned out to be slow for filling it with millions of entities. This work presents the open source tool RaiseWikibase for speeding up data filling and knowledge graph construction by inserting data directly into the database. We test its performance for creating the items and wikitexts and share a reusable example for knowledge graph construction.

Keywords: Knowledge graph construction · Wikidata · Wikibase

1 Introduction

Motivation. German company data are spread over many providers, registers and time spans. The company identifiers in Germany are sadly famous for their lack of uniqueness, inconsistent representations and multiple registrations per legal entity[1]. The modern data for millions of German companies were scraped and unchained by OpenCorporates [9]. The collection was supported by the TheyBuyForYou project [8] and is used in euBusinessGraph [6]. Historical information about German companies is still confined within many undigitized documents as reported by the EurHisFirm project [5]. Only some of the documents were digitized, processed and structured [2,3]. All this makes knowledge graph construction for German companies difficult, urgent and necessary.

Wikibase and Wikidata. We chose Wikibase for creating a knowledge graph. Its benefits are a live Blazegraph-based SPARQL endpoint, RDF export, an API, data science tools and the promising strategy for the decentralized Wikibase Ecosystem [4]. The general-purpose Wikidata knowledge graph [10] (the main Wikibase instance) can help with ontology development for new instances.

---

[1] https://blog.opencorporates.com/2019/02/19/wait-what-the-problems-of-company-numbers-in-germany-and-how-were-handling-them.

ⓒ Springer Nature Switzerland AG 2021
R. Verborgh et al. (Eds.): ESWC 2021 Satellite Events, LNCS 12739, pp. 60–64, 2021.
https://doi.org/10.1007/978-3-030-80418-3_11

Related work. An ontology and data can be filled into a Wikibase instance manually or using the wrappers of the Wikibase API. WikidataIntegrator [1], wikibase-cli, Wikidata-Toolkit, WikibaseIntegrator, Pywikibot, QuickStatements and many other tools are excellent for data filling during the collaborative knowledge graph development. However, they can insert roughly 1–6 entities per second, making data filling and knowledge graph construction with a fresh Wikibase instance lengthy. A solution is to insert data directly into the database, but a ready-to-use tool for it does not yet exist. The only relevant work [11] provides code in Java for Wikibase 1.34. Unfortunately, its reuse requires changing hard-coded values and restructuring of the code. Instead, we implemented RaiseWikibase in Python for Wikibase 1.35.

Our Contribution and Structure. We present the tool RaiseWikibase for speeding up data filling and knowledge graph construction with Wikibase. Next, we describe RaiseWikibase, raise our BERD instance, and make conclusions.

2 Raising Wikibase

RaiseWikibase is written in Python, uses the version "1.35" of the Wikibase Docker image, and connects to the MariaDB database using the mysqlclient library. The open source code is shared at https://github.com/UB-Mannheim/RaiseWikibase.

The main functions are **page** and **batch**. The **page** function executes inserts into the database but does not commit them. Multiple **page** functions are wrapped into a transaction inside the **batch** function. Creating a million of items is as simple as batch('wikibase-item',items), where the first argument specifies a content model and **items** is a list of JSON representations of the items.

To create or edit the JSON representation of an entity, we added the following functions for the Wikibase data model[2]: entity, claim, snak, label, alias and description. They return the suitable template dictionaries. Eighteen datatypes are implemented in the snak function. The JSON representation of an item with an English label, aliases, description and one claim is given by:

```
item = entity(labels=label('en', 'organization'),
              aliases=alias('en', ['organisation', 'org']),
              descriptions=description('en','social entity'),
              claims=claim(prop='P2101',
                           mainsnak=snak(datatype='string',
                                         value='org',
                                         prop='P2101')),
              etype='item')
```

RaiseWikibase inserts data into the nine tables according to the database schemas of Mediawiki and Wikibase. While this is sufficient in case of unstructured data, for structured data some of the secondary tables are also changed.

---

[2] https://www.mediawiki.org/wiki/Wikibase/DataModel.

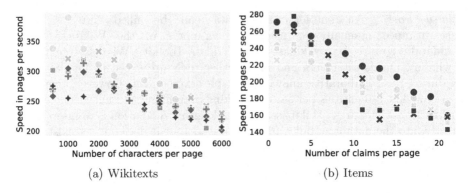

Fig. 1. RaiseWikibase performance in the batch mode of page creation.

Figure 1 shows the results of our performance analysis. Every data point is based on a batch of ten thousands pages. Figure 1a illustrates the results of six repeated experiments indicated by differently-shaped data points. In Fig. 1b two colors represent repeated experiments and three shapes of a data point stand for: ● – a claim lacks qualifiers and references, ✖ – a claim has one qualifier and no reference, and ■ – a claim has one qualifier and one reference. The insert rate decreases approximately linearly with increasing number of characters per wikitext and with increasing number of claims per item. Small pages can be uploaded at rates of 250–350 wikitexts per second (Fig. 1a) and 220–280 items per second (Fig. 1b). The source codes and technical details about our tests can be found on GitHub.

The ElasticSearch index and some of the secondary tables are built after data filling. Queries on the "page" and "text" tables can be made. A bot account, needed for the wrappers of the Wikibase API, is created automatically.

3 Raising BERD

A fresh Wikibase instance contains only the main page. An ontology, templates, modules, structured and unstructured data have to be filled into the database. Some extensions have to be installed and many parameters have to be configured.

We prepared the configuration files, modules and extensions, created the templates, changed the sidebar, a style of pages (skin) and the main page. The page with SPARQL examples, shown at the query frontend, is also created. These files are stored in the "texts" folder of RaiseWikibase, are quickly uploaded using the **page** function and can be easily adapted to a new use case.

The Wikidata properties are reused. Unfortunately, the federated properties in Wikibase are still under development and the extension WikibaseImport does not work as expected and turned out to be slow. We created three properties with IDs "P1"[3], "P2" and "P3" shown in Table 1a. Then, the Wikidata endpoint

---

[3] This is only the last and unique part of ID. The full URLs are omitted for brevity.

is queried for all (8600+) properties with labels, descriptions, aliases, datatypes, formatter URLs and formatter URIs for RDF resources. Those properties containing the triples with "P1"-"P3" are then created locally, see Table 1b.

Table 1. (a) Four properties created manually, (b) more than 8600 properties queried from the Wikidata endpoint, (c) the properties matched automatically by the semantic annotator "bbw", and (d) the properties matched manually.

(a) **Four properties created manually**		
BERD ID	Wikidata ID	English label
P1	-	Wikidata ID
P2	P1630	formatter URL
P3	P1921	formatter URI for RDF resource
P4	-	native company number
(b) **More than 8600 properties queried from the Wikidata endpoint**		
P5	P6	head of government
...	...	...
P8656	P9448	introduced on
(c) **Automatically matched properties by semantic annotator "bbw"**		
P1020	P1320	Open Corporates ID
P91	P159	headquarters location
(d) **Manually matched properties**		
P5699	P6375	street address
P588	P813	retrieved

The German company dataset[4], donated to the Open Knowledge Foundation Deutschland by OpenCorporates, is converted to a CSV file. To automate ontology learning with Wikidata, the open source semantic annotator "bbw" [7] is applied to a part of the "company" table. The properties matched automatically are listed in Table 1c. Table 1d shows the properties matched manually. Additionally, we created a property for a native company number with ID "P4" as shown in Table 1a. It corresponds to the registration authority (court), the code related to a legal form and the number which is unique for the given court.

To reduce memory requirements, the JSON representations of entities are created using RaiseWikibase while reading the data from a CSV file line by line and the `batch` function is executed for lists with 100000 entities. Each entity has at most three claims with one qualifier and one reference. A million entities of German companies are filled into the BERD instance in seventy minutes.

---

[4] https://offeneregister.de.

Note that ElasticSearch indexing and building some of the secondary tables take additional time. We plan to add a multiprocessing implementation to improve on those issues.

4 Conclusions

We presented the open source tool RaiseWikibase for speeding up data filling and knowledge graph construction using Wikibase and shared it at https://github.com/UB-Mannheim/RaiseWikibase. Up to a million entities and wikitexts per hour can be filled. A reusable example of knowledge graph construction is provided.

Acknowledgments. This work was funded by the Ministry of Science, Research and Arts of Baden-Württemberg through the project "Business and Economics Research Data Center Baden-Württemberg". We thank Jesper Zedlitz for [11].

References

1. Burgstaller-Muehlbacher, S., et al.: SuLab/WikidataIntegrator 0.5.1 (2020). https://doi.org/10.5281/zenodo.3621065
2. Gehrlein, S., Kamlah, J., Pintsch, M., Schumm, I., Weil, S.: Vom Papier zur Datenanalyse. "Neue" historische Forschungsdaten für die Wirtschaftswissenschaften. In: Heuveline, V. (ed.) E-Science-Tage 2019 : Data to Knowledge, vol. 598, pp. 140–152. heiBOOKS (2020). https://doi.org/10.11588/heibooks.598.c8423
3. Gram, D., Karapanagiotis, P., Krzyzanowski, J., Liebald, M., Walz, U.: An extensible model for historical financial data with an application to German company and stock market data. SAFE Working Paper No. 300 (2020). http://dx.doi.org/10.2139/ssrn.3770607
4. Pintscher, L., Voget, L., Koeppen, M., Aleynikova, E.: Strategy for the Wikibase Ecosystem (2019). https://w.wiki/334L
5. Poukens, J.: EURHISFIRM D4.2: Report on the Inventory of Data and Sources (2018). https://doi.org/10.5281/zenodo.3246457
6. Roman, D., et al.: A bird's-eye view of euBusinessGraph: a business knowledge graph for company data. In: ISWC 2020 Demos and Industry Tracks, vol. 2721, pp. 39–44 (2020). http://ceur-ws.org/Vol-2721/paper493.pdf
7. Shigapov, R., Zumstein, P., Kamlah, J., Oberländer, L., Mechnich, J., Schumm, I.: bbw: matching CSV to Wikidata via meta-lookup. In: Semantic Web Challenge on Tabular Data to Knowledge Graph Matching (SemTab 2020) at ISWC 2020, vol. 2775, pp. 17–26 (2020). http://ceur-ws.org/Vol-2775/paper2.pdf
8. Soylu, A., et al.: An overview of the TBFY knowledge graph for public procurement. In: ISWC 2019 Satellite Tracks (Posters & Demonstrations), vol. 2456, pp. 53–56 (2019). http://ceur-ws.org/Vol-2456/paper14.pdf
9. Taggart, C., Hanley, M., Skene, A.: Creating the German open company data: how we did it (2019). https://blog.opencorporates.com/2019/02/07/creating-the-german-open-company-data-how-we-did-it
10. Vrandečić, D., Krötzsch, M.: Wikidata: a free collaborative knowledgebase. Commun. ACM **57**(10), 78–85 (2014). https://doi.org/10.1145/2629489
11. Zedlitz, J.: Filling a Wikibase instance with millions of data (2020). https://blog.factgrid.de/archives/2013

Do Judge an Entity by Its Name! Entity Typing Using Language Models

Russa Biswas[1,2(✉)], Radina Sofronova[1,2], Mehwish Alam[1,2], Nicolas Heist[3], Heiko Paulheim[3], and Harald Sack[1,2]

[1] FIZ Karlsruhe – Leibniz Institute for Information Infrastructure,
Eggenstein-Leopoldshafen, Germany
{russa.biswas,radina.sofronova,mehwish.alam,harald.sack}@fiz-karlsruhe.de
[2] Karlsruhe Institute of Technology, Institute AIFB, Karlsruhe, Germany
[3] University of Mannheim, Mannheim, Germany
{nico,heiko}@informatik.uni-mannheim.de

Abstract. The entity type information in a Knowledge Graph (KG) plays an important role in a wide range of applications in Natural Language Processing such as entity linking, question answering, relation extraction, etc. However, the available entity types are often noisy and incomplete. Entity Typing is a non-trivial task if enough information is not available for the entities in a KG. In this work, neural language models and a character embedding model are exploited to predict the type of an entity from only the name of the entity without any other information from the KG. The model has been successfully evaluated on a benchmark dataset.

Keywords: Entity type prediction · Knowledge graph completion · Deep neural networks

1 Introduction

Entity Typing is a vital task in Knowledge Graph (KG) completion and construction. The entity types in KGs such as DBpedia, YAGO, Wikidata, etc. are either extracted automatically from structured data, generated using heuristics, or are human-curated. These factors lead to incomplete and noisy entity type information in the KGs. More specifically, in case of DBpedia, the Wikipedia infoboxes are the primary source of information. The types of the entities in Wikipedia infoboxes are mapped to the classes in DBpedia. Recent years have witnessed research in the automated prediction of entity types in KGs using heuristics [5] as well as neural network-based models [1,3,4]. The existing state-of-the-art (SOTA) models exploit the triples in the KGs whereas others consider the textual entity descriptions as well. While those approaches work well if there is a lot of information about an entity, it is still a challenge to type entities for which there is only scarce information. This paper focuses on predicting the entity types solely from their label names, e.g., *Is it possible to predict that*

© Springer Nature Switzerland AG 2021
R. Verborgh et al. (Eds.): ESWC 2021 Satellite Events, LNCS 12739, pp. 65–70, 2021.
https://doi.org/10.1007/978-3-030-80418-3_12

the entity `dbr:Berlin` *is a place only from its name?*. To do so, the SOTA continuous space-based Neural Language Models (NLM) such as Word2Vec, GloVe, Wikipedia2Vec [11], BERT [6] as well as a character embedding model are exploited. This work tackles the challenge of insufficient information for the entities. Since the NLMs are trained on a huge amount of textual data, they provide implicit contextual information about the entities in their corresponding latent representations. In this work, the task of entity typing is considered as a classification problem in which a neural network-based classifier is applied on top of the NLMs. Furthermore, an analysis of the performance of the different NLMs for this task is provided.

2   Related Work

A heuristic based approach SDType [5] leverages the relations between the instances to predict the types of the entities. In [3,4], the authors propose embedding based entity typing models considering the structural information in the KG as well as the textual entity descriptions. The word embedding models such as Word2Vec, GloVe, FastText are trained on KGs in [1] to generate the entity vectors to predict the types of entities. Other language model based entity typing models are proposed in MuLR [10] and FIGMENT [9] in which multi-level representations of entities are learned by using character, word, and entity embeddings. However, these entity type prediction models based on NLMs do not restrict themselves to only the label names and consider the other information available in the KGs. In [8], the authors propose a model in which the pre-trained RDF2Vec vectors are used to predict the entity types using a classifier. Also, the meaningfulness of the entity names in Semantic Web has been studied in [7]. However, unlike the SOTA models, in this work, the NLMs are leveraged to generate the entity embeddings from the names of the entities for the task of entity type prediction.

3   Model

This section discusses the NLMs and the classifiers used for the task of entity typing only from the names of the entities.

Word2Vec. It aims to learn the distributed representation for words reducing the high dimensional word representations in a large corpus. The CBOW Word2Vec model predicts the current word from a window of context words and the skip-gram model predicts the context words based on the current word.

GloVe. GloVe exploits the global word-word co-occurrence statistics in the corpus with the underlying intuition that the ratios of word-word co-occurrence probabilities encode some form of the meaning of the words.

BERT. **B**idirectional **E**ncoder **R**epresentations from **T**ransformers is a contextual information based embedding approach in which pretraining on bidirectional representations from unlabeled text by using the left and the right context in all the layers is performed.

Wikipedia2vec. The model jointly learns word and entity embeddings from Wikipedia where similar words and entities are close to one another in the vector space. It uses three submodels to learn the representation namely: Wikipedia Link Graph Model, Word-based skip-gram model, and Anchor context model.

Character Embedding. Character embedding represents the latent representations of characters trained over a corpus which helps in determining the vector representations of out-of-vocabulary words.

Embeddings of the Entity Names. In this work, pre-trained Word2Vec model on Google News dataset[1], GloVe model pre-trained on Wikipedia 2014 version and Gigaword 5[2], Wikipedia2Vec model pre-trained on English Wikipedia 2018 version[3], and pre-trained English character embeddings derived from GloVe 840B/300D dataset[4] are used with a vector dimension of 300. The average of all word vectors in the entity names is taken as the vector representation of the entities. For BERT, the average of the last four hidden layers of the model is taken as a representation of the names of entities and the dimension used is 768.

Classification. In this work, entity typing is considered a classification task with the types of entities as classes. Two classifiers have been built on top of the NLMs: (**i**) Fully Connected Neural Network (FCNN), and (**ii**) Convolutional Neural Network (CNN). A three-layered FCNN model consisting of two dense layers with ReLU as an activation function has been used on the top of the vectors generated from the NLMs. The softmax function is used in the last layer to calculate the probability of the entities belonging to different classes. The CNN model consists of two 1-D convolutional layers followed by a global max-pooling layer. `ReLu` is used as an activation function in the convolutional layers and the output of the pooling layer is then passed through a fully connected final layer, in which the softmax function predicts the classes of the entities.

4 Evaluation

This section consists of a detailed description of the datasets used for evaluating the models, followed by an analysis of the results obtained.

Datasets. The experiments are conducted on the benchmark dataset DBpedia630k [12] extracted from DBpedia consisting of 14 non-overlapping classes[5]

---

[1] https://code.google.com/archive/p/word2vec/.
[2] http://nlp.stanford.edu/data/glove.6B.zip.
[3] https://wikipedia2vec.github.io/wikipedia2vec/pretrained/.
[4] https://github.com/minimaxir/char-embeddings/blob/master/output/.
[5] https://bit.ly/3bBgjiV.

Table 1. Results on the DBpedia630k dataset (in accuracy %)

Embedding models	Types in labels		No types in labels		CaLiGraph test set	
	FCNN	CNN	FCNN	CNN	FCNN	CNN
word2vec	80.11	46.71	72.08	44.39	48.93	25.91
GloVe	83.34	54.06	82.62	53.41	61.88	31.3
wikipedia2vec	91.14	60.47	90.68	57.36	75.21	36.97
BERT	67.37	62.27	64.63	60.4	53.42	35.55
Character embedding	73.43	58.13	72.66	58.3	54.91	45.73

with 560,000 train and 70,000 test entities. However, predicting fine-grained type information of an entity only from its name is a non-trivial task. For e.g. identifying dbr:Kate_Winslet as an *Athlete* or *Artist* from only the entity name is challenging. Therefore, seven coarse-grained classes of the entities in this dataset are considered: *dbo:Organisation, dbo:Person, dbo:MeanOfTransportation, dbo:Place, dbo:Animal, dbo:Plant*, and *dbo:Work*. Also, 4.656% of the total entities in the train set and 4.614% entities in the test set have their type information mentioned in their RDF(S) labels. For example, *dbr:Cybersoft_(video_game_company)* has the label *Cybersoft (video game company)* stating that it is a *Company*. Therefore, the experiments are conducted both with and without the type information in the names for the DBpedia630k dataset. To evaluate the approaches independently of DBpedia, we use an additional test set[6] composed of entities from CaLiGraph [2]. The latter is a Wikipedia-based KG containing entities extracted from tables and enumerations in Wikipedia articles. It consists of 70,000 entities that are unknown to DBpedia and evenly distributed among 7 classes.

Results. The results in Table 1 depict that for all the NLMs, FCNN works better compared to the CNN model. This is because the CNN model does not work well in finding patterns in the label names of the entities. Also, BERT performs the worst in predicting the type of the entities from their label names. Further error analysis shows that only 4.2% of the total person entities in the test set *with Types in Labels* variation of the dataset have been correctly identified as dbo:Person for BERT. Since the names of persons can be ambiguous and BERT is a contextual embedding model, the vector representations of the entities generated only from their label names do not provide a proper latent representation of the entity. However, FCNN achieves an accuracy of 84.74% on the same dataset without the class dbo:Person for BERT. On the other hand, Wikipedia2Vec works best amongst all the NLMs for FCNN with an accuracy of 91.14% and 90.68% on the *Types in Labels* and *no Types in Labels* variants of the dataset respectively. Also, on removal of the class dbo:Person from the dataset, it achieves an accuracy of 91.01% on *Types in Labels* vari-

[6] http://data.dws.informatik.uni-mannheim.de/CaLiGraph/whats-in-a-name/ whats-in-a-name_caligraph_test-balanced70k.csv.bz2.

ant. Therefore, the decrease of 0.13% in the accuracy infers that entities of the class `dbo:Person` are well represented in the entity vectors obtained from the pre-trained Wikipedia2Vec model.

However, after removing the type information from the name labels, a slight drop in the accuracy for each model has been observed for both the classifiers. Wikipedia2Vec and the character embedding model experience the smallest drop in accuracy of 0.46% and 0.77% with the FCNN classifier. This is because DBpedia entities are extracted from Wikipedia articles, therefore the vectors of the entities are well represented by the Wikipedia2Vec model. Also for character embedding, removal of the type information from their labels has low impact because the vector representation of the entity names depends on the corresponding character vectors and not word vectors. Furthermore, an unseen test set from CaLiGraph has been evaluated on the classification model trained on the *no Types in Labels* variation of the dataset. On the CaLiGraph test set, the FCNN model achieves the best results with the Wikipedia2Vec model with an accuracy of 75.21%. The entities in the CaLiGraph test set are not contained in DBpedia, hence the representations of these entities are not learned during the training of the Wikipedia2Vec model. This depicts the robustness of the proposed model and the entity vectors generated by taking average of the word vectors present in the names of the entities provides a better latent representation.

5   Conclusion and Future Work

In this paper, different NLMs for entity typing in a KG have been analyzed. The achieved results imply that NLMs can be exploited to get enough information to predict the types of entities in a KG only from their names. In the future, fine-grained type prediction using other features from the KG using the NLMs is to be explored.

References

1. Biswas, R., Sofronova, R., Alam, M., Sack, H.: Entity type prediction in knowledge graphs using embeddings. DL4KG @ ESWC2020 (2020)
2. Heist, N., Paulheim, H.: Entity extraction from Wikipedia list pages. In: ESWC (2020)
3. Jin, H., Hou, L., Li, J., Dong, T.: Attributed and predictive entity embedding for fine-grained entity typing in knowledge bases. In: COLING (2018)
4. Jin, H., Hou, L., Li, J., Dong, T.: Fine-grained entity typing via hierarchical multi graph convolutional networks. In: EMNLP-IJCNLP (2019)
5. Paulheim, H., Bizer, C.: Type inference on noisy RDF data. In: ISWC (2013)
6. Peters, M.E., et al.: Deep contextualized word representations. In: NAACL-HLT (2018)
7. de Rooij, S., Beek, W., Bloem, P., van Harmelen, F., Schlobach, S.: Are names meaningful? Quantifying social meaning on the semantic web. In: Groth, P., et al. (eds.) ISWC 2016. LNCS, vol. 9981, pp. 184–199. Springer, Cham (2016). https://doi.org/10.1007/978-3-319-46523-4_12

8. Sofronova, R., Sack, H.: Entity typing based on RDF2Vec using supervised and unsupervised methods. In: The Semantic Web: ESWC 2020 Satellite Events: ESWC 2020 Satellite Events, Heraklion, Crete, Greece, 31 May–4 June 2020, Revised Selected Papers, p. 203 (2020)
9. Yaghoobzadeh, Y., Adel, H., Schütze, H.: Corpus-level fine-grained entity typing. J. Artif. Intell. Res. **61**, 835–862 (2018)
10. Yaghoobzadeh, Y., Schütze, H.: Multi-level representations for fine-grained typing of knowledge base entities. In: Proceedings of the 15th Conference of the European Chapter of the Association for Computational Linguistics, EACL 2017, Valencia, Spain, 3–7 April 2017, Volume 1: Long Papers (2017)
11. Yamada, I., et al.: Wikipedia2Vec: an efficient toolkit for learning and visualizing the embeddings of words and entities from Wikipedia. arXiv preprint Arxiv:1812.06280v3 (2020)
12. Zhang, X., Zhao, J.J., LeCun, Y.: Character-level convolutional networks for text classification. In: NIPS (2015)

Towards a Domain-Agnostic Computable Policy Tool

Mitchell Falkow⬤, Henrique Santos[✉]⬤, and Deborah L. McGuinness⬤

Tetherless World Constellation, Rensselaer Polytechnic Institute, Troy, NY, USA
{falkom,oliveh}@rpi.edu, dlm@cs.rpi.edu

Abstract. Policies are often crucial for decision-making in a wide range of domains. Typically they are written in natural language, which leaves room for different individual interpretations. In contrast, computable policies offer standardization for the structures that encode information, which can help decrease ambiguity and variability of interpretations. Sadly, the majority of computable policy frameworks are domain-specific or require tailored customization, limiting potential applications of this technology. For this reason, we propose ADAPT, a domain-agnostic policy tool that leverages domain knowledge, expressed in knowledge graphs, and employs W3C standards in semantics and provenance to enable the construction, visualization, and management of computable policies that include domain knowledge to reduce terminology inconsistencies, and augment the policy evaluation process.

1 Introduction

Policies (often referred to as *guidelines*) are sets of rules that describe the preferred responses to a given set of conditions, and typically are used to support practitioners with making decisions. Policies are often expressed using natural language. Natural language encodings are often ambiguous and sometimes incomplete, thus allowing for a potential range of interpretations. In contrast, computable policies (CPs) are typically written using frameworks that govern policy structures to ensure machine-readability, and allow for automatic evaluation using evaluation engine software. CPs are found in many contexts such as access control (e.g. XACML [1]) and healthcare (e.g. GEM [11], SAGE [14]).

Many frameworks are domain-specific, and using one outside its intended domain(s) often requires extensive configuration and/or the creation of customized extensions to the framework. Furthermore, the required changes can create unintended consequences, and sometimes errors.

One solution would be to make use of declarative domain knowledge expressed in an extensible and machine-understandable format stored within CPs. Besides preserving machine-readability and mitigating inconsistencies, this approach would enable the use of domain knowledge during policy evaluation.

Code and demo video: https://tetherless-world.github.io/adapt/.

© Springer Nature Switzerland AG 2021
R. Verborgh et al. (Eds.): ESWC 2021 Satellite Events, LNCS 12739, pp. 71–75, 2021.
https://doi.org/10.1007/978-3-030-80418-3_13

Very few frameworks are capable of using domain knowledge during evaluation, and of the frameworks that provide this capacity, even fewer provide user-friendly tools to help work within those frameworks.

For these reasons we introduce ADAPT, a domain-agnostic policy tool that leverages the domain knowledge stored in knowledge graphs (KGs). ADAPT represents CPs by extending KGs and by using recommended standards for ontologies (OWL) and provenance (PROV). Our solution enables the construction, visualization, and management of CPs that include machine-understandable domain knowledge. This approach can be used to reduce terminology inconsistencies and augment the policy evaluation process.

2   ADAPT Architecture

The ADAPT architecture (shown in Fig. 1) consists of a web-based user interface (UI), a RESTful backend API, and an RDF store that manages all policy and KG data. The role of the RDF store is fulfilled by the Tetherless World Knowledge Store[1].

Policies created in ADAPT use a generalization of the CP framework outlined in [9]. CPs that use this framework are capable of using existing OWL 2 reasoners to perform evaluation.

When creating policies, the UI makes HTTP requests to the backend API, which in turn uses SPARQL queries to extract attributes from the RDF store. The API processes the attributes and returns them as rule structures to the UI for use in policy construction. The API also wraps the standard HTTP method endpoints (e.g. GET, POST) for policies in the RDF store. These are used for tasks such as policy visualization and management.

ADAPT also aims to allow users to configure their domain by supplying their own domain KGs, and edit, browse, and visualize policies that they create.

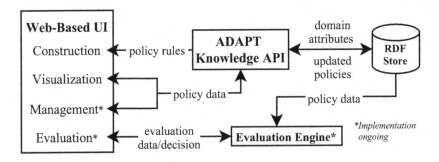

Fig. 1. ADAPT architecture diagram

---

[1] https://github.com/tetherless-world/twks.

3   Demonstration: Healthcare Guidelines

We will illustrate the utility of ADAPT by creating a CP based on a guideline for diabetes patients from the American Diabetes Association [2]. Consider Recommendation 5.32, which reads:

> *Advise all patients not to use cigarettes and other tobacco products or e-cigarettes. (Evidence Rating = A)*

A policy author must interpret the policy, extracting the necessary information that composes the policy's rules. Policy *rules* are restrictions placed on PROV classes (`Activity`, `Entity`, `Agent`). The Semanticscience Integrated Ontology (SIO) [4] is used for attribute rules, which are restrictions defined with `sio:hasAttribute`. Terms from existing KGs can be reused by adding assertions.

Here, we assume a background KG where Smoking/NotRecommended and Diabetes are assumed to be subclasses of prov:Activity and sio:Attribute, respectively. We use EvidenceRating to denote policy precedence.

```
1  Class: Recommendation-5.32
2    EquivalentTo: SmokingCigarettes and (wasAssociatedWith some
3      (hasAttribute some Type1Diabetes))
4    SubClassOf: EvidenceRating-A, NotRecommended
```

Listing 1.1. Example Policy (Manchester Syntax)

To construct the policy (Listing 1.1), we first load the required KGs and definitions into the RDF store. ADAPT discovers and generates the valid rule structures. We then take these steps in the UI (see Fig. 2): (1) enter the *Source, ID, Label,* and *Description*; (2) specify *Smoking* for the action; (3) add a rule under *Rules* and select *Type 1 diabetes*; (4) select *Evidence Rating A* for *Precedence*; and lastly, (5) choose *Not Recommended* for the *Effect*. Once we click *Save*, ADAPT saves the policy to the RDF store and displays a graph view of the policy.

Fig. 2. Screenshots of ADAPT UI for policy construction

4   ADAPT and Other Computable Policy Tools

CP tools exist to aid in creating and editing policies. Many CP frameworks provide their own, as seen with GEM [5], SAGE [14]. Still these frameworks are domain-specific, and while there is potential for reuse, significant changes would be needed from the user. In contrast, users configure ADAPT by providing domain knowledge from KGs. The benefit of this approach is that users can leverage domain knowledge from pre-existing domain KGs.

As for leveraging KGs, XACML does not readily provide this feature. Most frameworks in the medical domain make use of medical domain knowledge in the form of KGs [8], but users cannot necessarily supply their own domain KGs.

Torres et al. [13] propose a domain-independent tool for creating the medical equivalent of a CP. Similar to ADAPT, the tool uses KGs to support the authoring process. However, the resulting CP uses a domain-specific syntax Arden, so customization is needed for reuse, and reasoning via standard OWL reasoners would not be supported.

KAoS [15], Rei [6], and PROTUNE [3] are established frameworks that use Semantic Web technology. Approaches by Lopes et al. [7] and by Speiser et al. [12] are more recent Semantic Web approaches. Santos et al. [10] introduce a tool for building CPs in the dynamic spectrum access (DSA) domain, and uses the framework from [9]. ADAPT improves upon this tool by enabling usage in domains beyond DSA. Our choice for using the generalized framework in the latter is that it builds on previous works by matching the cross-domain policy expression semantics, enabling the implementation of a wide variety of attribute-based policies across domains.

5   Conclusion

We introduced ADAPT: a domain-agnostic tool for creating and visualizing computable policies that leverage domain knowledge from knowledge graphs. By employing Semantic Web standards, ADAPT permits users to create policies that maintain standards for terminology and augment policy evaluation by incorporating domain knowledge during the policy evaluation process.

The limitations of ADAPT in its current state include the dependency on users supplying ontologies that align with PROV and SIO, with limited flexibility. Santos et al. [10] combat this by allowing users to create terms on the fly. ADAPT should consider a similar approach going forward. Additional language support is necessary – currently ADAPT does not support the *union* of rules (e.g. (`Smoking ...`) or `Drinking`), which constrains the expressiveness of rules that can be created.

Finally, we are pursuing the incorporation of a policy evaluation engine, as indicated in Fig. 1, which will support the capacity to enforce policies.

References

1. eXtensible Access Control Markup Language (XACML) Version 3.0. http://docs.oasis-open.org/xacml/3.0/xacml-3.0-core-spec-os-en.html
2. American Diabetes Association: Facilitating behavior change and well-being to improve health outcomes: standards of medical care in diabetes–2020. Diabetes Care **43**(Supplement 1), S48–S65 (2020)
3. Bonatti, P.A., Coi, J.L.D., Olmedilla, D., Sauro, L.: PROTUNE: A Rule-based PROvisional TrUst NEgotiation Framework (2010)
4. Dumontier, M., et al.: The Semanticscience Integrated Ontology (SIO) for biomedical research and knowledge discovery. J. Biomed. Semant. **5**, 14 (2014)

5. Hajizadeh, N., Kashyap, N., Michel, G., Shiffman, R.N.: GEM at 10: a decade's experience with the guideline elements model. In: AMIA Annual Symposium Proceedings 2011, pp. 520–528 (2011)
6. Kagal, L., Finin, T., Joshi, A.: A policy language for a pervasive computing environment. In: Proceedings POLICY 2003. IEEE 4th International Workshop on Policies for Distributed Systems and Networks, pp. 63–74, June 2003
7. Lopes, N., Kirrane, S., Zimmermann, A., Polleres, A., Mileo, A.: A logic programming approach for access control over RDF. In: Dovier, A., Costa, V.S. (eds.) Technical Communications of the 28th International Conference on Logic Programming (ICLP'12). Leibniz International Proceedings in Informatics (LIPIcs), vol. 17, pp. 381–392. Schloss Dagstuhl-Leibniz-Zentrum fuer Informatik, Dagstuhl, Germany (2012)
8. Peleg, M.: Computer-interpretable clinical guidelines: a methodological review. J. Biomed. Inform. **46**(4), 744–763 (2013)
9. Santos, H., et al.: A semantic framework for enabling radio spectrum policy management and evaluation. In: Pan, J.Z., et al. (eds.) ISWC 2020. LNCS, vol. 12507, pp. 482–498. Springer, Cham (2020). https://doi.org/10.1007/978-3-030-62466-8_30
10. Santos, H., et al.: The dynamic spectrum access policy framework in action. In: ISWC 2020 Posters, Demos, and Industry Tracks (2020)
11. Shiffman, R.N., Karras, B.T., Agrawal, A., Chen, R., Marenco, L., Nath, S.: GEM: a proposal for a more comprehensive guideline document model using XML. J. Am. Med. Inform. Assoc. **7**(5), 488–498 (2000)
12. Speiser, S., Studer, R.: A self-policing policy language. In: Patel-Schneider, P.F., et al. (eds.) ISWC 2010. LNCS, vol. 6496, pp. 730–746. Springer, Heidelberg (2010). https://doi.org/10.1007/978-3-642-17746-0_46
13. Torres, J., Artola, G., Muro, N.: A domain-independent semantically validated authoring tool for formalizing clinical practice guidelines. Stud. Health Technol. Inform. **270**, 517–521 (2020)
14. Tu, S.W., et al.: The SAGE guideline model: achievements and overview. J. Am. Med. Inform. Assoc. **14**(5), 589–598 (2007)
15. Uszok, A., et al.: KAoS policy management for semantic Web services. IEEE Intell. Syst. **19**(4), 32–41 (2004)

Towards an Evaluation Framework for Expressive Stream Reasoning

Pieter Bonte$^{(\boxtimes)}$ ⓘ, Filip De Turck ⓘ, and Femke Ongenae ⓘ

IDLab, Ghent University – imec, Ghent, Belgium
`Pieter.Bonte@UGent.be`

Abstract. Stream Reasoning, and more particularly RDF Stream Processing (RSP), has focused on processing data streams in a timely manner, while expressive reasoning techniques, such as OWL2 DL, allow to fully model and interpret their domain knowledge. However, expressive reasoning techniques have thus far mostly focused on static data, as it tends to become slow with growing datasets. Expressive Stream Reasoning aims to combine these fields and evaluate expressive reasoning techniques in a timely manner over volatile data streams through various reasoning optimizations. Both expressive reasoning and RSP have benchmarks and frameworks for evaluating and comparing proposed solutions. However, no benchmarks or evaluation frameworks for Expressive Stream Reasoning are currently available.

In this paper, we propose *OWL2Streams*, a resource framework for the evaluation of Expressive Stream Reasoning solutions. We identified challenges and opportunities for optimizations when dealing with expressive reasoning over the combination of streams and static data. *OWL2Streams* proposes three streaming scenarios, each tackling different challenges.

Keywords: Stream reasoning · Evaluation · Benchmark

1 Introduction

Due to the increasing rate at which data is being produced, the Stream Reasoning community has investigated how to process heterogeneous data streams in a timely manner. RDF Stream Processing (RSP), a part of the Stream Reasoning initiative, is focusing specifically on the timely processing of RDF data streams.

However, to extract meaningful insights from these data streams, the streams should be combined with domain knowledge [2,6]. Many domains rely on rich background knowledge to fully capture the domain, such as Pervasive Health [5] or the Internet of Things (IoT) [4]. Expressive reasoning, such as OWL2 DL, allows to fully capture this domain knowledge. Recent study shows that most IoT labeled ontologies on Linked Open Vocabularies[1] require expressive reasoning techniques, such as OWL2 DL, to be fully interpreted. However, until now, such

---

[1] https://lov.linkeddata.es/.

© Springer Nature Switzerland AG 2021
R. Verborgh et al. (Eds.): ESWC 2021 Satellite Events, LNCS 12739, pp. 76–81, 2021.
https://doi.org/10.1007/978-3-030-80418-3_14

reasoning techniques have mostly focussed on rather static data [12]. Expressive stream reasoning aims at optimizing and exploiting trade-offs to speed up the slower expressive reasoning techniques, such that they can be used for streaming scenarios [3]. However, currently, there are no benchmarks or evaluation frameworks available to evaluate and push the research field forward. The RSP community has investigated multiple benchmarks for low expressive streaming tasks [1], while the reasoning community has proposed benchmarks and evaluation frameworks for highly expressive static tasks [11]. Currently, a benchmark or evaluation framework that bridges the two is still missing.

In this paper, we propose *OWL2Streams*, the first initiative towards an expressive reasoning evaluation framework resource. Similar to the OWL2Bench benchmark [11], we provide challenges for each of the OWL2 profiles. Furthermore, we highlight additional challenges when performing expressive reasoning over volatile data. Each of the challenges can be used to optimize different parts of the expressive stream reasoning process. We propose three use cases, i.e. a Smart City, Smart Building, and a University Management scenario, each tackling a different combination of challenges. Next to the streaming data, each scenario provides an ontology TBox and an ABox describing the static data. *OWL2Streams* builds upon prominent Semantic Web resources, such as RML [7] to map raw data to the semantic model, TripleWave [9] to publish the streams, and VoCaLS [15] to describe the data streams.

2 Framework Setup

For the setup of the *OWL2Streams* evaluation framework, we use TripleWave [9] for the publishing of the streams and VoCaLS [15] for the stream description. We use the idea of a *Test Stand* [13], where the framework controls the input and validates the output of the engine under evaluation. *OWL2Streams* consists of the following building blocks:

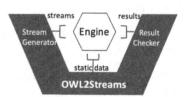

Fig. 1. The OWL2Streams test stand

- The *Stream Generator* generates data streams and makes them accessible to the engine under evaluation.
- The *Result Checker* functions as an *oracle*, that has an overview of which results to expect. It joins forces with the *Stream Generator* to realize this.
- The framework also provides the *static data*, which needs to be taken into account during the evaluation.

OWL2Streams is publicly available on Github².

---

² https://github.com/IBCNServices/OWL2Streams.

3   Expressive Stream Reasoning Challenges

When performing expressive reasoning over the combination of both static and streaming data, there are additional challenges to tackle, fortunately each challenge also contains opportunities for further optimizations:

– *Size of the static data*: the larger the size of the static data, the slower the reasoning. Optimizations can focus on only extracting relevant parts of the static data [4].
– *Expressivity of the ontology*: the expressivity negatively impacts the reasoning time, optimizations can focus on extracting only relevant statements from the ontology TBox.
– *Frequency of the stream*: the faster the updates in the stream, the faster the reasoning process needs to be able to provide results. Optimizations can focus on first filtering relevant facts from the data [3].
– *Number of parallel streams*: More streams imply more data, however, challenges arise when data from various streams need to be correlated.
– *Numeric data streams*: in domains such as the IoT, many streams contain numeric data. However, data property reasoning is not supported by many OWL2 reasoners. Optimizations could focus on filtering out events with numeric values that are not useful.
– *Data Expiration*: next to reasoning over the addition of data, the removal of data is even more complex. Optimizations could investigate adapted incremental reasoning techniques for expressive reasoning. (Currently, none exist for OWL2 DL.)

The inference influence between the static and streaming data imposes different challenges as well. We identify four influence cases, as visualized in Fig. 2:

– *Static enrichment:* the influence of events in the data stream on the static data. The addition of the events causes additional inferences on the static data, e.g., inference that a *Room* is an *AlarmRoom* (which could be defined as a *Room* that has a *Sensor* that mode at least one *AlarmObservation*).
– *Event enrichment:* the influence of the static data on events. The enrichment of the events with static data allows to infer additional facts about the events. For example, an *AlarmObservation* could be defined as an *Observation* measuring a value above 100 by a sensor that observes the property CO2. The sensor description is typically part of the static data.
– *Window enrichment:* the influence of multiple events on the static data. To infer additional facts about the static data, multiple events from the streams need to be considered. Therefore, events cannot be processed one at a time and need to be combined together in a time window. For example, an *ActiveSensor* could be defined as a *Sensor* that had at least two *Observations* (in a certain time frame).

We make these distinctions, as it allows optimization in each area.

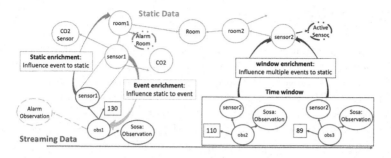

Fig. 2. Different levels of inference influences between static and streaming data.

4   Streaming Scenarios

OWL2Streams currently supports three scenarios, each focusing on different challenges presented above. The challenges tackled by each scenario are presented in Table 1. Note that for some scenarios, the size of the static data, or the number of streams can be generated and can thus vary in size.

S1 An adaptation of the OWL2Bench benchmark [11]. This scenario consists of a university where students register and enroll in a certain program. The data stream consists of the enrollment of the students.

S2 An extension of the CityBench benchmark [1], containing more elaborate background knowledge. This scenario describes a typical Smart City case.

S3 A new Smart building COVID-19 scenario, consisting of sensors that measure the air quality in various rooms. The domain knowledge allows to infer if certain rooms have higher probabilities for COVID-19 infections, based on the air quality and the activities in each room [10].

Table 1. Mapping of the various challenges on the three Scenarios. (D+: discretization)

	Static size	Expressivity	Stream frequency	Number parallel streams	Numeric streams	Data expiration	Inference influence
S1	Small to very large	High	Slow	1	No	No	Static & Event
S2	Small to medium	Medium	High	1–10	Yes & D+	Yes	All
S3	Small	Low	High	1–100	Yes	Yes	All

5   Related Work

In the realm of RSP, many benchmarks exists, such as LSBench [8], SRBench [16] and CityBench [1]. However, these benchmark focus mainly on the continuous evaluation of RDF data, with minimal focus on reasoning capabilities. Only CityBench and SRBench require very limited hierarchical reasoning, i.e. evaluation of subClassOf statements. LASS [14] is a stream reasoning benchmark for the social media domain. Compared to OWL2Streams, LASS supports a single scenario and fixed the ontological complexity to OWL2 RL, while OWL2Stream can target the various OWL2 profiles and different combinations of challenges in the various scenarios.

6   Conclusion

In this paper, we present *OWL2Streams*, a first evaluation framework for expressive stream reasoning. We have identified various challenges that arrise when performing expressive reasoning over volatile data streams. *OWL2Streams* consist of three scenarios that each tackle a different combination of challenges.

In future work, we will evaluate existing Stream Reasoners using OWL2Streams. Further more, we will explore additional scenarios to tackle different combinations of the challenges and aim at including additional reasoning challenges such as temporal reasoning.

Acknowledgments. Pieter Bonte is funded by a postdoctoral fellowship of Fonds Wetenschappelijk Onderzoek Vlaanderen (FWO) (1266521N).

References

1. Ali, M.I., Gao, F., Mileo, A.: CityBench: a configurable benchmark to evaluate RSP engines using smart city datasets. In: Arenas, M., et al. (eds.) ISWC 2015. LNCS, vol. 9367, pp. 374–389. Springer, Cham (2015). https://doi.org/10.1007/978-3-319-25010-6_25
2. Bonte, P., et al.: The MASSIF platform: a modular and semantic platform for the development of flexible IoT services. KAIS **51**(1), 89–126 (2017)
3. Bonte, P., et al.: Streaming MASSIF: cascading reasoning for efficient processing of IoT data streams. Sensors **18**(11), 3832 (2018)
4. Bonte, P., Ongenae, F., De Turck, F.: Subset reasoning for event-based systems. IEEE Access **7**, 107533–107549 (2019)
5. De Brouwer, M., et al.: Towards a cascading reasoning framework to support responsive ambient-intelligent healthcare interventions. Sensors **18**(10), 3514 (2018)
6. Della Valle, E., Dell'Aglio, D., Margara, A.: Taming velocity and variety simultaneously in big data with stream reasoning: tutorial. In: DEBS, pp. 394–401 (2016)
7. Dimou, A., et al.: RML: a generic language for integrated RDF mappings of heterogeneous data. In: LDOW (2014)

8. Le-Phuoc, D., Dao-Tran, M., Pham, M.-D., Boncz, P., Eiter, T., Fink, M.: Linked stream data processing engines: facts and figures. In: Cudré-Mauroux, P., et al. (eds.) ISWC 2012. LNCS, vol. 7650, pp. 300–312. Springer, Heidelberg (2012). https://doi.org/10.1007/978-3-642-35173-0_20

9. Mauri, A., et al.: TripleWave: spreading RDF streams on the web. In: Groth, P., et al. (eds.) ISWC 2016. LNCS, vol. 9982, pp. 140–149. Springer, Cham (2016). https://doi.org/10.1007/978-3-319-46547-0_15

10. Peng, Z., Jimenez, J.L.: Exhaled CO2 as COVID-19 infection risk proxy for different indoor environments and activities. medRxiv (2020)

11. Singh, G., Bhatia, S., Mutharaju, R.: OWL2Bench: a benchmark for OWL 2 reasoners. In: Pan, J.Z., et al. (eds.) ISWC 2020. LNCS, vol. 12507, pp. 81–96. Springer, Cham (2020). https://doi.org/10.1007/978-3-030-62466-8_6

12. Stuckenschmidt, H., et al.: Towards expressive stream reasoning. In: Dagstuhl Seminar Proceedings. Schloss Dagstuhl-Leibniz-Zentrum für Informatik (2010)

13. Tommasini, R., Della Valle, E., Balduini, M., Dell'Aglio, D.: Heaven: a framework for systematic comparative research approach for RSP engines. In: Sack, H., Blomqvist, E., d'Aquin, M., Ghidini, C., Ponzetto, S.P., Lange, C. (eds.) ESWC 2016. LNCS, vol. 9678, pp. 250–265. Springer, Cham (2016). https://doi.org/10.1007/978-3-319-34129-3_16

14. Tommasini, R., et al.: Towards a benchmark for expressive stream reasoning. In: RSP+ QuWeDa@ ESWC, pp. 26–36 (2017)

15. Tommasini, R., et al.: VoCaLS: vocabulary and catalog of linked streams. In: Vrandečić, D., et al. (eds.) ISWC 2018. LNCS, vol. 11137, pp. 256–272. Springer, Cham (2018). https://doi.org/10.1007/978-3-030-00668-6_16

16. Zhang, Y., Duc, P.M., Corcho, O., Calbimonte, J.-P.: SRBench: a streaming RDF/SPARQL benchmark. In: Cudré-Mauroux, P., et al. (eds.) ISWC 2012. LNCS, vol. 7649, pp. 641–657. Springer, Heidelberg (2012). https://doi.org/10.1007/978-3-642-35176-1_40

Schema-Backed Visual Queries over Europeana and Other Linked Data Resources

Kārlis Čerāns[(✉)], Jūlija Ovčiņņikova, Uldis Bojārs, Mikus Grasmanis, Lelde Lāce, and Aiga Romāne

Institute of Mathematics and Computer Science, University of Latvia, Riga, Latvia
karlis.cerans@lumii.lv

Abstract. We describe and demonstrate the process of extracting a data-driven schema of the Europeana cultural heritage Linked data resource (with actual data classes, properties and their connections, and cardinalities) and application of the extracted schema to create a visual query environment over Europeana. The extracted schema information allows generating SHACL data shapes describing the actual data endpoint structure. The schema extraction process can be applied also to other data endpoints with a moderate data schema size and a potentially large data triple count, as e.g., British National Bibliography Linked data resource.

Keywords: RDF · SPARQL · Linked data · Europeana · Visual Queries · SHACL

1 Introduction

Europeana[1] is a cultural heritage information aggregator that provides access to millions of digitized books, films, paintings, and other types of cultural heritage objects [1] (cf. also [2]). This information is gathered from hundreds of cultural institutions and is presented in a unified user interface.

Availability of the Europeana data as a SPARQL endpoint[2] allows the interested parties to issue multiple-entity and aggregated queries over its data, as well as to integrate Europeana within the Linked data landscape, where the queries can be asked about multiple data sets simultaneously (e.g., as federated SPARQL queries).

To ask the data queries efficiently, knowing the data schema is essential, and a support of a tool that can help an end-user by suggesting a schema-based information for query completion would be a major advantage. The tools relying on some sort of a schema information for a data endpoint involve visual query systems as Optique VQs [3] and ViziQuer [4], as well as facet-based [5] and natural-language based [6] systems.

The definition of the Europeana Data model[3] (including the Mapping Guidelines) provides the description of the classes and properties that characterize the available data;

---

[1] https://www.europeana.eu/.

[2] http://sparql.europeana.eu/.

[3] Europeana Data Model, https://pro.europeana.eu/page/edm-documentation.

© Springer Nature Switzerland AG 2021
R. Verborgh et al. (Eds.): ESWC 2021 Satellite Events, LNCS 12739, pp. 82–87, 2021.
https://doi.org/10.1007/978-3-030-80418-3_15

however, these may not be fully in sync with the actual data structure necessary for the query creation support. A similar situation is typical for Linked data resources in general, as their provision is not necessarily schema based.

Although SPARQL has instructions for the schema retrieval from the data, running these on a large-scale endpoint such as Europeana (holding more than 2.8 billion data triples), is not always technically feasible without explicit arrangements for performance.

The novel contributions of the paper are the following:

- a generic method for extracting a moderately sized data schema, suitable for a visual query environment creation, from a large SPARQL endpoint such as Europeana or British National Bibliography (BNB)[4], and
- automated generation of SHACL [7] descriptions of the actual endpoint data structure from the extracted data schemas.

We demonstrate the visual query environment creation in the ViziQuer tool[5] [4], however, we expect that the schema information can be easily restructured also to support other use cases, as demonstrated by the SHACL description generation.

In what follows, Sect. 2 describes the data schema extraction process, Sect. 3 sketches an obtained visual query environment, Sect. 4 comments on SHACL generation, provides some further discussion and concludes the paper. The resources supporting the paper are available at https://viziquer.lumii.lv/examples/europeana2021.

2 Data Schema Extraction

A data schema shall contain the information about the classes and properties in the data model, and their interconnection. The cardinality information and the data and object property separation shall also be recorded in the schema, where possible.

Given a SPARQL endpoint, one can write queries for collecting the schema information, however, for endpoints of substantial data size (as the Europeana endpoint is), the execution of such queries may not be possible technically. To overcome the limitations (where possible), we propose the following schema extraction process:

1) determine the **list of classes**, together with the **instance count**, if possible (instance count can be asked in the joint query, or for each class separately),
2) determine the **list of properties**, together with the **triple count**, if possible (triple count can be asked in the joint query, or for each property separately),
3) determine the **subclass relation**, where possible (to check if A is a subclass of B, ask, if A and B have a joint instance, then, if none of A instances is outside B). As an example, a SPARQL query template used here would be:
   SELECT ?x WHERE { ?x a <classA>. OPTIONAL { ?x a ?value.
   FILTER (?value = <classB>)} FILTER (!BOUND(?value))} LIMIT 1
4) count (look for existence of) **data and object triples of a property**, obtaining a (non-strict) separation of properties as (primarily) data and object properties.

---

[4] https://bnb.data.bl.uk/sparql.
[5] https://github.com/LUMII-Syslab/viziquer, http://viziquer.lumii.lv/.

5) determine the **class and property map**: for each property and each class check, if there is a class instance that is a subject of a property triple and if there is an instance that is an object of a property triple; if possible, count the respective triples. If a single query over all properties fails, go class by class, if that fails, go property by property, then go by individual (class, property) pairs, if needed,

6) for a property that has data triples, compute the **property and datatype map** – find the datatypes that are types of the property triple object values,

7) compute the **minimum and maximum cardinality** (check, if any of these is 1) for each property in the context of each its subject class, as well as for the **inverse** of each property in the context of each its object class,

8) for each object property p compute its **most important target class set** to cover as much of p triple objects, as possible by a limited size class set. We order all p target classes c descending by their (p,c)-count (the count of p objects that are instances of c), then by the c size ascending. We walk through the ordered class list and mark a class important, if it contains a p object that is not an instance of any class marked already as important. A SPARQL template for determining if to mark a class $<newc>$ as an important target class for a property $<p>$ in the presence of classes $<cc1>$, .., $<ccn>$ already marked as important, would be:

    SELECT ?y WHERE { ?x <p> ?y. ?y a <newc>.
    OPTIONAL{?y a ?cc. FILTER(?cc = <cc1> || ?cc = <cc2> ||.. || ?cc = <ccn>)}
    FILTER (!BOUND(?cc))} LIMIT 1

    The process can be continued through all p target classes, or a pre-defined important target class set size limit (e.g., 5 or 7) can be introduced. In each case we note, if the union of all important target classes found is a proper **range** of p (i.e., it covers all p objects).

    The **most important source class set** for any property is computed similarly; we check, if it is a **domain** of p.

9) compute the **class-property-class triples** (pairs of subject and object classes for each property from the class/property map; this corresponds *to type-property paths* in terms of [8]), with triple count (*frequency* [8]), where possible,

10) if possible, compute **the most important target class set** for each property in the **context of each source class** and **the most important source class set** for each property in the **context of each target class** (following the schema of p. 8).

The most important target/source class set and range/domain information is an essential part of the data schema for suggesting properties in a class context together with their "other end" classes. For instance, in Europeana the property *edm:rights* relates *ore:Aggregation* and *cc:License* classes, however, only 32K of 65M *edm:rights* triple objects are of type *cc:License* (the others do not have any type assertion), so it is important to offer in UI also the option to introduce the *edm:rights* property into the query without the object class information (since *cc:License* is not a range for *edm:rights*).

The schema information can be used for the visual query environment creation in ViziQuer tool [4] and for generation of the dataset description in SHACL [7].

An initial implementation of the schema extraction algorithm is available in the open source ViziQuer-related OBIS-SchemaExtractor service[6]. The supporting page provides the queries asked to retrieve the schema for Europeana (from the server log).

3 Visual Query Environment

The data schemas obtained by the schema extraction algorithm, described in Sect. 2, can be loaded into the open source ViziQuer tool environment [4]. Figure 1 shows a visual query environment fragment over Europeana SPARQL endpoint, involving a class list (right) and two versions of a simple query: a direct visual rendering of Example 3 from [9] and its class-enriched variant. Both visual queries can be translated into SPARQL and executed over the Europeana SPARQL endpoint by the tool.

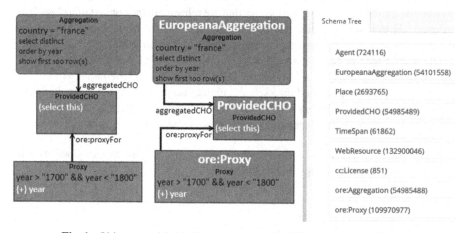

Fig. 1. Objects provided to Europeana from the 18th century from France

The query environment provides text completion options for the class and property names in the query, including the property path construction.

The visual query presentation can be seen to have appearance benefits if compared to the textual query presentation form [9] by virtue of structuring the query across several interlinked graph nodes. The schema-based environment facilitates using of the class-enriched option that has further readability benefits, as the class names provide the conceptualization of different nodes in the query (using class-name like variable names do not always succeed in such presentation and can be even misleading).

The papers' supporting resource page provides visual presentations of SPARQL queries corresponding to [9], together with access to a live query creation environment.

---

[6] https://github.com/LUMII-Syslab/obis-schemaextractor.

4 Discussion and Conclusions

SPARQL query access to cultural heritage and other Linked data resources is important for enabling rich ad hoc data enquiry options. Schema information availability and visual query presentation/composition style can ease the query composition task (cf. [10]).

The generic data schema extraction process described here would allow retrieving the actual data schema that can be used to support the visual query creation over the data heavy and moderate schema size Linked data resources such as Europeana or British National Bibliography SPARQL endpoint. The actual data schemas extracted from the endpoints can be saved also in SHACL [7] format enabling their use in other contexts, as well. There can be various level of detail the SHACL descriptions of a data set could provide. Regarding the Europeana endpoint the most informative is a manually created specification in [11]. Our contribution here is the ability to obtain the SHACL description of the data set structure (involving cardinalities) automatically from the data set. We also introduce descriptions of inverse properties that are relevant in the context of a class. The generated SHACL schemas can also be extended e.g., by the triple count information for a property in a class context, that can be useful in UI generation.

The related approaches of data schema retrieval by SPARQL queries, as e.g. [8, 12] do not reach the capability of retrieving the full Europeana data schema.

A limitation of the proposed data schema extraction process is that it would not be suitable for endpoints with very large actual data schemas, as DBPedia and Wikidata; data schema extraction and visual query support for these endpoints is further work.

Acknowledgements. This work has been partially supported by a Latvian Science Council Grant lzp-2020/2–0188 "Visual Ontology-Based Queries".

References

1. Isaac, A., Haslhofer, B.: Europeana linked open data – data.europeana.eu. Semantic Web **4**(3), 291–297 (2013). https://eprints.cs.univie.ac.at/3732/1/main.pdf
2. Freire, N., Meijers, E., de Valk, S., Raemy, J.A., Isaac, A.: Metadata aggregation via linked data: results of the Europeana Common Culture project. In: Garoufallou, E., Ovalle-Perandones, M.-A. (eds.) MTSR 2020. CCIS, vol. 1355, pp. 383–394. Springer, Cham (2021). https://doi.org/10.1007/978-3-030-71903-6_35
3. Soylu, A., Giese, M., Jimenez-Ruiz, E., Vega-Gorgojo, G., Horrocks, I.: Experiencing OptiqueVQS: a multi-paradigm and ontology-based visual query system for end users. Univ. Access Inf. Soc. **15**(1), 129–152 (2016)
4. Čerāns, K., et al.: ViziQuer: a web-based tool for visual diagrammatic queries over RDF data. In: Gangemi, A., et al. (eds.) ESWC 2018. LNCS, vol. 11155, pp. 158–163. Springer, Cham (2018). https://doi.org/10.1007/978-3-319-98192-5_30
5. Khalili, A., Meroño-Peñuela, A.: WYSIWYQ—What you see is what you query. In: Voila!2017, CEUR, vol. 1947, pp.123–130 (2017). http://ceur-ws.org/Vol-1947/paper11.pdf
6. Ferré, S.: Sparklis: an expressive query builder for SPARQL endpoints with guidance in natural language. Semantic Web **8**, 405–418 (2017)
7. Shapes Constraint Language (SHACL), W3C Recommendation (2017). https://www.w3.org/TR/shacl/

8. Dudáš, M., Svátek, V., Mynarz, J.: Dataset summary visualization with LODSight. In: The 12th Extented Semantic Web Conference (ESWC2015).

9. Europeana SPARQL API. https://pro.europeana.eu/page/sparql. Accessed 03 Mar 2021

10. Čerāns, K., et al.: ViziQuer: a visual notation for RDF data analysis queries. In: Garoufallou, E., Sartori, F., Siatri, R., Zervas, M. (eds.) MTSR 2018. CCIS, vol. 846, pp. 50–62. Springer, Cham (2019). https://doi.org/10.1007/978-3-030-14401-2_5

11. https://github.com/hugomanguinhas/europeana_shapes

12. Weise, M., Lohmann, S., Haag, F.: LD-VOWL: extracting and visualizing schema information for linked data. In: Voila!2016, pp. 120–127 (2016)

CLiT: Combining Linking Techniques for Everyone

Kristian Noullet(✉)📵, Samuel Printz📵, and Michael Färber📵

Karlsruhe Institute of Technology (KIT), Karlsruhe, Germany
{kristian.noullet,michael.faerber}@kit.edu, samuel.printz@student.kit.edu

Abstract. While the path in the field of Entity Linking (EL) has been long and brought forth a plethora of approaches over the years, many of these are exceedingly difficult to execute for purposes of detailed analysis. In many cases, implementations are available, but far from being a *plug-and-play* experience. We present Combining Linking Techniques (CLiT), a framework with the purpose of executing singular linking techniques and complex combinations thereof, with a higher degree of reusability, reproducibility and comparability of existing systems in mind. Furthermore, we introduce protocols for the exchange of sub-pipeline-level information with existing and novel systems for heightened out-of-the-box compatibility. Among others, our framework may be used to consolidate multiple systems in combination with meta learning approaches and increase support for backwards compatibility of existing benchmark annotation systems.

Keywords: Entity linking · Meta-learning · Reproducibility · NLP · Semantic Web

1 Introduction

The domain of Entity Linking (EL) deals with the interlinkage of textual mentions in text-based documents to corresponding entities in knowledge graphs. Researching and developing EL systems is a highly time-consuming process, encompassing a multitude of considerations at each step, including a plethora of moving parts – each capable of affecting the final results. Therefore, singling out the reason for the success – or failure – through ablation studies oftentimes constitutes a complex task, as any part of the processing pipeline may entail major changes. Consequently, comparability to other systems is effectively rendered *impossible* without tremendous research efforts. Even if such efforts are put in for a single system, being able to make use of these for novel research may pose an issue. In order to address these issues, we have worked on developing CLiT as a highly modular and flexible framework, allowing for an ease of adoption into existing systems and ones to come.

While research efforts allowing for performance evaluation of annotation tools have been developed, easing the centralised execution of said systems for the

© Springer Nature Switzerland AG 2021
R. Verborgh et al. (Eds.): ESWC 2021 Satellite Events, LNCS 12739, pp. 88–92, 2021.
https://doi.org/10.1007/978-3-030-80418-3_16

purpose of further processing results has been mostly untouched. We intend to further extend the philosophy of increasing comparability between annotators through predefined evaluation data sets and computed metrics presented in [7,8,10], by enabling the use of complex workflows and in-depth analyses. In contrast to GERBIL [10], CLiT executes pipelines to a more granular degree, as well as combine the aforementioned, creating novel workflows. Further, the Silk framework [11] provides a *comparable* workflow, made up of various kinds of components interacting with each other. While the level of granularity is similar, to the best of our knowledge, CLiT introduces a larger degree of distributed customization and specialises more directly on the task of entity linking. In alignment with the vision of the Web of Data, all of our workflow's components and output provide and consume machine-readable data formats, in particular NIF 2.0 and JSON.

We intend to lead the research towards being able to answer the following research questions:

1. How can the research community **leverage** (sub-)component-level results from **existing systems**?
2. Can we increase result **explainability** for (mostly) black-box systems?
3. How may approaches be compared in an in-depth fashion? (**Comparability**)
4. How to properly reproduce existing systems? (**Reproducibility**)

To the best of our knowledge, no execution system attempting to fill the gaps of maximising reusability and comparability, additionally to minimising future development efforts for annotation approaches, exists. As such, we introduce CLiT, our means of simplifying life for and pleasing researchers as well as practitioners in the field of entity linking.

We advance the state-of-the-art by:

1. Introducing novel concepts for EL workflows, including compatibility with existing paradigms;
2. Allowing for nigh-infinite configurability of supported components in complex pipelines;
3. Enabling down-stream processing of annotation results rather than metrics;
4. Improving reusable components from existing systems and ones to come, increasing degree of system support;
5. Providing a knowledge graph agnostic and potentially multi-knowledge graph-supporting annotation service (through *translator*-subcomponents);
6. Defining open exchange protocols based on the Agnos [6] framework, JSON and NIF 2.0 for Mention Detection (MD), Candidate Generation (CG), Entity Disambiguation (ED) as well as *pre- and post-processing subcomponents* acting logically between the aforementioned;
7. Allowing simple introduction of existing systems through RESTful standards.

For further details on CLiT including a demonstration video, we refer interested parties to our Github page (https://github.com/kmdn/CLiTESWC2021).

Fig. 1. Classical Pipeline for an EL system. Consisting of mention detection (MD), candidate generation (CG) and entity disambiguation (ED).

2   System Design

Classical Pipeline. While EL systems vary in terms of approaches and potential steps within respective pipelines, we identify the most commonly-employed ones as the *classical pipeline*. We use said pipeline as a template for our framework in order to reach compatibility with as many existing systems as possible. In Fig. 1, we present our understanding of the functioning of a classical pipeline for a single system.

CLiT Framework. Currently, CLiT has integrated six annotators, namely Babelfy [3], DBpediaSpotlight [5], AIDA [4], FOX [9], EntityClassifierEU [2] and OpenTapioca [1] – with more on the way. In order to allow for customised experiences and configurations, in addition to elements pertaining to the *classical pipeline* and entire annotators, we introduce further processing capabilities with the intent of allowing for nigh-infinite combinations of system components (see Fig. 2). We refer to them as *processors* or *subcomponents*, handling post-processing of structures' output from prior tasks, preparing them for being, in turn, potentially further processed by subsequent steps in the chosen workflow. In this paper, we define 4 types of processors: *splitters*, *combiners*, *filters* and *translators*.

Splitter. Allowing for processing of items prior to passing them on to a subsequent step, a splitter is utilised in the case of a *single* stream of data being sent to *multiple* components, potentially warranting specific splitting of data streams (e.g. people-related entities being handled by one system, while another processes movies). This step encompasses both a post-processing step for a prior component, as well as a pre-processing step for a following one. A potential post-processing step may be to filter information from a prior step, such as eliminating superfluous candidate entities or unwanted mentions.

Combiner. As a counterpart to a splitter, a *combiner* subcomponent must be utilised in case multiple components were utilised in a prior step and are meant to be consolidated through a variety of possible combination actions (e.g. union and intersection). It combines results from multiple inputs into a single output, passing merged partial results on to a subsequent component.

Filter. In order to allow removal of particular sets of items through user-defined rules or dynamic filtering, we introduce a subcomponent capable of processing results on binary classifiers: a *filter*. The truth values evaluated on passed

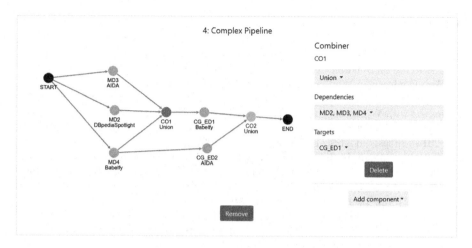

Fig. 2. GUI of CLiT with an example of a *complex* EL pipeline.

partial results define which further outcomes may be detected by a subsequent component or translator.

Translator. Enabling seamless use of annotation tools regardless of underlying Knowledge Graph (KG), the translator subcomponent is meant as a processing unit capable of *translating* entities and potentially other features, allowing further inter-system compatibility. It may be employed at any level and succeeded by any (sub-)component due to its ubiquitous characteristics and necessity when working with heterogeneous systems.

3 Conclusion and Future Work

In this paper, we introduced CLiT, a framework for the combination and execution of multiple entity linking approaches, both novel and existing. We show how components classically interact with each other based on a commonly-adopted pipeline and how they may be utilised, as well as extended through our framework. Currently our framework supports six end-to-end entity linking systems for execution in their entirety, as well as in combination with each other. Furthermore, we will introduce semi-automated in-depth analysis features in the future, allowing for collaborative evaluation, yielding a more fine-granular evaluation view on both annotators as well as data sets. Our contributions also increase the ease to train meta learning annotation classifiers with advanced degrees of flexibility and adaptability in relation to textual features.

References

1. Delpeuch, A.: OpenTapioca: lightweight entity linking for Wikidata. In: Proceedings of the 1st Wikidata Workshop Co-located with the 19th International Semantic Web Conference. Wikidata 2020, vol. 2773. CEUR-WS.org (2020)
2. Dojchinovski, M., Kliegr, T.: Entityclassifier.eu: real-time classification of entities in text with Wikipedia. In: Blockeel, H., Kersting, K., Nijssen, S., Železný, F. (eds.) ECML PKDD 2013. LNCS (LNAI), vol. 8190, pp. 654–658. Springer, Heidelberg (2013). https://doi.org/10.1007/978-3-642-40994-3_48
3. Flati, T., Navigli, R.: Three birds (in the LLOD Cloud) with one stone: BabelNet, Babelfy and the Wikipedia Bitaxonomy. In: Proceedings of the Posters and Demos Track of 10th International Conference on Semantic Systems. SEMANTiCS 2014, vol. 1224, pp. 10–13. CEUR-WS.org (2014)
4. Hoffart, J., et al.: Robust disambiguation of named entities in text. In: Proceedings of the 2011 Conference on Empirical Methods in Natural Language Processing. EMNLP 2011, pp. 782–792. ACL (2011)
5. Mendes, P.N., Jakob, M., García-Silva, A., Bizer, C.: DBpedia spotlight: shedding light on the web of documents. In: Proceedings the 7th International Conference on Semantic Systems. I-SEMANTICS 2011, pp. 1–8. ACM (2011)
6. Noullet, K.: KG-agnostic entity linking orchestration. In: Proceedings of the Doctoral Consortium at ISWC 2020 co-located with 19th International Semantic Web Conference. ISWC 2020, vol. 2798, pp. 41–48. CEUR-WS.org (2020)
7. Rizzo, G., van Erp, M., Troncy, R.: Benchmarking the extraction and disambiguation of named entities on the semantic web. In: Proceedings of the Ninth International Conference on Language Resources and Evaluation. LREC 2014, pp. 4593–4600. European Language Resources Association (ELRA) (2014)
8. Rizzo, G., et al.: NERD: a framework for unifying NERD extraction tools. In: Proceedings of the Demonstrations at the 13th Conference of the European Chapter of the Association for Computational Linguistics
9. Speck, R., Ngomo, A.N.: Named entity recognition using FOX. In: Proceedings of the ISWC 2014 Posters and Demonstrations Track of the 13th International Semantic Web Conference. ISWC 2014, vol. 1272, pp. 85–88. CEUR-WS.org (2014)
10. Usbeck, R., et al.: GERBIL: general entity annotator benchmarking framework. In: Proceedings of the 24th International Conference on World Wide Web. WWW 2015, pp. 1133–1143. ACM (2015)
11. Volz, J., Bizer, C., Gaedke, M., Kobilarov, G.: Silk - A link discovery framework for the web of data. In: Proceedings of the WWW 2009 Workshop on Linked Data on the Web. LDOW 2009, vol. 538. CEUR-WS.org (2009)

SANTé: A Light-Weight End-to-End Semantic Search Framework for RDF Data

Edgard Marx[1,2(✉)] ⓘ, André Valdestilhas[1], Hannah Beck[2], and Tommaso Soru[1]

[1] Institute of Computer Science, AKSW, University of Leipzig, Leipzig, Germany
{marx,valdestilhas,soru}@informatik.uni-leipzig.de
[2] Leipzig University of Applied Science (HTWK), Leipzig, Germany
{edgard.marx,hannah.beck}@stud.htwk-leipzig.de

Abstract. Natural language interfaces are one of the most powerful technologies to enable content access. It is a diverse and thriving topic that tackles a multitude of challenges ranging from designing better ranking models to user interfaces. Developing or adapting search engines is a very time-demanding and resource-consuming task. We present SANTé, a semantic search framework that facilitates publishing, querying, and browsing RDF data sets. We show the different interfaces implemented by SANTé through guided steps from raw RDF data to the search result using keyword queries. We demonstrate how SANTé can be used to publish and consume RDF data.
Repository: http://github.com/AKSW/sante
License: https://www.apache.org/licenses/LICENSE-2.0
FOAF demo: http://foaf.aksw.org/
Pokémon demo: http://pokemon.aksw.org/

1 Introduction

There is an enormous amount of machine-readable data published on the Web ranging from a variety of serialization formats and domains. Among the most used serialization formats lies the W3C standard Resource Description Framework (RDF).[1] RDF advocates for a flexible-schema approach that allows publishers to curate content (re-)using self-descriptive metadata. Many institutions such as Google[2] and the German National Library[3] have adopted the W3C standard either for consuming or publishing information. To date, over 600 thousand RDF data sets [8] are openly accessible on the Web over interfaces that facilitate its access such as SPARQL[4] and Comunica [7]. However, most of these initiatives require lay users to be familiar with RDF standards and domain-specific languages. Additionally, many of the RDF data available on the Web

---

[1] https://www.w3.org/RDF.
[2] https://developers.google.com/search/docs/data-types/product.
[3] https://wiki.dnb.de/pages/viewpage.action?pageId=68060017.
[4] https://www.w3.org/TR/sparql11-query.

© Springer Nature Switzerland AG 2021
R. Verborgh et al. (Eds.): ESWC 2021 Satellite Events, LNCS 12739, pp. 93–97, 2021.
https://doi.org/10.1007/978-3-030-80418-3_17

has no equivalent human-friendly format such as web pages or relies on third-party search engines such as Google for content access and discovery. Over the last years, several approaches such as question answering [2], search [4] and user interfaces [1] have been proposed to address this problem. In this article, we demonstrate SANTé, an open-source semantic search framework that aims to democratize RDF access by providing an end-to-end semantic search framework. SANTé is a result of several years of research [4,5] and is designed for enabling RDF data publishing, browsing, and search through keyword queries. SANTé can be used to leverage complex applications such as SPARQL query building capabilities using natural language queries [3] and facet search [6]. In this work, we show SANTé's different built-in functionalities and demonstrate how to publish arbitrary RDF data in the following section. We conclude with an outlook on future work.

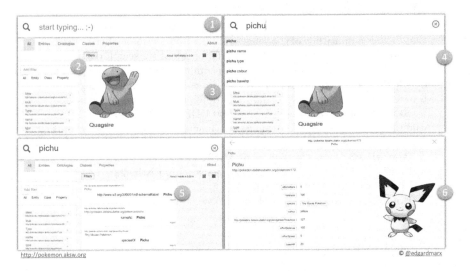

Fig. 1. An overview of six different features available in SANTé User Interface over the Pokémon data set: (1) Search bar; (2) Faceted Filter: enables to refine the search and to perform faceted navigation through the addition of graph pattern based filters; (3) Knowledge cards: simplifies the information visualization; (4) Autocomplete: offers automatic suggestions based on the user's query; (5) Structured Highlights: highlights the search result accordingly to the best match property-object(s) and generates concise snippets; (6) Data browser: allows to explore and browse content and search results.

2   Demonstration

The goal of this demonstration is to cover the necessary steps of making an arbitrary RDF data set accessible using keyword queries. We showcase a practical example of instantiation using standard ontologies. We aim to promote a community discussion around the topic and to gather relevant feedback. In the following, we provide a guided outline of the publishing pipeline and access interfaces. SANTé's code and releases are openly available at https://github.com/ AKSW/sante. To facilitate the assessment and evaluation, a short animation and video demonstrating SANTé's capabilities are also available on the Git repository.

2.1 Indexing and Instantiating

The RDF framework allows users to model concepts and their relations in a structured manner. Ontologies such as OWL and RDFS are powerful tools for creating metadata. One of the most distinguishable RDF features is the possibility of using reasoners to infer unexplicit hierarchies and relations. SANTé relies on triple stores for index creation, which can support different levels of reasoning. In the following running example, we show how to instantiate a KBox[5] endpoint containing the FOAF ontology and its dependencies (Listing 1.1) as well as how to create an index from there using a command line (Listing 1.2).

```
1 java -jar kbox.jar -server -kb "http://xmlns.com/foaf/0.1,
    https://www.w3.org/2000/01/rdf-schema,http://www.w3.org
    /2002/07/owl,http://www.w3.org/1999/02/22-rdf-syntax-ns
    ,http://purl.org/dc/elements/1.1/,http://purl.org/dc/
    terms/,http://purl.org/dc/dcam/,http://purl.org/dc/
    dcmitype/" -install
2 Loading Model...
3 Publishing service at http://localhost:8080/kbox/sparql
4 Service up and running ;-) ...
```

Listing 1.1. Instantiating an endpoint using FOAF ontology and its dependencies.

```
1 java -jar sante-vXXX.jar index -endpoint http://localhost
    :8080/kbox/sparql -path \foaf
```

Listing 1.2. Indexing the FOAF ontology and its dependiencies instantiated in Listing 1.1.

After indexing, the content can be published using SANTé's Web Service WAR file as follows.

```
1 java -jar sante-vXXX.jar server -war sante-vXXX.war -path \
    foaf -port 9090
```

Listing 1.3. Instantiating SANTé's webserver with the FOAF ontology and its dependencies previously indexed (see Listing 1.2).

If all steps above have been successfully followed, the Web search interface will be accessible at http://localhost:9090.

Searching & Browsing. Figure 1 gives an overview of SANTé's search and browsing capabilities. It is possible to refine the search with graph pattern filters or explore and navigate through the metadata over user-friendly web pages.

---

[5] https://github.com/AKSW/KBox.

SANTé works with customizable Knowledge Cards. Knowledge Cards are *rich cards*[6] that contain useful information about something and could be enriched with links, pictures, and other types of media accordingly to the necessity (③ in Fig. 1). Another SANTé's feature is dubbed *Structured Highlights* (⑤ in Fig. 1). Common search engines display results using `feature snippets` and `OneBox results` (see Footnote 4) [6]. They present relevant web page text blocks in case of the former or an inline answer in case of the latter. Structured Highlights are knowledge-card-snippets automatically generated using the most likely property-objects containing the information sought. Structured Highlights works as a cognitive activity snapshot giving an outlook on every available relevant information through highly activated graph connections—using *P [4].

2.2 Access Interfaces

To facilitate integration and information consumption, SANTé allows to search through four different `REST` APIs and a command-line interface:

/API/lookup exposes a `JSON` REST interface that allows to access the indexed data using the DBpedia `lookup` API.[7]

/API/reconcile implements the Reconcile Service API Specification Version 0.1.[8] with limited support to `queries`[9] over `HTTP GET`.

/API/search and */API/suggest* exposes resp. the search and auto-suggestion REST APIs, allowing to restrict results by class, URI- and URI-prefixes.

Command-line interface In addition to the four `REST` interfaces, it is also possible to search using a `command-line` interface as follows:

```
1 java -jar sante-vXXX.jar -query "resource" -path \foaf
```

Listing 1.4. Searching for all occurrences of the word *"resource"* in the FOAF ontology.

2.3 Showcases

SANTé's different capabilities are showcased in two live instances:

- http://foaf.aksw.org/ This is the live instance of the running example presented in this paper. The user can experience a real-time search where the result is computed while the query is being typed. It showcases SANTé's simple (search and data browser) interface on publishing the FOAF ontology.
- http://pokemon.aksw.org/ This instance showcases SANTé's full functionalities (search, autocomplete, REST APIs, facet search using graph pattern based filters, and data browser) over the Pokémon data set.

---

[6] https://developers.google.com/search/docs/advanced/appearance/search-result-features.

[7] https://wiki.dbpedia.org/lookup.

[8] https://www.w3.org/community/reconciliation/.

[9] https://reconciliation-api.github.io/specs/0.1/#reconciliation-queries.

3   Conclusion

In this work, we presented an open-source framework that enables publishing, browsing, and search RDF data through keyword queries. The presented framework is designed to facilitate lay users to access RDF data contents. The next efforts will consist of: (1) Facilitating content extraction, streaming, and access with query languages; (2) Improving the user interfaces; Integrate (3) entity recommendation, (4) versioning, and, (5) content curation. We see this work as the first step towards human- and machine-enabled content access. We are looking forward to fruitful collaborative engagement with RDF data set publishers and consumers.

References

1. Bast, H., Bäurle, F., Buchhold, B., Haußmann, E.: Semantic full-text search with broccoli. In: Proceedings of the 37th International ACM SIGIR Conference on Research & Development in Information Retrieval, pp. 1265–1266 (2014)
2. Diefenbach, D., Lopez, V., Singh, K., Maret, P.: Core techniques of question answering systems over knowledge bases: a survey. Knowl. Inf. Syst. **55**(3), 529–569 (2018)
3. Ferré, S.: Sparklis: an expressive query builder for SPARQL endpoints with guidance in natural language. Seman. Web **8**(3), 405–418 (2017)
4. Marx, E., Höffner, K., Shekarpour, S., Ngomo, A.-C.N., Lehmann, J., Auer, S.: Exploring term networks for semantic search over RDF knowledge graphs. In: Garoufallou, E., Subirats Coll, I., Stellato, A., Greenberg, J. (eds.) MTSR 2016. CCIS, vol. 672, pp. 249–261. Springer, Cham (2016). https://doi.org/10.1007/978-3-319-49157-8_22
5. Marx, E., et al.: DBtrends: publishing and benchmarking RDF ranking functions. In: SumPre 13th Extended Semantic Web Conference (2016)
6. Moreno-Vega, J., Hogan, A.: GraFa: scalable faceted browsing for RDF graphs. In: Vrandecic, D., et al. (eds.) ISWC 2018. LNCS, vol. 11136, pp. 301–317. Springer, Cham (2018). https://doi.org/10.1007/978-3-030-00671-6_18
7. Taelman, R., Van Herwegen, J., Vander Sande, M., Verborgh, R.: Comunica: a modular SPARQL query engine for the web. In: Proceedings of the 17th International Semantic Web Conference, October 2018
8. Valdestilhas, A., Soru, T., Nentwig, M., Marx, E., Saleem, M., Ngomo, A.-C.N.: Where is my URI? In: Gangemi, A., et al. (eds.) ESWC 2018. LNCS, vol. 10843, pp. 671–681. Springer, Cham (2018). https://doi.org/10.1007/978-3-319-93417-4_43

Coverage-Based Summaries for RDF KBs

Giannis Vassiliou[1], Georgia Troullinou[2], Nikos Papadakis[1], Kostas Stefanidis[3], Evangelia Pitoura[4], and Haridimos Kondylakis[1,2(✉)]

[1] Department of Electrical and Computer Engineering, Hellenic Mediterranean University, Heraklion, Greece
npapadak@hmu.gr
[2] FORTH-ICS, Heraklion, Greece
{troullin,kondylak}@ics.forth.gr
[3] Tampere University, Tampere, Finland
konstantinos.stefanidis@tuni.fi
[4] Computer Science and Engineering Department, University of Ioannina, Ioannina, Greece
pitoura@cs.uoi.gr

Abstract. As more and more data become available as linked data, the need for efficient and effective methods for their exploration becomes apparent. Semantic summaries try to extract meaning from data, while reducing its size. State of the art structural semantic summaries, focus primarily on the graph structure of the data, trying to maximize the summary's utility for query answering, i.e. the query coverage. In this poster paper, we present an algorithm, trying to maximize the aforementioned query coverage, using ideas borrowed from result diversification. The key idea of our algorithm is that, instead of focusing only to the "central" nodes, to push node selection also to the perimeter of the graph. Our experiments show the potential of our algorithm and demonstrate the considerable advantages gained for answering larger fragments of user queries.

1 Introduction

The rapid explosion of the available data in the web has led to an enormous amount of widely available RDF datasets [1]. However, these datasets often have extremely complex and large schemas, which are difficult to comprehend, limiting the exploitation potential of the information they contain. One method for condensing and simplifying such datasets is through semantic summaries. According to our recent survey [1], a semantic summary is a compact information, extracted from the original RDF graph. Summarization aims at extracting meaning from data, and also at offering compact representations which some applications can exploit instead of the original graph to perform certain tasks.

State of the art works in the area of structural summarization [2–5] first try to identify the most important nodes of the schema graph, and then to optimally link them, producing a connected schema sub-graph. As such, the size of the presented schema graph is reduced to a minimum size, so that end-users are easier to understand the contents of the generated summary, while in parallel the most important nodes are selected and presented to the user.

© Springer Nature Switzerland AG 2021
R. Verborgh et al. (Eds.): ESWC 2021 Satellite Events, LNCS 12739, pp. 98–102, 2021.
https://doi.org/10.1007/978-3-030-80418-3_18

The Problem. The problem with the state-of-the-art structural semantic summaries is that the selected, most important nodes, are in most of the cases nodes located centrally to the graph, missing exploration opportunities for the nodes that are located at the perimeter of the graph. For example, consider the graph shown on the left of Fig. 1, which shows a summary from the state-of-the-art tool on structural summaries, i.e. the RDFDigest+ [3]. We can see that the summary focuses on a central part of the entire graph and all nodes are connected to a central one, i.e. the *Agent* class. Although such a summary would be really useful for queries around the *Agent*, for a non-homogeneous query workload, a summary like the one presented on the right of Fig. 1 would arguably be better, as it is able to give us more insights on the specific dataset at it not focus only on the *Agent* class but also to other more diverse nodes.

Contribution. To this direction, result diversification has also attracted considerable attention as a means of enhancing the quality of the exploration results presented to the users, as it offers, intuitively more informative results than a homogeneous result [6]. However, to the best of our knowledge, those ideas, although notably useful and interesting, have not yet migrated into structural semantic summaries. In this paper, we focus on summaries that try to maximize query coverage, exploiting ideas from the result diversification field. The idea is to combine semantic and structural diversity in order to further improve the generated summary, by first ordering the nodes based on their importance, and then iteratively starting from the nodes with the longest shortest paths, eliminate the nodes in the ranking within a specific radius, till the desired number of nodes is selected.

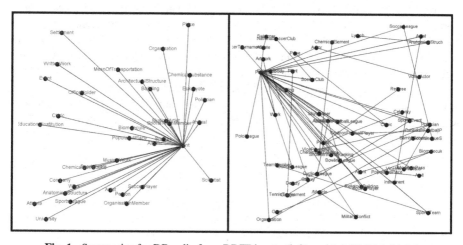

Fig. 1. Summaries for DBpedia from RDFDigest+ (left) and 1-LSP-Disc (right)

2 Schema Summarization

Schema summarization aims to highlight the most representative concepts of a schema, preserving important information and reducing the size and the complexity of the whole schema. Central questions to summarization are (i) how to select the schema nodes for generating the summary, and (ii) how to link selected nodes in order to produce a valid sub-schema graph [1]. To answer the first question, existing works so far exploit centrality measures, selecting the k nodes with the highest value of the specific centrality measure used (e.g. betweenness). To link those nodes, Graph Steiner-Tree [7] approximation algorithms are used, by introducing the minimum number of additional nodes to the summary - as introducing many additional nodes would shift the focus of the summary and decrease summary's quality.

In this work, we separate between the schema and instances of an RDF/S KB, represented in separate graphs, G_S and G_I as similarly done in the bibliography [1, 3] and as the schema graph offer the first level of abstraction for an RDF/S KB. The schema graph contains all classes and the properties they are associated with. The instance graph contains all individuals, and the corresponding properties. In our approach, we focus specifically on the schema graph and more specifically on *how to select the most important schema nodes so that summary's utility for query answering is maximized*. As such, assuming a query log, we would like to *maximize the fragments of queries that are answered by the summary*. More specifically, having a summary, we can calculate for each query that can be partially answered by the summary, the percentage of the classes and properties that are included in the summary, i.e. the success classes and the success properties. The *query coverage is the weighted sum of these percentages*.

Now, having defined the coverage for a given query workload Q, *a coverage-based summary is the one maximizing the coverage for the queries in Q*. As the problem of computing the summary with the maximum coverage for Q is NP-complete, in this paper we propose a heuristic algorithm for computing it. The algorithm, named 1-LSP-DisC, starts by ranking all nodes based on the betweenness centrality measure (lines 3–5) and then it calculates all shortest paths for the top $k/2$ nodes in that list (lines 6–7). It selects the ones with the maximum distance and eliminates from the betweenness list their neighbors in a radius r. Then it continues visiting the remaining nodes in the list, removing each time, the neighbors of the selected nodes and so on (lines 9–15). The novelty of the algorithm lies in the fact that it combines shortest paths for only $k/2$ nodes, selecting the ones with the maximum shortest path and uses them as a seed to eliminate neighbors and so on.

Algorithm 1: 1-LSP-DisC(G_S,k, r)
Input: An RDF/S schema graph G_S, k the number of nodes to select, r the radius of the nodes to be excluded.
Output: A set of nodes N.
1. N:= $\emptyset$; N_{LSP}:= $\emptyset$
3. **for each** *node* in G_S **do**
4.   *betweenness[node]*:=calculate_betweenness(G_S, *node*)
5. sort_nodes(*betweenness*)
6. N_{BET}:=Select top $k/2$ nodes from *betweenness*
7. *LSP* := Calculate_all_pairs_shortest_paths(N_{BET}, G_S)
8. N_{LSP} := Select the two nodes from *LSP* with maximum shortest path
9. **for each** *node* in N_{LSP} **do**
10.   **Add** *node* to N
11.   **Remove** *node and node's* neighbors in a radius r from the *betweenness* list
12. **while** *betweenness* != $\emptyset$ and $|N| < k$ **do**
14.   **Add** *top node* in *betweenness* to N
15.   **Remove** *node* neighbors in a radius r from the *betweenness* list
16. **Return** N

---

3   Evaluation and Conclusions

Next, we present a preliminary evaluation. We use as a baseline LSP and contrast our results with the state-of-the-art approach on structural summaries, the RDFDigest+ [3]. **LSP** selects k schema nodes with *the maximum shortest path distance to be included in the summary*, whereas **RDFDigest+** selects the k schema nodes *with the highest betweenness value*. For **1-LSP-DisC**, we set the radius to one, as this is the only case were we could get in the summary the 10% of the available nodes (for r > 1, many neighbors were excluded from the list and as such only few nodes were eventually left). In addition, as we are focusing on node-based summaries, for calculating coverage, we use 0.8 for the weight on classes and 0.2 for the weight on properties. For the evaluation, we use DBpedia v3.8 (422 classes, 1323 properties and more than 2.3M instances) and Semantic Web Dog Food (SWDF) KBs (120 classes, 72 properties and more than 300K triples) exploiting user query logs from the corresponding SPARQL endpoints (902 queries for SWDF and 56K queries for DBpedia). In each case, we request a 10% summary (16 nodes for SWDF and 36 for DBpedia). In this paper due to lack of space we only report results for 10% but results are similar for 5% as well.

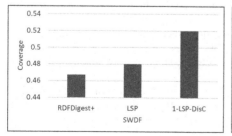 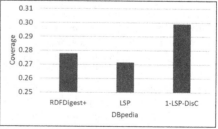

Fig. 2. Coverage for the various algorithms for the SWDF (left) and DBpedia (right) datasets.

As shown in Fig. 2, in both cases out algorithm outperforms both LSP and RDFDigest+. In the case of SWDF, the RDFDigest+ generates a summary with a coverage of 47%, the LSP achieves a coverage of 48% whereas the 1-LSP-DisC method achieves a coverage of 52%. The same is happening for DBpedia, where our approach achieves a coverage of 30%. Note that the difference in the coverage between the DBpedia and the SWDF dataset is attributed to the significantly larger size of DBpedia and to the large number of queries we had available for the DBpedia dataset.

Overall, our experiments confirm that the produced summaries indeed maximize the coverage of thousands of user queries, although they have been constructed, without using the specific workload. In our next steps, we intend to focus on properties selection, so that we not only select the ones minimizing addition of extra nodes in the summary, but also the most important ones, maximizing further the result coverage. Finally, we intend to exploit summaries for RDF query answering [8] as having summaries that maximize coverage has the potential to use those summaries for query answering instead of the original graph.

Acknowledgements. This research project was supported by the Hellenic Foundation for Research and Innovation (H.F.R.I.) under the "2nd Call for H.F.R.I. Research Projects to support Post-Doctoral Researchers" (iQARuS Project No. 1147).

References

1. Kondylakis, H., Plexousakis, D.: Ontology evolution: assisting query migration. In: Atzeni, P., Cheung, D., Ram, S. (eds.) ER 2012. LNCS, vol. 7532, pp. 331–344. Springer, Heidelberg (2012). https://doi.org/10.1007/978-3-642-34002-4_26
2. Čebirić, Š, et al.: Summarizing semantic graphs: a survey. VLDB J. **28**(3), 295–327 (2018). https://doi.org/10.1007/s00778-018-0528-3
3. Pappas, A., Troullinou, G., Roussakis, G., Kondylakis, H., Plexousakis, D.: Exploring importance measures for summarizing RDF/S KBs. In: Blomqvist, E., Maynard, D., Gangemi, A., Hoekstra, R., Hitzler, P., Hartig, O. (eds.) ESWC 2017. LNCS, vol. 10249, pp. 387–403. Springer, Cham (2017). https://doi.org/10.1007/978-3-319-58068-5_24
4. Troullinou, G., Kondylakis, H., Stefanidis, K., Plexousakis, D.: Exploring RDFS KBs using summaries. In: Vrandečić, D., et al. (eds.) ISWC 2018. LNCS, vol. 11136, pp. 268–284. Springer, Cham (2018). https://doi.org/10.1007/978-3-030-00671-6_16
5. Troullinou, G., Kondylakis, H., Daskalaki, E., Plexousakis, D.: RDF digest: ontology exploration using summaries. In: International Semantic Web Conference (Posters & Demos) (2015)
6. Drosou, M., Pitoura, E.: DisC diversity: result diversification based on dissimilarity and coverage. Proc. VLDB Endow. **6**(1), 13–24 (2012)
7. Voß, S.: Steiner's problem in graphs: heuristic methods. Discrete Appl. Math. **40**(1), 45–72 (1992)
8. Agathangelos, G., Troullinou, G., Kondylakis, H., Stefanidis, K., Plexousakis, D.: RDF query answering using apache Spark: review and assessment. In: IEEE 34th International Conference on Data Engineering Workshops (ICDEW), pp. 54–59 (2018)

Named Entity Recognition as Graph Classification

Ismail Harrando$^{(\boxtimes)}$ and Raphaël Troncy

EURECOM, Sophia Antipolis, Biot, France
{ismail.harrando,raphael.troncy}@eurecom.fr

Abstract. Injecting real-world information (typically contained in Knowledge Graphs) and human expertise into an end-to-end training pipeline for Natural Language Processing models is an open challenge. In this preliminary work, we propose to approach the task of Named Entity Recognition, which is traditionally viewed as a *Sequence Labeling* problem, as a *Graph Classification* problem, where every word is represented as a node in a graph. This allows to embed contextual information as well as other external knowledge relevant to each token, such as gazetteer mentions, morphological form, and linguistic tags. We experiment with a variety of graph modeling techniques to represent words, their contexts, and external knowledge, and we evaluate our approach on the standard CoNLL-2003 dataset. We obtained promising results when integrating external knowledge through the use of graph representation in comparison to the dominant end-to-end training paradigm.

Keywords: Named Entity recognition · Graph Classification

1 Introduction

Transformer-based language models such as BERT [2] have tremendously improved the state of the art on a variety of Natural Language Processing tasks and beyond. While it is hard to argue against the performance of these language models, taking them for granted as the fundamental building-block for any NLP application stifles the horizon of finding new and interesting methods and approaches to tackle quite an otherwise diverse set of unique challenges related to specific tasks. This is especially relevant for tasks that are known to be dependent on real-world knowledge or domain-specific and task-specific expertise. Although these pre-trained language models have been shown to internally encode some real-world knowledge (by virtue of being trained on large and encyclopedic corpora such as Wikipedia), it is less clear which information is actually learnt and how it is internalized, or how one can inject new external information (e.g. from a knowledge base) into these models in a way that it does not require retraining them from scratch.

In this work, we propose a novel method to tackle Named Entity Recognition, a task that has the particularity of relying on both the linguistic understanding

© Springer Nature Switzerland AG 2021
R. Verborgh et al. (Eds.): ESWC 2021 Satellite Events, LNCS 12739, pp. 103–108, 2021.
https://doi.org/10.1007/978-3-030-80418-3_19

of the sentence as well as some form of real-world information, as what makes a Named Entity is the fact that it refers to an entity that is generally designated by a proper name. Since graphs are one of the most generic structures to formally represent knowledge (e.g. Knowledge Graphs), they constitute a promising representation to model both the linguistic (arbitrarily long) context of a word as well as any external knowledge that is deemed relevant for the task to perform. Graph connections between words and their descriptions seems to intuitively resemble how humans interpret words in a sentence context (how they relate to preceding and following words, and how they relate external memorized knowledge such as being a "city name" or "an adjective"). Hence, we propose to cast Named Entity Recognition as a Graph Classification task, where the input of our model is the representation of a graph that contains the word to classify, its context, and other external knowledge modeled either as nodes themselves or as node features. The output of the classification is a label corresponding to the entity type of the word (Fig. 1).

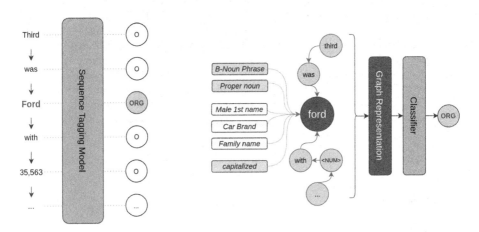

Fig. 1. Left: Traditional sequence tagging model. Right: Each *word* in a sentence becomes the central node of a graph, linked to the words from its context, as well as other task-related features such as grammatical properties (e.g. "Proper Noun"), gazetteers mentions (e.g. "Car Brand") and task-specific features (e.g. "Capitalized"). The graph is then embedded which is passed to a classifier to predict an entity type.

2   Approach

In order to perform Named Entity Recognition as a Graph Classification task, the "word graph" needs to be transformed into a fixed-length vector representation, that is then fed to a classifier, e.g. a feed-forward neural network (see Fig. 1). This graph representation needs to embed the word to classify (the *central node*), as well as its *context* – words appearing before and after it – and its related *tags* (properties such as gazetteers mention, grammatical role, etc.). This formalization is interesting because it allows to represent the entire context of the word (as graphs can be arbitrarily big), to explicitly model the left and the right context separately, and to embed different descriptors to each word seamlessly (either as node features or as other nodes in the graph) and thus help the model to leverage knowledge from outside the sentence and the closed training process. This is a first difference with the traditional sequence labeling methods that only consider a narrow window the tokens to annotate. While we posit that this method can integrate any external data in the form of new nodes or node features in the input graph, we focus on the following properties that are known to be related to the NER task:

- **Context:** which is made of the words around the word we want to classify.
- **Grammatical tags:** we use the Part of Speech tags (POS) e.g. 'Noun', as well as the shallow parsing tags (chunking) e.g. 'Verbal Phrase'.
- **Case:** in English, capitalization is an important marker for entities. We thus add tags such as: 'Capitalized' if the word starts with a capital letter, 'All Caps' if the word is made of only uppercase letters, and so on.
- **Gazetteers:** we generate lists of words that are related to potential entity types by querying Wikidata for labels and synonyms corresponding to entities belonging to types of interest such as *Family Name*, *Brand*, etc.

The literature on Graph Representations shows a rich diversity in approaches [1,4], but for our early experiments, we choose one candidate from each of the main representation families: a neural auto-encoder baseline, Node2Vec for node embeddings, TransE for Entity Embeddings, and a Graph Convolutional Network based on [4]. This is admittedly a small sample of the richness that can be further explored in the future, both in terms of the models and the way the input graph is constructed (how to model the context and the added knowledge).

3   Experiments and Results

3.1   Experimental Protocol

To train each of the aforementioned models, we construct a dataset[1] by going through every word in every document from the CoNLL training dataset, and build its graph (Fig. 1). Each of these graphs is then turned into a fixed-length vector that is fed to a neural classifier (Sect. 3.2). For each of the representations, we fine-tune the hyper-parameters using the ConLL validation (dev) set. We report the Micro-F1 and Macro-F1 scores for all trained models in Table 1 for both the validation and test sets together with the best currently reported performance approach from the state of the art[2].

---

[1] https://github.com/Siliam/graph_ner/tree/main/dataset/conll.
[2] See also http://nlpprogress.com/english/named_entity_recognition.html.

3.2 Methods

To evaluate the approach, we selected the following methods to generate graph embeddings:

1. `Binary Auto-encoder`: we represent the word graph as a binary vector. We concatenate one-hot embeddings of the word, its left and right context, and all other extra tags in the vocabulary (e.g. POS tags, gazetteers mention, etc.). We use this "flat" representation of the graph as a baseline that incorporates all the external data without leveraging the graph structure. We first train a neural encoder-decoder (both feed-forward neural networks with one hidden layer) to reconstruct the input binary representation of the graph. We then use the encoder part to generate a graph embedding to feed to our final classifier.

2. `Node2Vec`: we generate the graph representing all nodes in the training set (all words as related to their context, with the external knowledge tags also represented as nodes), and then we use `Node2Vec` [3] to generate embeddings for all nodes. The final input graph representation is obtained by averaging all nodes representations, i.e. the word, its context and its tags.

3. `TransE`: we generate the graph as with the `Node2Vec` method, except that the edges between the different nodes (entities) are now labeled relations such as 'before', 'after', 'pos'. We average the representations of each of these nodes to obtain a graph embedding.

4. `GCN`: unlike the previous approaches where a graph embedding is generated before the training phase, we can directly feed the graph data into a GCN and train it end-to-end, thus allowing the network to learn a task-specific graph representation. We base our model on GraphSAGE-GCN [4], using an architecture based on this model from the PyTorch Geometric library[3] that we modify to account for additional node features (tags, gazetteers classes, etc.). This allows the network to learn a graph representation that is specific to this task.

3.3 Results

In Table 1, we observe a significant decrease in performance for all models between the evaluation and test sets (with a varying intensity depending on the choice of the model) that is probably due to the fact that the test set contains a lot of out-of-vocabulary words that do not appear in the training set. Thus, they lack a node representation that we can feed to the network in inference time. We also see that adding the external knowledge consistently improve the performance of the graph models on both Micro-F1 and Macro-F1 for all models considered. Finally, while the performance on the test set for all graph-only models is still behind LUKE, the best performing state of the art NER model on ConLL 2003, we observe that these models are significantly smaller and thus faster to train (in matters of minutes once the graph embeddings are generated), when using a simple 2-layers feed-forward neural as a classifier.

---

[3] https://github.com/rusty1s/pytorch_geometric/blob/master/examples/proteins_topk_pool.py.

Table 1. NER results with different graph representations (CoNLL-2003 dev and test sets). The entries marked with "+" represent the models with external knowledge added to the words and their context.

Method	Dev m-F1	Dev M-F1	Test m-F1	Test M-F1
Auto-encoder	91.0	67.3	90.3	63.2
Auto-encoder+	91.5	71.7	91.5	70.4
Node2Vec	93.3	81.6	90.0	68.3
Node2Vec+	94.1	82.1	91.1	72.6
TransE	91.8	75.0	91.7	70.0
TransE+	93.6	78.8	91.9	74.5
GCN	96.1	86.3	92.9	78.8
GCN+	96.5	88.8	94.1	81.0
LUKE [5]				**94.3**

These preliminary results show promising directions for additional investigations and improvements.

4   Conclusion and Future Work

While the method proposed in this paper shows some promising results, the performance on the ConLL 2003 test set is still significantly lower than the best state-of-the-art Transformer-based method as of today. However, we have made multiple design choices to limit the models search space and we believe that additional work on the models themselves (different architectures, hyper-parameters fine-tuning, adding attention, changing the classifier) can improve the results. The drop of performance from the validation to the test set is probably due to the lack of any external linguistic knowledge outside of the training set, which can be overcome by enriching the nodes with linguistic features such as Word Embeddings. We will further study the gain from each of the added external knowledge, and test the method on other specialized datasets in order to demonstrate its value for domain-specific applications (fine-grained entity typing). To facilitate reproducibility, we published the code of our experiments at https://github.com/D2KLab/GraphNER.

Acknowledgments. This work has been partially supported by the French National Research Agency (ANR) within the ASRAEL (ANR-15-CE23-0018) and ANTRACT (ANR-17-CE38-0010) projects, and by the European Union's Horizon 2020 research and innovation program within the MeMAD (GA 780069) project.

References

1. Chami, I., Abu-El-Haija, S., Perozzi, B., Ré, C., Murphy, K.: Machine Learning on Graphs: A Model and Comprehensive Taxonomy. arxiv:2005.03675 (2021)
2. Devlin, J., Chang, M., Lee, K., Toutanova, K.: BERT: pre-training of deep bidirectional transformers for language understanding. In: NAACL-HLT (2019)
3. Grover, A., Leskovec, J.: Node2vec: scalable feature learning for networks. In: 22nd ACM International Conference on Knowledge Discovery and Data Mining (2016)
4. Hamilton, W.L., Ying, Z., Leskovec, J.: Inductive representation learning on large graphs. In: NeurIPS (2017)
5. Yamada, I., Asai, A., Shindo, H., Takeda, H., Matsumoto, Y.: Luke: deep contextualized entity representations with entity-aware self-attention. In: EMNLP (2020)

Exploiting Transitivity for Entity Matching

Jurian Baas$^{(\boxtimes)}$, Mehdi M. Dastani, and Ad J. Feelders

Utrecht University, Heidelberglaan 8, 3584 CS Utrecht, Netherlands
{j.baas,m.m.dastani,a.j.feelders}@uu.nl

Abstract. The goal of entity matching in knowledge graphs is to identify sets of entities that refer to the same real-world object. Methods
for entity matching in knowledge graphs, however, produce a collection
of pairs of entities claimed to be duplicates. This collection that represents the sameAs relation may fail to satisfy some of its structural
properties such as transitivity. We show that an ad-hoc enforcement of
transitivity on the set of identified entity pairs may decrease precision.
We therefore propose a methodology that starts with a given similarity
measure, generates a set of entity pairs, and applies cluster editing to
enforce transitivity, leading to overall improved performance.

1 Introduction

Many datasets use different identifies to refer to the same real life entities, or may
contain duplicates themselves. Automated methods for identifying and linking
duplicate entities, also known as entity matching, in the knowledge graphs are
necessary. A considerable difficulty with entity matching is that the total number
of possible entity pairs is much larger than the number of actual (duplicate)
entity pairs, also known as the problem of skewness [1,10]. This extreme skewness
can cause false positive results to overwhelm the true positives, even for highly
accurate classifiers. This has caused many other works to use ranking techniques,
and their associated metrics, to sort the possible entity pairs with some similarity
measure, where duplicate entity pairs are expected to appear on top of the
ranking [4,8,9,11]. Other works, such as Saeedi et al. [7], perform blocking in the
first stages to reduce the number of pairs that are evaluated. Furthermore, Raad
et al. [5] start with a set of sameAs relations, and use a community detection
algorithm to associate an error degree for each sameAs relation. They show that
when only taking sameAs relations with an error degree ≤ 0.4, they achieve
100% accuracy within their random sample.

The identified set of pairs are generally required to satisfy some structural
properties, in particular transitivity. However, taking the transitive closure of
the entity pairs identified by entity matching techniques may not work as this
may possibly conclude many spurious entity pairs.

We propose the application of cluster editing for entity matching and set
up a number of experiments to evaluate our proposal. We show that compared

R. Verborgh et al. (Eds.): ESWC 2021 Satellite Events, LNCS 12739, pp. 109–114, 2021.
https://doi.org/10.1007/978-3-030-80418-3_20

to an ad-hoc enforcement of transitive closure on identified pairs, our approach always results fewer distinct entity pairs (i.e. they have a higher precision) while retaining duplicate entity pairs (i.e. recall is not lowered).

The experiments are performed on semi-synthetic datasets that are generated by introducing duplicates in an existing dataset in a controlled manner. This results in a range of different cluster distributions, where we measure the effects of the number of clusters and different cluster sizes.

2   Applying Cluster Editing on Matched Entities

An overview of our overall method is given in Fig. 1. We start with an embedding of a set of entities E, some of which may be duplicates, and use Euclidean distance to measure their proximity (panel A of Fig. 1). For each entity $e_i \in E$, we make k candidate pairs (e_i, e_j), where e_j is the k-nearest neighbor of e_i, thereby addressing skewness by ruling out the vast majority of pairs.

The dotted lines in panel B illustrate the candidate pairs for $k = 1$. Moreover, we assume that a (small) subset of these candidate pairs is labeled by a domain expert (blue lines in panel B). The labeled pairs are used to train a probabilistic classifier. This classifier is used to determine, for each candidate pair (e_i, e_j), the fitted probability p_{ij} that e_i and e_j are duplicates. Depending on the features used by the classifier, and its complexity, the fitted probabilities need not be proportional to the distance between entities. We do however assume that the features used by the classifier are symmetric so that $p_{ij} = p_{ji}$, and therefore we can indeed regard a pair of entities as unordered. We then use a cut-off value θ so that if $p_{ij} > \theta$, then e_i and e_j are predicted to be duplicates (panel C). This "raw outcome" of the pairwise classifier, which represents te sameAs relation, may however violate the expected transitivity constraint. Obviously, an ad-hoc application of transitive closure to the links predicted by the classifier never removes any links, but can only add new links (panel G). This may result many spurious entity pairs. A more principled method to restore transitivity is to use the cluster editing technique [3]. Here, we compute a weight $w(i,j) = \log(\frac{p_{ij}}{1-p_{ij}}) - \log(\frac{\theta}{1-\theta})$ for each pair of entities (e_i, e_j) within the same connected component (regardless of whether it is a candidate pair or not), such that $w(i,j)$ is positive if $p_{ij} > \theta$, and negative otherwise (panel D). If $w(i,j)$ is positive (negative), a link between i and j is provisionally assumed to be present (absent). The resulting set of links may however again violate the transitivity constraint. Cluster editing is used to restore transitivity by adding and/or removing links in such a way that the total score $\sum_{(i,j)} w(i,j) x_{ij}$ is maximized, where $x_{ij} = 1$ if a link between i and j is present in the solution, and $x_{ij} = 0$ otherwise (panels E and F). Finally, more information about our method is available at [2].

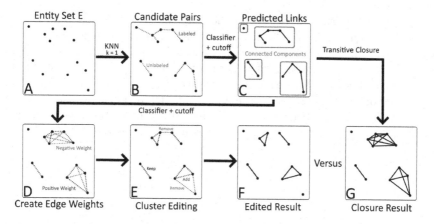

Fig. 1. An overview of the entity matching process.

3   Results

The data source we use is an RDF version of Ecartico[1], a comprehensive collection of biographical data about, among others, painters, engravers and book sellers. These people worked in the Low Countries at the time of the 16th and 17th century. This data source is actively curated so we can be sure there are no duplicate records of persons. From the Ecartico graph, we have constructed a new graph containing all `schema:Person` entities that have values for the properties – `schema:name`, – `schema:workLocation`, and – `schema:hasOccupation`. For each of these entities, we also copy the property-value pairs for – `schema:birthDate`, – `schema:deathDate`, – `schema:birthPlace`, and – `schema:deathPlace` when they are present. This resulted in a graph with, including `rdf:type` for the class `schema:Person`, eight properties, all centered around that one RDF class.

Then we introduce duplicates by uniformly sampling a percentage of entities and altering their respective URI's. For example, when sampling entities, an entity with URI `www.data.uu.nl/1234` will be modified to `www.data.uu.nl/1234/3`. We create three cluster distributions $\mathcal{D}_{10}$, $\mathcal{D}_{25}$ and $\mathcal{D}_{50}$, which are determined by the percentage of entities that is sampled, which can be either 10, 25 or 50%. Figure 2 shows the resulting distributions of clusters, where, for instance with 10%, we expect most entities to be in a cluster of size 1, meaning they were not duplicated. When modifying 50%, of entities, however, this results in most entities being duplicated at least once, and the largest proportion being duplicated twice. In this case non-duplicate entities are in the minority, making the entity matching problem considerably harder.

Table 1 shows the results of our experiments. We denote the application of transitive closure with the subscript TC and the application of cluster editing with the subscript CE. For every value of $\theta \in (0, 1)$ (in steps of 0.01) we generate an associated $F\frac{1}{2}$-score, as it is our experience that a low precision has a larger

---

[1] http://www.vondel.humanities.uva.nl/ecartico.

negative impact (than low recall) on the performance of downstream systems such as SPARQL engines. The $F_{\frac{1}{2}}$-score weights precision twice as heavy as recall. We average the $F_{\frac{1}{2}}$-score for all values of θ (100 values between 0 and 1) to denote the performance of a given combination of cluster distribution, classifier and features. We experimented with a logistic regression (LR) and support vector machine (SVM) classifier. All were trained using cosine similarity as the sole feature. Furthermore, we used just 100 pairs to train each classifier, limiting the burden on the domain expert as much as possible.

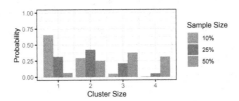

Fig. 2. Generated probability distributions of entity clusters of size 1 to 4 in the synthetic data. The values of a color sum to one.

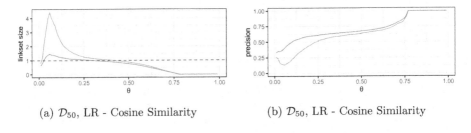

(a) $\mathcal{D}_{50}$, LR - Cosine Similarity   (b) $\mathcal{D}_{50}$, LR - Cosine Similarity

Fig. 3. Left: relative number of pairs predicted vs actual number (red dotted line). Right: precision for transitive closure (red lines) and edited closure (blue lines). (Color figure online)

In all cases we observe that the application of cluster editing improves the resulting set of duplicates over the application of transitive closure. Furthermore, the optimal value for θ is in most cases reduced when cluster editing is applied, suggesting that a more lenient cutoff can be used, while at the same time improving performance. Furthermore, Fig. 3a shows how closure of the entity pair set tend to overestimate the number of duplicate pairs for low values of θ, where the number of predicted pairs is more than 4 times the number of actual pairs. Finally, Fig. 3b shows that the cluster editing method consistently outperforms transitive closure in precision.

Table 1. A comparison of the mean and maximum $F\frac{1}{2}$-scores, and associated value for θ for transitive closure (TC) and cluster editing (CE), per classifier and cluster distributions ($\mathcal{D}_{10}, \mathcal{D}_{25}, \mathcal{D}_{50}$)

Classifier	Dataset	θ_{TC}	θ_{CE}	Mean$_{TC}$	Mean$_{CE}$	Max$_{TC}$	Max$_{CE}$
LR	$\mathcal{D}_{10}$	0.43	0.51	0.46	0.50	0.69	0.70
	$\mathcal{D}_{25}$	0.40	0.35	0.37	0.41	0.62	0.64
	$\mathcal{D}_{50}$	0.51	0.41	0.38	0.44	0.62	0.64
SVM	$\mathcal{D}_{10}$	0.72	0.83	0.61	0.64	0.68	0.70
	$\mathcal{D}_{25}$	0.70	0.66	0.43	0.51	0.62	0.64
	$\mathcal{D}_{50}$	0.78	0.67	0.45	0.54	0.62	0.64

4 Conclusion and Future Work

In practice, entity matching methods are applied and the resulting entity pairs are used by, e.g., a reasoner in a SPARQL engine, which applies the transitive closure. This may introduce many spurious links, potentially creating large clusters of unrelated entities. We propose to apply cluster editing to create a set of links that is closed under transitivity and show that the application of cluster editing, compared to the transitive closure, always results in a set of duplicates that contains fewer distinct entity pairs (i.e. they have a higher precision) while retaining duplicate entity pairs (i.e. recall is not lowered). The NP-Hardness of cluster editing limits us to solving only relatively small connected components. There are, however, heuristic methods which enables larger components to be solved. These heuristic methods can effectively reduce the instance size of the problem and are fast in case a small number of edits is allowed [6]. Additionally, the Louvain community detection technique proposed by Raad et al. [5] for detecting erroneous links can be applied to the connected components formed by the candidate pairs. It would be interesting to see how it compares to other (heuristic) clustering techniques.

References

1. Al Hasan, M., Zaki, M.J.: A survey of link prediction in social networks. In: Aggarwal, C. (ed.) Social Network Data Analytics, pp. 243–275. Springer, Boston (2011). https://doi.org/10.1007/978-1-4419-8462-3_9
2. Baas, J., Dastani, M., Feelders, A.: Exploiting transitivity constraints for entity matching in knowledge graphs. arXiv:2104.12589 (2021)
3. Böcker, S., Baumbach, J.: Cluster editing. In: Bonizzoni, P., Brattka, V., Löwe, B. (eds.) CiE 2013. LNCS, vol. 7921, pp. 33–44. Springer, Heidelberg (2013). https://doi.org/10.1007/978-3-642-39053-1_5
4. Chen, M., Tian, Y., Chang, K.W., Skiena, S., Zaniolo, C.: Co-training embeddings of knowledge graphs and entity descriptions for cross-lingual entity alignment. arXiv preprint arXiv:1806.06478 (2018)

5. Raad, J., Beek, W., van Harmelen, F., Pernelle, N., Saïs, F.: Detecting erroneous identity links on the web using network metrics. In: Vrandečić, D. (ed.) ISWC 2018. LNCS, vol. 11136, pp. 391–407. Springer, Cham (2018). https://doi.org/10.1007/978-3-030-00671-6_23
6. Rahmann, S., Wittkop, T., Baumbach, J., Martin, M., Truss, A., Böcker, S.: Exact and heuristic algorithms for weighted cluster editing. In: Computational Systems Bioinformatics, vol. 6, pp. 391–401. World Scientific (2007)
7. Saeedi, A., Nentwig, M., Peukert, E., Rahm, E.: Scalable matching and clustering of entities with famer. Complex Syst. Inform. Model. Q. **16**, 61–83 (2018)
8. Sun, Z., Hu, W., Li, C.: Cross-lingual entity alignment via joint attribute-preserving embedding. In: d'Amato, C., Fernandez, M., Tamma, V., Lecue, F., Cudré-Mauroux, P., Sequeda, J., Lange, C., Heflin, J. (eds.) ISWC 2017. LNCS, vol. 10587, pp. 628–644. Springer, Cham (2017). https://doi.org/10.1007/978-3-319-68288-4_37
9. Trisedya, B.D., Qi, J., Zhang, R.: Entity alignment between knowledge graphs using attribute embeddings. In: Proceedings of the AAAI Conference on Artificial Intelligence, vol. 33, pp. 297–304 (2019)
10. Weiss, G.M.: Mining with rarity: a unifying framework. ACM Sigkdd Explorations Newsletter **6**(1), 7–19 (2004)
11. Zhu, H., Xie, R., Liu, Z., Sun, M.: Iterative entity alignment via joint knowledge embeddings. IJCAI **17**, 4258–4264 (2017)

The Nuremberg Address Knowledge Graph

Oleksandra Bruns[1,2(✉)], Tabea Tietz[1,2], Mehdi Ben Chaabane[2],
Manuel Portz[2], Felix Xiong[2], and Harald Sack[1,2]

[1] FIZ Karlsruhe – Leibniz Institute for Information Infrastructure,
Karlsruhe, Germany
{oleksandra.bruns,tabea.tietz,harald.sack}@fiz-karlsruhe.de
[2] Karlsruhe Institute of Technology, Institute AIFB, Karlsruhe, Germany

Abstract. The research of European history across various time layers
gives insights about the development of the European cultural identity.
Nuremberg as one of the great European metropolises during the Middle
Ages experienced a number of transformations throughout the centuries.
Within the TRANSRAZ research project, Nuremberg and the development of its architecture and culture is recreated from the 17th to the 21st
century. It will be available for researchers and the public by means of an
interactive 3D environment. Goal of this poster paper is to discuss the
ongoing work of connecting heterogeneous historical data from sources
previously hidden in archives to the 3D model using knowledge graphs
for a scientifically accurate exploration of Nuremberg. The contribution
of this paper is the Nuremberg Address Knowledge Graph (NA-KG)
which contains information of people and organizations in Nuremberg
from unstructured data of Nuremberg address books.

Keywords: Knowledge graphs · Cultural heritage · History

1 Introduction

The exploration of European cities and their development throughout history
contributes to our understanding of the European cultural identity. However,
to explore our city histories including the cultures within on the Web, historical records have to be collected and transformed into a structured format
which can be integrated into intelligent user interfaces. Nuremberg was one of
the great European metropolises in the Middle Ages and beyond. Since then,
the city experienced numerous transformations, including the almost complete
destruction during the Second World War. Therefore, a systematic and scientific reconstruction of the city in different time periods is necessary to preserve
this important part of the European cultural heritage and make it accessible
for research. Nuremberg's reconstruction was first initiated with the TOPORAZ
project [2], in which a virtual research environment (VRE) was created linking a scholarly sound 3D model of the main market of the city of Nuremberg

© Springer Nature Switzerland AG 2021
R. Verborgh et al. (Eds.): ESWC 2021 Satellite Events, LNCS 12739, pp. 115–119, 2021.
https://doi.org/10.1007/978-3-030-80418-3_21

Fig. 1. A digitized page from "Addressbuch von Nürnberg 1910"

to a database in four different time layers. In this paper, parts of the ongoing project TRANSRAZ [3] (a successor of TOPORAZ) are presented. As part of TRANSRAZ, the Nuremberg History Knowledge Graph is being developed and integrated into the 3D VRE for exploration by researchers and the public. In order to provide means of exploration for Nuremberg, historical resources have to be collected and integrated into the KG. Address books provide one of the most comprehensive and valuable sources to extract knowledge about Nuremberg's citizens across different time periods. The Nuremberg address books date back to 1792 and are available annually since 1890. They form one part of a number of resources used to create the *Nuremberg History Knowledge Graph*. Prior projects integrating historical data into user interfaces to explore city histories include Amsterdam Time Machine[1] and the Time Traveler Berlin application [4]. Furthermore, notable recent efforts involving the creation of Linked Data resources from unstructured OCR data in the cultural heritage domain include [1,5].

Goal of this poster paper is to report on the ongoing work of integrating heterogeneous historical data sources into the *Nuremberg History Knowledge Graph* as part of the TRANSRAZ research project. The contribution of this paper is the *Nuremberg Address Knowledge Graph (NA-KG)* containing 860 K triples on persons and organizations in the Nuremberg address book of 1910. NA-KG is publicly available[2]. This contribution is valuable for historical scientists and digital humanists intending to study citizens' names, historical occupations as well as companies and their distribution in Nuremberg. After its integration into the 3D VRE, the address book data can be explored by researchers as well as the general public.

2   Nuremberg Address Knowledge Graph

This section presents the main contribution of the paper and discusses the workflow to populate the *Nuremberg Address Knowledge Graph (NA-KG)* as a part of the *Nuremberg History Knowledge Graph*.

---

[1] https://amsterdamtimemachine.nl/.
[2] https://github.com/ISE-FIZKarlsruhe/Transraz.

Data. The NA-KG is based on data from the 1910 address book of Nuremberg. The book contains information about 1) historical residents, e.g. their names, occupations, addresses, granted civil rights, 2) historical organizations, e.g. names and types of companies, ownership information and addresses. Starting point are scanned images of the address book in JPEG format (see Fig. 1) and their transcribed version in plain TXT format. Due to low paper quality, distortion of pages, poor inking, historic gothic fonts, ligatures, archaic terms and typos in the original sources, the resulting transcribed documents are rather noisy and require significant error correction as described below.

Segmentation. Based on the syntactic structure of the text, the data was divided into person entries and company entries. By developing a set of regular expressions the entries were further segmented into their individual components, e.g. last name, company name, street name, occupation. The missing information, e.g. omitted last names in case of namesakes and family members, was inserted.

Normalization. The errors in the individual components of the entries were resolved by leveraging reference vocabularies and lookup matching of potential candidates in the lexicon for correction, based on the Levenshtein distance. For addressing orthographic errors in last and first names a list of all first names of Cologne[3] and indexed data from Books of Nuremberg's Twelve Brothers[4] were exploited. For correcting the occupations the lists of German occupations[5] and German historical occupations[6][7] were extracted. The street names were normalized according to the urban space that is covered by TRANSRAZ project.

The Nuremberg Address Knowledge Graph. The NA-KG builds upon OWL[8], VCARD[9], FOAF[10], SCHEMA[11] and DBPEDIA[12]. It contains 5 classes: *vcard:Individual*, *vcard:Address*, *vcard:Organization*, *schema:Occupation* and *dbo:Street*; 6 object properties that describe relations between instances of these classes, e.g. *dbo:owningOrganization* and *vcard:hasAddress* ; and 10 datatype properties that provide information about instances, e.g. *vcard:organizationname* and *transraz:abbreviatedName*. The NA-KG includes 860 K RDF triples based on 165 K entities that were extracted from the address book. It consists of structured data about 1403 historical companies and 67 K residents of Nuremberg.

Being based on one of the fullest sources of Nuremberg citizens in 1910, the NA-KG makes it possible to develop hypotheses and draw reliable conclu-

---

[3] https://offenedaten-koeln.de/dataset/vornamen.
[4] https://hausbuecher.nuernberg.de/index.php?do=page&mo=5.
[5] https://de.wikipedia.org/wiki/Kategorie:Beruf.
[6] https://de.wikipedia.org/wiki/Kategorie:Historischer_Beruf.
[7] https://www.guenteroppitz.at/berufe/alte-berufsbezeichnungen-in-matzleinsdorf/.
[8] https://www.w3.org/OWL/.
[9] https://www.w3.org/TR/vcard-rdf/.
[10] http://xmlns.com/foaf/spec/.
[11] https://schema.org/.
[12] https://www.dbpedia.org/.

sions of the population and subsequently to extend and to enrich the knowledge about life in historical Nuremberg. For example, the existing KG is able to answer the following questions: *What was the ratio of persons with civil rights to persons without civil rights?* (Fig. 2), *What was the most common profession in 1910?* (Fig. 3), or *What was the central business district of Nuremberg? (Fig. 4)*[13]. Thus, the provided address book data allows to explore not only the whereabouts of Nuremberg inhabitants but also their social status, family relations and business developments.

```
PREFIX transraz: <http://transraz/addressbook#>
PREFIX rdf: <http://www.w3.org/1999/02/22-rdf-syntax-ns#>
PREFIX vcard: <http://www.w3.org/2006/vcard/ns#>
SELECT ?civilRight (COUNT(?civilRights) as ?counter_cvR)
WHERE { ?Individual rdf:type vcard:Individual   ;
            transraz:civilRights ?civilRights   . }
GROUP BY ?civilRights
ORDER BY DESC (?counter_cvR)
```

Fig. 2. The SPARQL query targeting the number of citizens who were granted civil rights.

```
PREFIX rdfs: <http://www.w3.org/2000/01/rdf-schema#>
PREFIX schema: <http://schema.org/>
SELECT ?name (COUNT(?name) as ?frequency)
WHERE { ?Individual schema:hasOccupation ?Occupation   .
        ?Occupation rdfs:label ?name   .}
GROUP BY ?name
ORDER BY DESC (?frequency)
```

Fig. 3. The SPARQL query targeting the frequency of occupations mentioned in "Addressbuch von Nürnberg 1910".

3   Discussion

Although the NA-KG is part of ongoing work to create a scientifically sound Nuremberg History Knowledge Graph, the contribution of the first version of NA-KG already provides a valuable structured resource for researchers in historical science, digital humanities and cultural heritage in general.

However, the current version of NA-KG also has shortcomings which will be addressed in future work. For example, in the address books, names and occupations are abbreviated inconsistently which complicates the normalization of the data. Furthermore, the NA-KG will be populated with data from address books

---

[13] See more example SPARQL queries under https://github.com/ISE-FIZKarlsruhe/
Transraz/tree/main/NurembergAddressKG/SPARQL_Queries.

```
PREFIX rdfs: <http://www.w3.org/2000/01/rdf-schema#>
PREFIX schema: <http://schema.org/>
SELECT ?Streetname (COUNT(?Streetname) as ?frequency)
WHERE {?Organization rdf:type vcard:Organization    ;
                      vcard:hasAddress ?AddressID    .
       ?AddressID vcard:hasStreetAddress ?Street     .
       ?Street rdfs:label ?Streetname    . }
GROUP BY ?Streetname
ORDER BY DESC(?frequency)
```

Fig. 4. The SPARQL query targeting the amount of companies for every street in Nuremberg.

of different time periods, thus, entity disambiguation and entity linking across different time layers will be required. To accomplish this, the historical data from address books will be enriched by mapping the entities to external data sources like Wikidata and national authority files. Moreover, for future exploration of such temporal changes the reasonable representation of time component will be considered.

4   Conclusion

This paper presents the *Nuremberg Address Knowledge Graph* which contains persons and organizations in the historical city of Nuremberg based on scanned and transcribed address book data. NA-KG is a substantial part of an ongoing work towards a *Nuremberg History Knowledge Graph* aiming to connect heterogeneous historical data about Nuremberg to a 3D virtual research environment. The presented KG allows to draw conclusions about the citizens and businesses of Nuremberg in 1910 and is available publicly on the Web.

Acknowledgement. This work is funded by the Leibniz Association under project number SAW-2020-FIZ KA-4-Transraz.

References

1. Koho, M., Ikkala, E., Leskinen, P., Tamper, M., Tuominen, J., Hyvönen, E.: Warsampo knowledge graph: Finland in the second world war as linked open data. Semant. Web (Preprint), 1–14 (2019)
2. Razum, M., et al.: Ein digitales raum-zeit-modell für vernetzte forschung am beispiel nürnberg. Inf. Wissenschaft Praxis **71**(4), 185–194 (2020)
3. Tietz, T., Bruns, O., Göller, S., Razum, M., Dessi, D., Sack, H.: Knowledge graph enabled curation and exploration of Nuremberg's city heritage [to be published]. In: Proceedings of the Conference on Digital Curation Technologies, CEUR-WS (2021)
4. Tolstoi, P.: A framework for location-based augmented reality content on mobile devices (2019)
5. van Erp, M., Wevers, M., Huurdeman, H.: Constructing a recipe web from historical newspapers. In: Vrandečić, D., et al. (eds.) ISWC 2018. LNCS, vol. 11136, pp. 217–232. Springer, Cham (2018). https://doi.org/10.1007/978-3-030-00671-6_13

SaGe-Path: Pay-as-you-go SPARQL Property Path Queries Processing Using Web Preemption

Julien Aimonier-Davat[✉][iD], Hala Skaf-Molli[iD], and Pascal Molli[iD]

LS2N, University of Nantes, Nantes, France
{julien.aimonier-davat,hala.skaf,pascal.molli}@univ-nantes.fr

Abstract. SPARQL property path queries allow to write sophisticated navigational queries on knowledge graphs (KGs). However, the evaluation of these queries on online KGs are often interrupted by fair use policies, returning only partial results. SaGe-Path addresses this issue by relying on the Web preemption and the concept of Partial Transitive Closure (PTC). Under PTC, the graph exploration for SPARQL property path queries is limited to a predefined depth. When the depth limit is reached, frontier nodes are returned to the client. A PTC-client is then able to reuse frontier nodes to continue the exploration of the graph. In this way, SaGe-Path follows a pay-as-you-go approach to evaluate SPARQL property path queries. This demonstration shows how queries that do not complete on the public Wikidata SPARQL endpoint can complete using SaGe-Path. An extended user-interface provides real-time visualization of all SaGe-Path internals, allowing to understand the approach overheads and the effects of different parameters on performance. SaGe-Path demonstrates how complex SPARQL property path queries can be efficiently evaluated online with guaranteed complete results.

Keywords: Semantic Web · SPARQL property path queries · Web preemption

1 Introduction

SPARQL property path queries provide a succinct way to write complex navigational queries over RDF knowledge graphs. However, the evaluation of these queries on online knowledge graphs such as DBPedia or Wikidata is often interrupted by quotas, returning no results or partial results. For example, the query $Q1$ depicted in Fig. 1, which returns all creative works with the list of fictional works that inspired them, is killed after 60s by the public Wikidata SPARQL endpoint. Consequently, only partial results are returned.

It is possible to get rid of quotas by evaluating path queries with Triple Pattern Fragment (TPF) [3,5] or Web Preemption [1]. However, as these approaches have no support for transitive closures on server-side, they materialize transitive closures on client-side. Then, they perform joins with the other parts of the

© Springer Nature Switzerland AG 2021
R. Verborgh et al. (Eds.): ESWC 2021 Satellite Events, LNCS 12739, pp. 120–125, 2021.
https://doi.org/10.1007/978-3-030-80418-3_22

PREFIX wd: <http://www.wikidata.org/entity/>
PREFIX wdt: <http://www.wikidata.org/prop/direct/>
SELECT ?creativeWork ?fictionalWork **WHERE** {
  ?creativeWork wdt:P144 ?fictionalWork .
  ?creativeWork wdt:P31/wdt:P279* wd:Q17537576 .
  ?fictionalWork wdt:P136 wd:Q8253}

Fig. 1. $Q1$: Creative works and the list of fictional works that inspired them on Wikidata

query, generating a huge data shipping that drastically degrades performances. For instance, SAGE[1], an online implementation of a web preemptive server, is able to complete query $Q1$ but the evaluation requires more than 17000 HTTP calls and takes 1100 s.

In [2], we presented a new approach to evaluate SPARQL property path queries by introducing the concept of Partial Transitive Closure (PTC). The PTC of a property path query Q corresponds to the evaluation of Q with a limited exploration depth. We demonstrated that a preemptable server [4] is able to fairly execute the PTC of any Basic Graph Patterns (BGPs) containing path expressions while returning complete results. When the PTC evaluation reaches the depth limit, frontier nodes are returned to a PTC-client, indicating where the graph exploration has been stopped. Thanks to this information, the PTC-client generates new path queries that restart the exploration from these frontier nodes. By iterating over frontier nodes, the PTC-client is able to go deeper and deeper in the graph exploration following a pay-as-you-go approach. Compared to the state of art, all transitive closures and BGPs are now executed on the preemptable server, only query results and control information are shipped to the clients. As described in [2], SAGE-PATH outperforms previous approaches both in terms of HTTP calls, data transfer and query execution time. For example, SAGE-PATH is able to complete the query $Q1$ in only 80s and 1500 HTTP calls for a depth set to 5.

For this demonstration, we build an interface that allows users to understand SAGE-PATH internals, how the evaluation of the SPARQL property path queries works, what are the underlying costs, what happens when changing the quanta of the web preemption and the depth limit of the Partial Transitive Closure. Finally, we show how SPARQL property path queries that cannot complete on public SPARQL endpoints can be easily terminated thanks to SAGE-PATH.

2   Overview of SAGE-PATH

SAGE-PATH relies on the *Web preemption* [4] to garantee complete results for any SPARQL property path queries. Web preemption is defined as the capacity of a web server to suspend a running SPARQL query after a fixed quantum of time and resume the next waiting query. When suspending a query Q, a

---

[1] SAGE is available at https://sage.univ-nantes.fr.

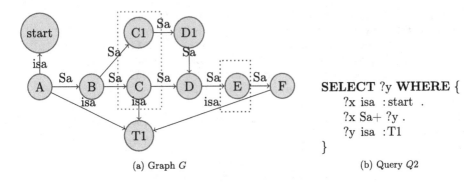

(a) Graph G (b) Query $Q2$

Fig. 2. Graph G and Query $Q2$

preemptable server saves the internal state of all operators of Q in a saved plan Q_s and sends Q_s to the client. The client can continue the execution of Q by sending Q_s back to the server. When reading Q_s, the server restarts the query Q from where it has been stopped. As a preemptable server can restart queries from where they have been stopped and makes a progress at each quantum, it eventually delivers complete results after a bounded number of quanta.

To compute property path queries with transitive closures, SaGe-Path extends the Web preemption with a PTC operator on server-side. The PTC of a property path query Q corresponds to the evaluation of Q where the exploration of the graph for transitive closures is limited to a maximum depth d. Under PTC, the evaluation of a property path query Q does not only return solution mappings, but also nodes visited by the PTC operators with their corresponding depths. Nodes visited at a depth equal to d are called *frontier nodes*.

To illustrate, consider the simple graph G defined in Fig. 2a and the query $Q2$ in Fig. 2b. Under a PTC semantics with $d = 2$, the evaluation of $Q2$ over G returns the solution $\{?y \mapsto C\}$ and the set of visited nodes $\{(B,1),(C,2),(C1,2)\}$ with their depths. Because C and $C1$ have been reached at depth 2, they are both marked as frontier nodes. In Fig. 2a, frontier nodes C and $C1$ are represented in a red dotted rectangle.

Q21: SELECT ?y WHERE {	Q22: SELECT ?y WHERE {	Q221: SELECT ?y WHERE {
BIND(:A as ?x).	BIND(:A as ?x).	BIND(:A as ?x).
:C1 Sa+ ?y.	:C Sa+ ?y.	:E Sa+ ?y.
?y isa :T1	?y isa :T1	?y isa :T1
}	}	}

Fig. 3. Expanded path queries

Because query $Q2$ terminates with 2 frontier nodes, the PTC-client generates two new queries $Q21$ and $Q22$ as depicted in Fig. 3. Queries $Q21$ and $Q22$ allow to continue the exploration of the graph G from the frontier nodes $C1$

and C, respectively. The execution of the query $Q21$ returns no solution mappings but two new visited nodes $\{(D1,1),(D,2)\}$ where D is a frontier node. As $Q21$, the query $Q22$ also returns no solution mappings but new visited nodes $\{(D,1),(E,2)\}$ where E is a frontier node. As we can see, D has been visited twice, leading to the transfer of a duplicate. The transfer of duplicates is clearly an overhead of the SaGe-Path approach [2]. Because the preemptable server does not remember visited nodes between quanta, it is possible to visit and transfer the same nodes several times. Small quanta are more likely to generate duplicates.

Node D has been visited by both $Q21$ and $Q22$, but $Q22$ reached D at a lowest depth than $Q21$. Consequently, after the execution of $Q22$, D is no longer considered as a frontier node and will not be expand by the PTC-client. As illustrated in Fig. 2a by the blue dotted rectangle, only E remains a frontier node and a new query $Q221$ is generated from $Q22$ to expand E. The execution of $Q221$ returns a new solution mapping $\{?y \mapsto F\}$ and a new visited node $(F,1)$. Because all frontier nodes have been explored, the query $Q2$ terminates. By merging results of $Q2$, $Q21$, $Q22$ and $Q221$, i.e. $\{?y \mapsto C\}$ and $\{?y \mapsto F\}$, we obtain complete results.

As we can see, PTC follows a pay-as-you-go approach that returns results with the shortest path first modulo d. This can be very interesting in interactive use-cases. Another advantage is that all joins are performed on the server. This is why SaGe-Path outperforms the state of art approaches [1]. These advantages come at the price of transferring visited nodes, perhaps multiple times. This overhead is highly dependent of the exploration depth d and the value of the quantum. The demonstration allows users to understand how these two parameters influence the overhead and the global performance.

3   Demonstration Scenario

The scenario is based on queries that do not terminate on the SPARQL endpoint of Wikidata, such as the query $Q1$ (of course, a visiter can try her own property path queries). The demonstration shows how SaGe-Path is able to complete such queries thanks to the PTC approach. The source-code of the demonstration and a video are available online at[2] and[3].

Figure 4 presents a fragment of the final result of the execution of query $Q1$ with the SaGe-Path user interface. Users can change the quantum and the MaxDepth parameters to see the effects on the evaluation of the query. A step-by-step execution allows to see all frontier nodes and expanded queries. Statistics allow to compare different runs for different values of quantum and MaxDepth. Each run is labeled according to the value of these parameters. For instance, in Fig. 4, $(1500, 5)$ corresponds to a run of $Q1$ with a quantum set to 1500 ms and a MaxDepth set to 5. As we can see, running $Q1$ with a MaxDepth of 5 generates

---

[2] Source Code: https://github.com/JulienDavat/ppaths-demo.
[3] Video: https://youtu.be/u47rbvIawkc.

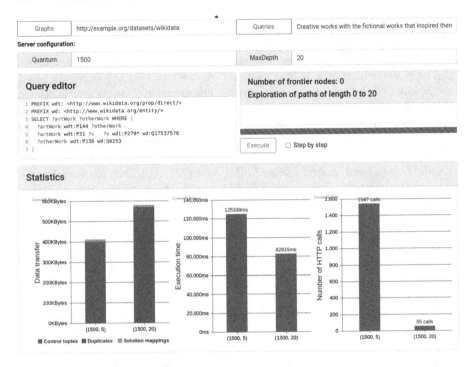

Fig. 4. User-Interface of SaGe-Path demonstration

less data transfer than a run with MaxDepth of 20, but the execution time and the number of HTTP calls are significantly increased.

4   Conclusion

In this demonstration, we presented SaGe-Path: a pay-as-you-go approach for processing SPARQL property path queries online and get complete results. The visualization of the progress of the query execution allows to observe how SaGe-Path servers provide a partial evaluation of a property path and how SaGe-Path clients use control information sent by the server to continue the execution until complete query execution. Compared to SPARQL endpoints, SaGe-Path always returns complete results and preserves the responsiveness of the server thanks to the web preemption. Compared to client-side approaches, SaGe-Path drastically improves performance in term of execution time and data transfer thanks to the PTC approach. As future works, in the current implementation, all expanded queries are executed sequentially. Executing them in parallel can significantly reduce execution times of SPARQL property path queries.

Acknowledgments. This work is supported by the national ANR DeKaloG (Decentralized Knowledge Graphs) project, ANR-19-CE23-0014, CE23 - Intelligence artificielle.

References

1. Aimonier-Davat, J., Skaf-Molli, H., Molli, P.: How to execute sparql property path queries online and get complete results? In: 4rth Workshop on Storing, Querying and Benchmarking the Web of Data (QuWeDa 2020) Workshop at ISWC2020 (2020)
2. Aimonier-Davat, J., Skaf-Molli, H., Molli, P.: Processing sparql property path queries online with web preemption. In: European Semantic Web Conference (2021)
3. Hartig, O., Letter, I., Pérez, J.: A formal framework for comparing linked data fragments. In: International Semantic Web Conference, pp. 364–382 (2017)
4. Minier, T., Skaf-Molli, H., Molli, P.: Sage: Web preemption for public sparql query services. In: The World Wide Web Conference, pp. 1268–1278 (2019)
5. Verborgh, R., et al.: Triple pattern fragments: a low-cost knowledge graph interface for the web. J. Web Semant. **37**, 184–206 (2016)

Ontology for Informatics Research Artifacts

Viet Bach Nguyen[✉] and Vojtěch Svátek

Department of Information and Knowledge Engineering,
Prague University of Economics and Business, Prague, Czech Republic
{nguv03,svatek}@vse.cz

Abstract. The IRAO ontology, as a new contribution to the network of ontologies for the scholarly domain, aims to model the most tangible aspect of research in computing disciplines – the research artifacts. It consists of parts focusing on the concepts of researcher, research artifact classification, research artifact meta information, relationships between artifacts, and research artifact quality evaluation benchmarks that are used to express the quality and maturity of each research artifact. We describe the ontology design requirements using competency questions and the evaluation of the ontology by the same questions that helped in defining the concept domain coverage.

Keywords: Competency question · Ontology building · Ontology competency · Ontology design · Research artifact · Research output

1 Introduction

Engineering disciplines such as informatics[1] tend to deliver, aside from the contribution to scientific knowledge by testing hypotheses and building theories, also compact, 'tangible' outputs, namely *artifacts*. Most typical examples are software prototypes, benchmark (or other) datasets, ontologies, as well as methodologies or managerial frameworks produced by Information Systems researchers. Notably, several computer science conferences (ISWC, ESWC, CIKM, BPM, SIGIR) and some journals have recently started to use the term 'resource paper' to denote a paper describing a reusable artifact aiming to serve the research (or, sometimes even practitioner) community; specific subclasses are then those of, e.g., 'software paper', 'dataset paper' or 'ontology paper'. Given this central role of artifacts in informatics research, it is rather surprising that no ontology has so far paid particular attention to this topic, by our recent survey [2].

---

[1] We use this concise term as largely interchangeable with 'computing disciplines', as discussed, e.g., in the new proposal for ACM/IEEE Computing Curricula, see https://cc2020.nsparc.msstate.edu/wp-content/uploads/2020/11/Computing-Curricula-Report.pdf.

Supported by IGA VŠE project № 56/2021.

R. Verborgh et al. (Eds.): ESWC 2021 Satellite Events, LNCS 12739, pp. 126–130, 2021.
https://doi.org/10.1007/978-3-030-80418-3_23

A research artifact is a tangible research output of a research project. This artifact is then circulated, shared, published, further developed, and may be reused to advance other research projects or applied in real-world scenarios. The motivation for carefully modeling informatics artifacts as a compact domain (rather than just specific kinds of artifacts in isolation) is manifold:

- The occurrence of different kinds of artifacts in research publications can be traced over time for particular sub-disciplines or venues, thus providing a broad picture of trends in informatics research.
- Networks of complementary or competitive artifacts (such as software tools being developed using a given methodology and applied on specific datasets backed on particular ontologies) can be connected together, thus allowing researchers to rapidly navigate from one to another and finding a reuse target (and even associated publications) more easily than by keyword search.
- Similarly, industrial companies can retrieve artifacts that they might consider transforming into deployed products.

In this poster paper, we introduce an ontology solution for the representation and management of informatics research artifacts. The goal of this ontology is to capture knowledge about research artifacts in the researcher environment and provide a reference model for the academic domain. This ontology is evaluated using competency questions that define the use cases for its functionalities.

Research/academia is gradually becoming a mainstream target domain for ontology-based applications. Recently we have published a comprehensive survey and analysis of academic and research-related ontologies [2]. We have retrieved and analyzed 43 ontologies and created a holistic model mapping for their coverage based on competency questions that focus on the academic domain from the perspective of a (primarily, senior) researcher's information needs. Among the reviewed resources, no ontologies focus on the description nor evaluation of research outputs or artifacts. There are, however: ontologies that include some general terms like *Resource*, in e.g., CCSO or DataCite;[2] ontologies that cover the project aspect of research with terms like *Project, License* or *Repository*, e.g., DOAP or SWRC;[3] ontologies that cover the publishing part of research with terms like *Deliverable* or *Output*, in e.g., VIVO or FRAPO.[4]

We have concluded that the artifact aspect of research needs an overarching formal conceptualization, which we identify as one of the missing features (gaps) in the existing ontology eco-system of the academic/researcher domain. By our survey, none of the current ontologies fully cover the requirement specification of our use cases, including the tangibility and quality assessment aspects. Another important requirement is the classification of research artifacts and the relationship between their types, which can be used to capture the interdependencies between artifacts within research projects.

---

[2] http://xworks.gr/ontologies/ccso, http://purl.org/spar/datacite.

[3] http://usefulinc.com/ns/doap, http://swrc.ontoware.org/ontology.

[4] http://vivoweb.org/ontology/core, http://purl.org/cerif/frapo.

2   Ontology Design and Competency Questions

Conforming to the NeOn ontology engineering methodology, we list out a set of competency questions (CQ) as part of our requirement specification document (ORSD) [3] to elicit relevant concepts, e.g., *CQ10 What type of artifact is it?* Both the CQs and the ORSD can be found in our GitHub repository.[5]

We first look up the terms 'research output' and 'research artifact' as defined on the websites of several academic institutions/universities (see the ORSD). From the definitions we collect the high-level entities such as *Researcher, Research Project* or *Research Artifact*. The *Informatics Research Artifact* as the direct output of a *Research Project* is the focal point of our ontology. To organize our competency questions, we divide the features of our ontology to four feature groups: for the research artifact itself, its development/readiness, its publishing/visibility and its quality.

Based on the gathered definitions of research output and competency questions, the ontology model should feature the following concepts:

- basic information about research artifacts, required for representing the artifact data gathered from repositories of theses, publications, software data repositories – incl. authorship, publication date, research field, topic, identifiers, etc.,
- types of research artifacts in terms of what they are useful for and how to use them,
- their development status, e.g., alpha, beta, release, or numbered version,
- their quality attributes, such as accessibility, use of an open standard, accessibility, or design principles,
- relationships between different types of artifacts, e.g., a dataset is described by a data model, a software uses a framework, etc.

3   Ontology Construction and Evaluation

Informatics Research Artifact Ontology (IRAO) was implemented in OWL using the Protégé editor. We also used OnToology [1] to automatically build the ontology using recommended metadata properties for self-documentation. The code and diagrams of IRAO can be found in our GitHub repository. The diagram in Fig. 1 shows the main entities of the ontology. The ontology documentation is available at https://w3id.org/def/InformaticsResearchArtifactsOntology.

IRAO consists of four parts that model the mentioned features. The artifact classification part lists out possible types of artifacts, e.g., *Dataset, Framework, Vocabulary,* and *Methodology*. All these types are defined as subclasses of the main concept. The meta information part includes relationships such as *hasAuthor, hasPublication, hasDomain* or *hasField*, having the range of *Researcher, Publication, Domain* and *Field*, respectively. The property *hasDevelopmentStatus* points to information about the maturity of the artifact. Properties *hasAccessibility, hasDesignQuality, isPublishedAt* and *hasStandard* are used

---

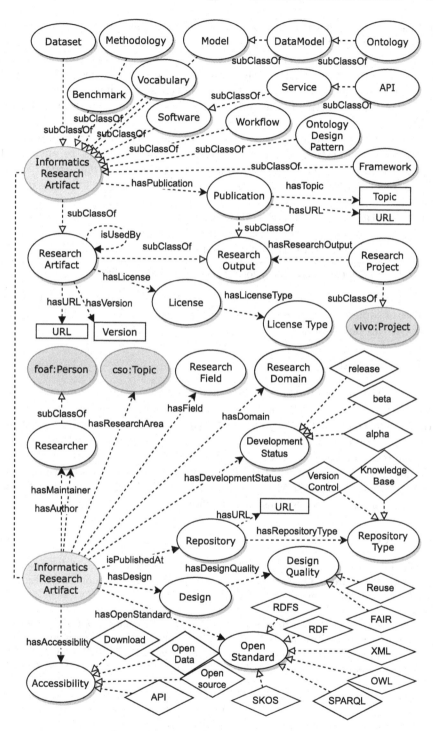

Fig. 1. Informatics research artifact ontology main diagram

to provide the artifact with classifying tags such as what types of standard was used to create the artifact and in what way is the artifact made available. The last part of our ontology deals with the relationships between different types of artifacts to describe situations such as when a research project can produce multiple types of artifacts in a way that some types of artifact can precede or follow other types of artifact. The diagram for these relationships is available on GitHub.

To ensure that the definitions correctly implement the ontology requirements and competency questions, we created several SPARQL queries to answer all competency questions. For example, to answer *CQ02 Who is the artifact's creator?* and *CQ11 Where was the artifact created?* we can use the following query:

```
SELECT * WHERE { ?artifact a irao:ResearchArtifact .
                 ?artifact irao:hasAuthor ?author .
                 ?author irao:hasAffiliation ?institution1 . }
```

Listing 1.1. Query for artifact author and affiliation

We also provide several examples of manually populated instance data for the use cases of conference resource track contributions and informatics dissertations in our GitHub repository.

4   Conclusion

The ontology described in this paper is envisioned to capture and manage informatics research artifacts. It can be used as a data model in a knowledge graph to track research artifacts along with their characteristics and meta-information, including relationship with other artifacts. It provides quality criteria for evaluating and recommending artifacts for researchers, reviewers and potential industrial adopters. The evaluation of the ontology was carried out by translating its competency questions to SPARQL queries, and examples from two different use cases were formulated to demonstrate its wider scope.

References

1. Alobaid, A., Garijo, D., Poveda-Villalón, M., Santana-Pérez, I., Fernández-Izquierdo, A., Corcho, Ó.: Automating ontology engineering support activities with OnToology. J. Web Semant. **57** (2019). https://doi.org/10.1016/j.websem.2018.09.003
2. Nguyen, V.B., Svátek, V., Rabby, G., Corcho, O.: Ontologies supporting research-related information foraging using knowledge graphs: literature survey and holistic model mapping. In: Keet, C.M., Dumontier, M. (eds.) EKAW 2020. LNCS (LNAI), vol. 12387, pp. 88–103. Springer, Cham (2020). https://doi.org/10.1007/978-3-030-61244-3_6
3. Suárez-Figueroa, M.C., Gómez-Pérez, A.: Ontology requirements specification. In: Suárez-Figueroa, M.C., Gómez-Pérez, A., Motta, E., Gangemi, A. (eds.) Ontology Engineering in a Networked World, pp. 93–106. Springer, Heidelberg (2012). https://doi.org/10.1007/978-3-642-24794-1_5

Non-named Entities – The Silent Majority

Pierre-Henri Paris$^{(\boxtimes)}$ and Fabian Suchanek

Télécom Paris, Institut Polytechnique de Paris, Palaiseau, France
{pierre-henri.paris,fabian.suchanek}@telecom-paris.fr

Abstract. Knowledge Bases (KBs) usually contain named entities. However, the majority of entities in natural language text are not named. In this position paper, we first study the nature of these entities. Then we explain how they could be represented in KBs. Finally, we discuss open challenges for adding non-named entities systematically to KBs.

1 Introduction

RDFS Knowledge Bases (KBs) such as DBpedia, YAGO, and Wikidata usually contain *named entities* – e.g., people, locations, and organizations. These entities are canonicalized, they are equipped with facts, and they belong to classes that are arranged in a taxonomy. The facts of a KB can be extracted, e.g., from natural language text. However, the majority of entities in real-world natural language text are not named. Consider for example the sentence "The Arab Spring resulted in a contentious battle between a consolidation of power by religious elites and the growing support for democracy" (taken from a Wikipedia article). This sentence is clearly factual, and thus interesting for information extraction. However, it contains only a single named entity. Many fact-extraction techniques will simply not consider the other entities. Thus, these entities remain "silent", and the statement stands no chance of making it into an RDFS KB.

The problem of extracting facts from such sentences is, of course, as old as information extraction itself. In this position paper, we look at the problem from a Semantic Web point of view. Technically, we look at *noun phrases*, i.e., sequences of words that take the grammatical function of a noun. In English, noun phrases can be the subject or object of a sentence, they fall under the *NP* node in phrase structure grammars, and they can contain determiners, adjectives (possibly modified by adverbs), one or several nouns (the last of which is the *head noun*), prepositional phrases (such as "in the Arab World"), relative clauses (introduced, e.g., by "which"), and other modifiers of the head noun. All noun phrases refer to *entities*. Some noun phrases are proper names (capitalized in English), and thus refer to *named entities* – but the vast majority are not. In a slight misuse of terms, and in line with [1,5], we call these noun phrases *non-named entities*.

In this article, we first study the nature of non-named entities manually on Wikipedia articles (Sect. 2). Then we discuss how they can be extracted and

R. Verborgh et al. (Eds.): ESWC 2021 Satellite Events, LNCS 12739, pp. 131–135, 2021.
https://doi.org/10.1007/978-3-030-80418-3_24

added to RDFS KBs (Sect. 3). Finally, we discuss what would have to be done to make non-named entities first-class citizens in RDFS KBs (Sect. 4).

2   Non-Named Entities

Several works have investigated the nature of non-named entities, albeit only as a side-product: The work of [5] studied Named Entity Recognition (NER) for resource-poor languages, and found that 86% of noun phrases in the studied corpus were non-named entities. The work of [1] studied the performance of NER models on different corpora, and manually annotated noun-phrases, classifying them into ACE categories. Due to the choice of literary texts, 67% of phrases refer to people.

To further investigate the nature of non-named entities, we conducted a manual analysis of noun-phrases in Wikipedia articles. Our choice is motivated by the fact that Wikipedia is a widely used standard reference, which also feeds KBs such as DBpedia and YAGO. We focus on the "featured articles", and choose one article from each of the 30 topics[1]. We automatically extract (and manually verify) noun phrases from the abstract of the article. We consider noun phrases that are sequences of nouns, adjectives, adverbs, prepositions, and determiners – 1924 in total.

We find that 78% of noun phrase heads are non-named entities. Of these, 63% are singular, and thus refer to a single entity ("a French book"). The others are plural, and could thus be understood as ad-hoc concepts ("French books"). Inspired by the YAGO 4 taxonomy [9], we annotated the noun phrases by the top-level classes of schema.org combined with the top-level classes of BioSchema.org. Unsurprisingly, a large part of the non-named entities are

Head of noun phrases		
Named	428	22%
Non-named	1496	78%
Total	1924	100%
Non-named: plurality		
Singular	937	63%
Plural	590	37%
Non-named: class		
Action	124	8%
Product	67	4%
Person	147	10%
Taxon	40	3%
Event	168	11%
Intangible	418	28%
Place	121	8%
Organization	75	5%
Medicalentity	3	0%
Creativework	310	21%
Biochementity	23	2%
Non-named: nature and modifiers		
Undetermined	590	39%
Determined	485	32%
Quantified	109	7%
Anaphora	92	6%
Qualified by an.	133	9%
Mass noun	288	19%
Preposition	503	34%
Contains named	167	11%
Adjective	571	38%
Adjacent nouns	188	13%
No modifiers	506	34%

Intangibles – such as "support", "gain", or "operation". Creative works (such as "song") and people ("singer") are also frequent. 32% of non-named entities

---

[1] https://en.wikipedia.org/wiki/Wikipedia:Featured_articles.

are determined ("the man"), which makes it more likely that they are central to the text. At 19%, mass nouns ("fame") are also rather frequent, while quantified expressions ("3 men") are not frequent. We counted as anaphoras any reference (by pronoun or determined noun phrase) to a preceding entity. They are rather infrequent. Some entities are qualified by an anaphora ("one of his siblings"). While one third of the noun phrases are unaccompanied, 38% are modified by an adjective, and 34% have a preposition. Inter-annotator agreement was 88%.

3   Adding Non-named Entities to RDFS KBs

Extracting Non-named Entities. Semantic parsers (such as FRED, K-Parser, Pikes, or Graphene), Abstract Meaning Representation systems, and structured discourse representation systems (such as [2]) build a semantic structure on top of a dependency parse of the input sentence. In this representation, non-named entities can figure just like named entities. The named entities can be mapped to existing entities in a KB, and the others remain unmapped. Some of these systems also perform co-reference resolution, so that anaphoras are resolved, and the semantic structure becomes a graph (as opposed to a tree). Open Information Extraction (IE) systems (such as OpenIE, StuffIE, NestIE, MinIE, or ClausIE) build triples of subject, predicate, and object, all of which can be arbitrary phrases (instead of canonicalized entities). Both representations can thus contain non-named entities (see, e.g., [4] or [6] for details about these systems).

Modeling Non-named Entities. The question is now how these non-named entities can be modeled in an RDFS KB. One possibility is by the means of classes: Plural phrases can become classes, and singular phrases can become anonymous instances of ad-hoc classes (so that two occurrences of "a French book" can be two instances of that class). These classes could then become subclasses of the superclass determined by the head noun ("French book" → "book"), or else directly the top-level class ("CreativeWork") – which could be determined by multi-class classification. Anaphoras (such as pronouns or determined nouns) would have to be replaced by their referents. Noun phrases that contain nested noun phrases would have to receive special treatment ("the gas in the balloon", e.g., would have to be linked to "the balloon"). Numbered noun phrases could be replicated appropriately. Mass nouns would have to become classes: Even if they do not allow a plural, they can still have instances (as in "the fame that Elvis achieved").

The Gap. Even if some non-named entities can be added straightforwardly to RDFS KBs, there is still a gap between the noun phrases in a text and the entities in an RDFS KB. There is currently no way that an RDFS KB can integrate a non-named entity such as "the growing support for democracy in many Muslim-majority states". Such an entity appears to combine several entities, it would be difficult to attach to a class other than "Intangible", it could semantically overlap in unspecified ways with other entities (such as "the support for democracy in

Muslim states"), and it is difficult to equip with facts, let alone axioms. Let us now detail these challenges.

4 Bridging the Gap

Knowledge Representation. The modeling of non-named entities depends on the modeling of classes and instances in the target KB. Currently, some KBs (such as ConceptNet, BabelNet, Quasimodo, and in general common sense KBs [7]) contain mainly classes. Others (such as WebIsALod, WebOfConcepts, NELL) make no difference between instances and classes. Again other KBs mix classes and instances (Wikidata makes "human" both an instance and a class). Some KBs duplicate classes and instances (DBpedia, e.g., contains a class and an instance called "book"), and others keep them separate (e.g., YAGO). These models may need to be reconsidered when non-named entities are added to the KB (see, e.g., [3] or [10] for surveys about such KBs).

Another challenge are plural phrases (such as "scientists", "many MLB batting records", or "hundreds of soldiers"), which generate an unspecified number of instances. These would potentially have to be modeled by axioms. OWL could provide the necessary semantics here. The same is true for all-encompassing noun phrases such as "all other non-ferrous metals". Some non-named entities would better be modeled as relations ("the knowledge of irrigation", "his invention of an early instant coffee process", or "the focus of their individual chapters"). Vagueness is another major challenge ("large-scale settlement" or "various notions"), as are noun phrases that reify statements ("the perception of hieroglyphs as purely odeographic") [8].

Canonicalization. Entities would have to be canonicalized, so that synonymous noun phrases are merged into one non-named entity ("the rise of the stock market" and "the surge of the stock market"), but distinct entities are kept apart (rises of different stock markets). This harbors challenges in the dimension of time (two different rises of the same stock market) and more generally in determining whether similar non-named entities in different contexts are the same (two stock market rises mentioned in different texts).

Facts. Non-named entities can require elaborate statements about classes (think of "pacific winds", "dormant volcano", or "his characteristic surrealist style"). A particular challenge are phrases that make sense only in connection to other phrases, especially comparatives, superlatives, and temporal comparisons ("the first woman to pilot her own baloon", "more powerful centers appearing to the south", "a growing hostility toward factual discussion", etc.). All of these may require elaborate axioms. Currently, instance-oriented KBs tend to make crisp boolean statements ("X was born in Y"), while class-oriented KBs tend to make weak statements ("Elephants are gray" means that elephants are typically gray, not necessarily all of them). To model non-named entities, one would probably need stricter relationships for instances and laxer ones for classes. This cohabitation, however, has not yet been studied.

5   Conclusion

In this position paper, we have argued that non-named entities make up a large majority of noun phrases in natural language text. We have analyzed their nature in a manual study of Wikipedia articles, and we have discussed how such noun phrases could be extracted and added to KBs. Finally, we have listed a number of challenges that still remain, indicating that we are still a long way from making full use of natural language text for RDFS KBs. All our data is available at https://phparis.net/posts/non-named_entities.

Acknowledgements. This work was partially funded by the ANR IA grant ANR-20-CHIA-0012 ("NoRDF").

References

1. Bamman, D., Popat, S., Shen, S.: An annotated dataset of literary entities. In: NAACL-HLT (2019)
2. Freitas, A., O'Riain, S., Curry, E., da Silva, J.C.P., Carvalho, D.S.: Representing texts as contextualized entity-centric linked data graphs. In: Workshop on Database and Expert Systems Applications (2013)
3. Hogan, A., et al.: Knowledge graphs. CoRR, abs/2003.02320 (2020)
4. Mahouachi, M.E., Suchanek, F.M.: Extracting complex information from natural language text: a survey. In: Semantic Journalism Workshop (2020)
5. Mbouopda, M.F., Melatagia Yonta, P.: Named entity recognition in low-resource languages using cross-lingual distributional word representation. ARIMA 33 (2020)
6. Niklaus, C., Cetto, M., Freitas, A., Handschuh, S.: A survey on open information extraction. In: COLING (2018)
7. Razniewski, S., Tandon, N., Varde, A.S.: Information to wisdom: commonsense knowledge extraction and compilation. In: WSDM (2021)
8. Suchanek, F.M.: The need to move beyond triples. In: Text2Story Workshop (2020)
9. Tanon, T.P., Weikum, G., Suchanek, F.M.: YAGO 4: a reason-able knowledge base. In: ESWC (2020)
10. Weikum, G., Dong, L., Razniewski, S., Suchanek, F.M.: Machine knowledge: creation and curation of comprehensive knowledge bases. In: Foundations and Trends in Databases (2021)

Unsupervised Relation Extraction Using Sentence Encoding

Manzoor Ali[1]([⊠]), Muhammad Saleem[2], and Axel-Cyrille Ngonga Ngomo[1]

[1] DICE Group, Department of Computer Science, Paderborn University,
Paderborn, Germany
manzoor@campus.uni-paderborn.de, axel.ngonga@upb.de
[2] AKSW, University of Leipzig, Leipzig, Germany
saleem@informatik.uni-leipzig.de

Abstract. Relation extraction between two named entities from unstructured text is an important natural language processing task. In the absence of labelled data, semi-supervised and unsupervised approaches are used to extract relations. We present a novel approach that uses sentence encoding for unsupervised relation extraction. We use a pre-trained, SBERT based model for sentence encoding. Our approach classifies identical sentences using a clustering algorithm. These sentences are used to extract relations between two named entities in a given text. The system calculates a confidence value above a certain threshold to avoid semantic drift. The experimental results show that without any explicit feature selection and independent of the size of the corpus, our proposed approach achieves a better F-score than state-of-the-art unsupervised models.

1 Introduction

Relation extraction (RE) is a salient Natural Language Processing (NLP) task, which aims to extract the semantic relation between two named entities from natural language text. Relation extraction plays an essential role for many NLP applications such as question answering systems, knowledge bases creation and completion [9], etc. Supervised approaches require labelled data for relation extraction, which is an expansive and tedious task. In the absence of labelled training data, unsupervised approaches are used to extract relations from natural language text.

State-of-the-art (SOTA) unsupervised approaches use different strategies such as word embeddings [5], entity-type information [10], convolutional neural network [8], etc. to extracts relations from unlabeled corpora. These approaches may fail to extract the correct and complete relations. For example, *"... Nephew George P. Bush – son of Florida Gov. Jeb Bush..."* from this sentence, the word embedding approach will extract *birthplace(George P. Bush, Florida)* relation. In contrast, the actual relations in this sentence are *governorOf (Jeb Bush, Florida)* and *sonOf(Jeb Bush, George P. Bush)*. In such situations, it is mandatory to

R. Verborgh et al. (Eds.): ESWC 2021 Satellite Events, LNCS 12739, pp. 136–140, 2021.
https://doi.org/10.1007/978-3-030-80418-3_25

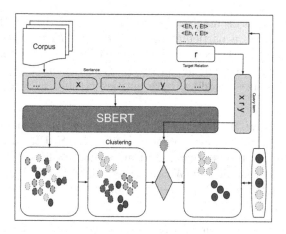

Fig. 1. The system architecture

know the context of the sentence instead of only using word embedding. Therefore, we use sentence encoding for relation extraction.

To the best of our knowledge, BERT-based [4] *sentence encoding* is yet not used for *unsupervised* relation extraction. This is because BERT-based sentence encoding and similarity is computationally expensive [7]. We propose a novel unsupervised approach dubbed **US-BERT** that uses the BERT-based sentence encoding [7] on a corpus that is already annotated for named entities (NE).

Our main contributions are as follow: we do not rely on any explicit feature selection for relation extraction; we achieve (SOTA) results for unsupervised relation extraction.

2   Our Approach

Figure 1 describes the US-BERT architecture. Input to our system is a target relation, named entities annotated corpus, and the two named entity types for the target relation. The system outputs all those sentences that include a target relation.

Our approach comprises four main modules. The candidate sentences selection module chooses all those sentences that contain two already specified named entity types. A sentence can also contain other entities and entity types. The sentence encoding module uses sentence-BERT to calculate 768-dimensional sentence encoding of the selected sentences. The clustering module creates clusters from similar vector representations of sentences. The relation extraction module uses a verb form to choose the most relevant cluster and extract semantically identical sentences based on cosine similarity.

Candidate Sentences Selection: The proposed approach chooses candidate sentences based on NE types for a particular relation for reducing the computation time. A set of candidate sentences is created from all annotated (named entity types annotation) sentences that include E_h and E_t, and the type of E_h and E_t is according to a particular relation. E_h and E_t represent the subject entity and object entity, respectively. For example, for a relation birthPlace, we only filter those sentences that include entity type Person (PER) and Location (LOC). Before sentence encoding, both entities E_h and E_t, are removed from the sentence.

Sentence Encoding: We consider the SBERT based pre-trained model that achieves SOTA performance for sentence encoding [7]. SBERT uses siamese and triplet network to produce sentences that are semantically meaningful and also comparable for cosine-similarity. We used pre-trained SBERT model, *distilbert-base-nli-stsb-mean-tokens*. It is trained on 570,000 sentences.

Clustering: To aggregate semantically similar vectors for a particular relation, we performed clustering. Clustering combines similar vectors and reduces the number of sentences for comparison to the query term. The system only selects those clusters that are semantically close to the query term.

Unsupervised algorithms like K-Mean and K-medoids require manual selection of the number of clusters. In relation extraction, two entities can have a variable number of relations in the real world. Therefore, we choose Affinity propagation for clustering. Affinity propagation does not need the number of cluster to be specified in advance. It selects an exemplar vector and creates a cluster around the exemplar.

Query Encoding and Relation Extraction: We adopt a query-based approach to extract a relation from a cluster. In our approach, a query is a sentence that contains two entities X and Y. Also, the query contains a relationship in phrasal verb form. For example, the complete query we use for the relation birthPlace is "X born in Y". We use sentence encoding to convert the query to a vector representation. We compute the cosine similarity between all the centroids and the query vector. If the cosine similarity between the centroid of a cluster and query vector crosses the threshold value, we select that cluster for further computation.

To increase recall and avoid semantic drift, we use two iterations. Semantic drift is the change in the actual meaning of a word with time [3]. In the first iteration, the system selects only those vectors from a cluster with a high cosine similarity score to the query term q. V_p represents the selected vectors in the first iteration. While in the second iteration, those vectors are selected that have high similarity with the list of selected vectors (V_p) in the first iteration. V_s represent the selected vectors in the second iterations. This two-step iteration increases the recall but sometimes causes semantic drift. To avoid semantic drift, we use a threshold value in the first iteration. In the second iteration, we score the vectors according to the following equation and only select those vectors with a P_{score} higher than zero.

$$P_{score} = Cosine(V_s, q) - (1 - Cosine(V_p, V_s))^2 \qquad (1)$$

Sometimes the sentences include semantically similar meanings, but the actual relation exists far from the two entities occurrences that cause a decrease in the precision [2]. To address this issue and increase the precision, our model uses a window-based approach like Snowball [1] to minimize the false-positive. The window consists of words around two entities, `Before` E_h, `Between` E_h and E_t, and `After` E_t. The system creates vectors representing the selected tokens using the sentence encoding module and finding the cosine similarity with the initially selected query term. Only those vectors are filtered, which have a higher score than a certain threshold.

3 Evaluation

We evaluate our proposed approach on the NYT-FB [6] dataset. The NYT-FB dataset is extracted from New York Times articles and aligned with freebase. The NYT-FB dataset consists of 253 relations. The initial evaluation result of our approach with the (SOTA) unsupervised systems is shown in Table 1. We run RelLDA1 on their reported parameter on the NYT-FB dataset for only StanfordNER based annotated sentences. In contrast, we run the other two models Simon and EType+, for both StanfordNER and AllenNLP NER.

Table 1. Precision (P) Recall (R) and F1 score of different systems using two NER annotation techniques on the NYT-FB.

Models	StanfordNER			AllenNLP NER		
	P	R	F1	P	R	F1
RelLDA1	0.30	0.47	0.36	–	–	–
Simon	0.32	0.50	0.39	0.334	0.497	0.399
EType+	0.30	**0.62**	**0.40**	0.31	**0.64**	0.417
US-BERT	**0.35**	0.45	0.39	**0.38**	0.61	**0.468**

Our proposed model (US-BERT) outperforms all the models in precision for StanfordNER based annotated sentences. However, the overall F1 score is less than the EType+. For AllenNLP NER based annotated sentences, our system achieves the highest F1 score. One of the reasons for the low recall we observed is the NER system. Wrongly annotated sentences reduce the recall. This did not penalize US-BERT since all evaluated systems were used with the same NER pre-processing steps.

4 Conclusion and Future Work

We used pre-trained sentence encoding to extract high-quality relations without any explicit features selection. We achieved the best F1, and precision score compares to the (SOTA) unsupervised methods. To further investigate the relation extraction, we will use some feature selection, compare the results with our work and see the impact also, we will compare our approach with some other (SOTA) approaches in our future work, mainly to the relation extraction systems based on language models.

Acknowledgement. This work has been supported by the EU H2020 Marie Skłodowska-Curie project KnowGraphs (860801), the BMBF-funded EuroStars projects E!113314 FROCKG (01QE19418) and E! 114154 PORQUE (01QE2056C).

References

1. Agichtein, E., Gravano, L.: *Snowball*: extracting relations from large plain-text collections. In: Proceedings of the Fifth ACM Conference on Digital Libraries. DL 2000, New York, NY, USA, pp. 85–94. Association for Computing Machinery (2000). https://doi.org/10.1145/336597.336644
2. Batista, D.S., Martins, B., Silva, M.J.: Semi-supervised bootstrapping of relationship extractors with distributional semantics. In: Proceedings of the 2015 Conference on Empirical Methods in Natural Language Processing, pp. 499–504 (2015)
3. Blank, A.: Why do new meanings occur? A cognitive typology of the motivations for lexical semantic change, pp. 61–90. De Gruyter Mouton (2013). https://doi.org/10.1515/9783110804195.61
4. Devlin, J., Chang, M.W., Lee, K., Toutanova, K.: BERT: pre-training of deep bidirectional transformers for language understanding (2019)
5. Elsahar, H., Demidova, E., Gottschalk, S., Gravier, C., Laforest, F.: Unsupervised open relation extraction. In: Blomqvist, E., Hose, K., Paulheim, H., Ławrynowicz, A., Ciravegna, F., Hartig, O. (eds.) ESWC 2017. LNCS, vol. 10577, pp. 12–16. Springer, Cham (2017). https://doi.org/10.1007/978-3-319-70407-4_3
6. Marcheggiani, D., Titov, I.: Discrete-state variational autoencoders for joint discovery and factorization of relations. TACL **4**, 231–244 (2016). https://www.aclweb.org/anthology/Q16-1017
7. Reimers, N., Gurevych, I.: Sentence-BERT: Sentence embeddings using siamese bert-networks. arXiv preprint arXiv:1908.10084 (2019)
8. Simon, É., Guigue, V., Piwowarski, B.: Unsupervised information extraction: Regularizing discriminative approaches with relation distribution losses. In: Proceedings of the 57th Annual Meeting of the Association for Computational Linguistics. pp. 1378–1387. Association for Computational Linguistics, Florence, Italy (Jul 2019). https://doi.org/10.18653/v1/P19-1133, https://www.aclweb.org/anthology/P19-1133
9. Surdeanu, M., Tibshirani, J., Nallapati, R., Manning, C.D.: Multi-instance multi-label learning for relation extraction. In: Proceedings of the 2012 Joint Conference on Empirical Methods in Natural Language Processing and Computational Natural Language Learning, Jeju Island, Korea, pp. 455–465. Association for Computational Linguistics (2012). https://www.aclweb.org/anthology/D12-1042
10. Tran, T.T., Le, P., Ananiadou, S.: Revisiting unsupervised relation extraction. In: Proceedings of the 58th Annual Meeting of the Association for Computational Linguistics, pp. 7498–7505. Association for Computational Linguistics, Online (2020). https://doi.org/10.18653/v1/2020.acl-main.669

evoKGsim+: A Framework for Tailoring Knowledge Graph-Based Similarity for Supervised Learning

Rita Torres Sousa$^{(\boxtimes)}$, Sara Silva, and Catia Pesquita

LASIGE, Faculdade de Ciências da Universidade de Lisboa, Lisbon, Portugal
{risousa,sgsilva,clpesquita}@ciencias.ulisboa.pt

Abstract. Knowledge graphs represent an unparalleled opportunity for machine learning, given their ability to provide meaningful context to the data through semantic representations. However, general-purpose knowledge graphs may describe entities from multiple perspectives, with some being irrelevant to the learning task. Despite the recent advances in semantic representations such as knowledge graph embeddings, existing methods are unsuited to tailoring semantic representations to a specific learning target that is not encoded in the knowledge graph.

We present evoKGsim+, a framework that can evolve similarity-based semantic representations for learning relations between knowledge graph entity pairs, which are not encoded in the graph. It employs genetic programming, where the evolutionary process is guided by a fitness function that measures the quality of relation prediction. The framework combines several taxonomic and embedding similarity measures and provides several baseline evaluation approaches that emulate domain expert feature selection and optimal parameter setting.

1 Introduction

Knowledge graphs (KGs) have been explored as providers of features and background knowledge in a wide variety of machine learning (ML) application scenarios [8]. One of these is predicting relations between KG entities that are not encoded in the KG, a problem cast as a classification task that takes as input a KG and a set of KG entity pairs. In the biomedical domain, ontologies are commonly employed to describe biological entities through semantic annotation. Tasks such as predicting protein-protein interactions using the Gene Ontology (GO) [12] or the mining of gene-disease associations on the Human Phenotype Ontology (HPO) [1] can be framed in this scenario.

In these cases, when we have a general-purpose KG (e.g., a KG that includes proteins and described their functions) that we aim to explore in the context of an independent and specific learning task (e.g., predicting if two proteins interact), it may very well be the case that large portions of the KG are irrelevant for the task. While in node/link/type prediction, instance representations such as embeddings [10] may be trained within the context of a particular learning task,

© Springer Nature Switzerland AG 2021
R. Verborgh et al. (Eds.): ESWC 2021 Satellite Events, LNCS 12739, pp. 141–146, 2021.
https://doi.org/10.1007/978-3-030-80418-3_26

in our scenario, no such tuning is possible since the classification targets are not a part of the KG. This problem is exacerbated in complex domains, such as the biomedical, where KGs represent multiple views (or semantic aspects) over the underlying data, some of which may be less relevant to train the model towards a specific target. For instance, the prediction of protein-protein interactions using the GO is more accurate if only a portion of the ontology is used [9] (in this case, the one concerning biological processes).

This brings us to the challenge of tailoring the semantic representation (SR) of the KG entities to an independent and specific classification task when the classification target is not encoded in the KG. A KG-based SR is a set of features describing a KG entity obtained by processing the KG and bridge the gap between KGs and the typical vector-based representations of entities used by most ML techniques. Most state-of-the-art KG-based numeric representations are based on graph embeddings [10], which produce feature vector (propositional) representations of the KG entities. Taxonomic semantic similarity [4] can also be used as an SR by comparing entities based on the properties they share and their taxonomic relationships. Both types of approaches are, in fact, methods for feature generation, but they also result in feature selection by the heuristics and approaches they employ in creating the representations.

To address the specific goal of predicting relations between KG entities when those relations are not encoded in the KG, we postulate that similarity between the entities is a suitable frame for SR to be used by downstream supervised learning approaches. Then, the problem is how to tailor a given semantic similarity representation to the classification task, i.e., classifying a pair of entities as related or not. Previously, we presented evoKGsim [9], a methodology that learns suitable semantic similarity-based SRs of data objects extracted from KGs optimized for supervised learning. This tailoring is achieved by evolving a suitable combination of semantic aspects using Genetic Programming (GP) using taxonomy-based semantic similarity measures.

In this work, we present an extension of evoKGsim into a full framework, evoKGsim+, that encompasses 10 KG-based similarity measures based on a selection of representative state-of-the-art KG embeddings and taxonomic similarity approaches. We evaluate the framework in its full extension in benchmark datasets devoted to protein-protein interaction (PPI) prediction.

2   Methodology

evoKGsim+ targets classification tasks that take as input a KG and a set of KG individual pairs for which we wish to learn a relation that is outside the scope of the KG. The models are trained using external information about the classification targets for each pair. The evoKGsim+ framework is able to: (1) compute semantic similarity-based representations of KG individuals according to different semantic aspects and using different similarity approaches; (2) employ GP to learn a suitable representation targeted to a supervised learning task by combining the different semantic aspects; and (3) evaluate the outcome of (2) against a set of static representations emulating experts. An overview of the framework is shown in Fig. 1.

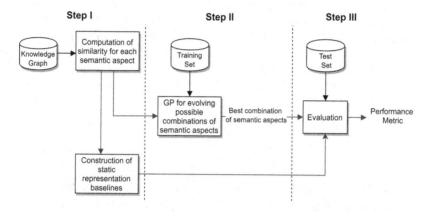

Fig. 1. Overview of the evoKGsim+ framework.

The first step of the framework is to represent each instance (i.e., a pair of KG entities) according to KG-based similarities computed for each semantic aspect. Currently, evoKGsim+ takes as semantic aspects the subgraphs rooted in the classes at a distance of one from the root class of the T-box in the KG, but this parameter can be easily adjusted. The second step is to employ GP to learn a suitable combination of the different aspect-based similarities, using a set of predefined operators, to address a given ML task. The last step is to evaluate the predictions made on the test set, and comparing them against optimized static representations that represent expert feature selection and parameter tuning.

This framework is independent of the specific implementation of KG-based similarity and the GP parameters employed to evolve the representations. Currently, evoKGsim+ supports 10 different KG-based similarity measures: 6 taxonomic similarity measures, derived by combining one of two information content approaches (IC_{Seco} and IC_{Resnik}) with one of three set similarity measures (ResnikMax, ResnikBMA, and SimGIC [6]); 4 measures based on cosine similarity over embeddings generated from TransE [2], distMult [11], RDF2Vec [7] and Owl2Vec [5].

3 Evaluation

PPI prediction was chosen as our evaluation domain for the following reasons: (1) it is backed by a large ontology with multiple semantic aspects, the GO; (2) there are gold-standard datasets [3]; (3) it is well known that the GO aspects biological process (BP) and cellular component (CC) describe properties that are stronger indicators for PPI than the molecular function aspect (MF) [9], which provides an ideal test bed for the need of adapting the SR to the learning task.

Table 1 presents the results obtained using different similarity-based SRs. As baselines, we have used five static SRs (the BP, CC and MF single aspects, and the average and maximum of the single aspect similarities). The static SRs are based on a simple threshold-based classifier, where a similarity score for a protein pair above the threshold predicts a positive interaction. For evaluating the quality of a predicted classification, the weighted average F-measure (WAF) was used for stratified 10-fold cross-validation.

Table 1. Median of WAF for 10-fold cross-validation.

Similarity measure	Static SRs					evoKGsim
	BP	CC	MF	Avg	Max	
ResnikMax + IC_{Seco}	0.760	0.713	0.646	0.749	0.743	**0.765**
ResnikMax + IC_{Resnik}	0.750	0.717	0.653	0.766	0.774	**0.776**
ResnikBMA + IC_{Seco}	0.753	0.715	0.643	0.771	0.744	**0.777**
ResnikBMA + IC_{Resnik}	0.753	0.714	0.648	0.777	0.772	**0.782**
SimGIC + IC_{Seco}	0.736	0.682	0.642	0.729	0.701	**0.746**
SimGIC + IC_{Resnik}	0.739	0.704	0.651	0.750	0.734	**0.758**
TransE	0.501	**0.534**	0.502	0.519	0.521	0.521
distMult	0.704	0.599	0.498	0.670	0.668	**0.712**
RDF2Vec	0.675	0.654	0.631	0.684	0.668	**0.685**
Owl2vec	0.678	0.662	0.621	**0.693**	0.686	**0.693**

evoKGsim with taxonomic similarity always achieves the best performance compared to the static SRs. Regarding the graph embedding approaches, TransE has performed worse than the other embedding methods. These differences are not unexpected since we are interested in learning which aspects of a KG are more relevant to the learning task, and most of the information to be processed is represented in the ontology portion of the KG, where taxonomic relations play an important role. Therefore, translational distance approaches that emphasize local neighbourhoods are less suitable than semantic matching methods, like disMult, or methods that capture longer-distance relations, such as path-based approaches (RDF2Vec and Owl2Vec).

When comparing the two SRs, evoKGsim with taxonomic similarity achieves a better performance than evoKGsim with embedding similarity. Although embeddings consider all types of relations, we hypothesize that taxonomic similarity can take into account class specificity that may give it the advantage over embedding similarity in more accurately estimating similarity.

4   Conclusion

We have developed a framework, evoKGsim+, that tailors KG-based similarity representations for supervised learning of relations between KG instances when the classification target is not encoded in the KG. We have shown that evoKGsim+ can generate tailored SRs that improve classification performance over static SRs both using embedding similarity and taxonomic semantic similarity. This framework can be readily generalized to other applications and domains, where KG-based similarity is a suitable instance representation, such as prediction of drug-target interactions and gene-disease association, KG link prediction or recommendations.

Acknowledgements. CP, SS, RTS are funded by the FCT through LASIGE Research Unit, ref. UIDB/00408/2020 and ref. UIDP/00408/2020. CP and RTS are funded by project SMILAX (ref. PTDC/EEI-ESS/4633/2014), SS by projects BINDER (ref. PTDC/CCI-INF/29168/2017) and PREDICT (ref. PTDC/CCI-CIF/29877/2017), and RTS by FCT PhD grant (ref. SFRH/BD/145377/2019). It was also partially supported by the KATY project which has received funding from the European Union's Horizon 2020 research and innovation programme under grant agreement No 101017453.

References

1. Asif, M., Martiniano, H.F., Vicente, A.M., Couto, F.M.: Identifying disease genes using machine learning and gene functional similarities, assessed through gene ontology. PLoS ONE **13**(12), e0208626 (2018)
2. Bordes, A., Usunier, N., Garcia-Duran, A., Weston, J., Yakhnenko, O.: Translating embeddings for modeling multi-relational data. In: Advances in Neural Information Processing Systems, pp. 2787–2795 (2013)
3. Cardoso, C., Sousa, R.T., Köhler, S., Pesquita, C.: A collection of benchmark data sets for knowledge graph-based similarity in the biomedical domain. Database **2020** (2020)
4. Harispe, S., Ranwez, S., Janaqi, S., Montmain, J.: Semantic Similarity from Natural Language and Ontology Analysis. Morgan & Claypool Publishers (2015)
5. Holter, O.M., Myklebust, E.B., Chen, J., Jimenez-Ruiz, E.: Embedding OWL ontologies with OWL2vec. In: CEUR Workshop Proceedings, vol. 2456, pp. 33–36. Technical University of Aachen (2019)
6. Pesquita, C., Faria, D., Bastos, H., Ferreira, A.E., Falcão, A.O., Couto, F.M.: Metrics for GO based protein semantic similarity: a systematic evaluation. BMC Bioinform. **9**, 1–16 (2008). https://doi.org/10.1186/1471-2105-9-S5-S4
7. Ristoski, P., Paulheim, H.: RDF2Vec: RDF graph embeddings for data mining. In: Groth, P., et al. (eds.) ISWC 2016. LNCS, vol. 9981, pp. 498–514. Springer, Cham (2016). https://doi.org/10.1007/978-3-319-46523-4_30
8. Ristoski, P., Paulheim, H.: Semantic Web in data mining and knowledge discovery: a comprehensive survey. J. Web Semant. **36**, 1–22 (2016)
9. Sousa, R.T., Silva, S., Pesquita, C.: Evolving knowledge graph similarity for supervised learning in complex biomedical domains. BMC Bioinform. **21**, 1–19 (2019)
10. Wang, Q., Mao, Z., Wang, B., Guo, L.: Knowledge graph embedding: a survey of approaches and applications. IEEE TKDE **29**(12), 2724–2743 (2017)

11. Yang, B., Yih, S.W., He, X., Gao, J., Deng, L.: Embedding entities and relations for learning and inference in knowledge bases. In: Proceedings of the ICLR (2015)
12. Zhong, X., Kaalia, R., Rajapakse, J.C.: GO2Vec: transforming GO terms and proteins to vector representations via graph embeddings. BMC Genomics **20**(9), 1–10 (2019)

Extraction of Union and Intersection Axioms from Biomedical Text

Nikhil Sachdeva$^{(\boxtimes)}$, Monika Jain , and Raghava Mutharaju

Knowledgeable Computing and Reasoning Lab, IIIT-Delhi, Delhi, India
{nikhil16061,monikaja,raghava.mutharaju}@iiitd.ac.in

Abstract. Many ontology, especially the ones created automatically by
the ontology learning systems, have only shallow relationships between
the concepts, i.e., simple subclass relations. Expressive axioms such as the
class union and intersection are not part of the ontology. These expressive axioms make the ontology rich and play an essential role in the
performance of downstream applications. However, such relations can
generally be found in the text documents. We propose a mechanism and
discuss our initial results in extracting union and intersection axioms
from biomedical text using entity linking and taxonomic tree search.

Keywords: Ontology learning · Ontology enrichment · Axiom
extraction

1 Introduction

Ontology learning [4] is the process of building ontologies automatically from
text. Several ontology learning systems [1,5] such as Text2Onto[1], Doodle OWL[2]
and DL-Learner[3] have been developed. Most of these systems support learning of
classes, subclasses and taxonomic relationships. But they do not support mining
of more expressive axioms from text such as union, intersection, quantifiers and
cardinality relation among the concepts. A richer and more expressive ontology
can be very useful to the downstream applications such as recommendation
systems and question and answering systems.

We propose a mechanism to extract union and intersection axioms from the
text with the help of an ontology. The extracted axioms are then added to
the ontology to enhance its expressivity. Examples of intersection and union
axioms are given in Axioms 1 and 2. Axiom 1 models the information that a
Mixed Glioma (type of tumor) is a combination of *Astrocytoma* and *Oligodendroglioma*. Axiom 2 captures the information that a *Tumor* can be either *Benign*
or *PreMalignant* or *Malignant*.

---

[1] http://neon-toolkit.org/wiki/1.x/Text2Onto.html.
[2] https://sourceforge.net/projects/doddle-owl/.
[3] http://dl-learner.org/.

© Springer Nature Switzerland AG 2021
R. Verborgh et al. (Eds.): ESWC 2021 Satellite Events, LNCS 12739, pp. 147–151, 2021.
https://doi.org/10.1007/978-3-030-80418-3_27

$$Mixed\ Glioma \sqsubseteq Astrocytoma \sqcap Oligodendroglioma \qquad (1)$$

$$Tumor \sqsubseteq Benign \sqcup PreMalignant \sqcup Malignant \qquad (2)$$

Although there have been attempts at identifying concepts and relations in the text with the help of an ontology [3] and word embeddings [6], to the best of our knowledge, this is the first attempt at extracting complex (non-taxonomic) ontology axioms from the text. In the next section, we describe the axiom extraction pipeline followed by the discussion of results.

2 Approach

Our system expects an ontology along with one or more text documents relevant to the ontology as input. The system identifies the named entities in the text that are of interest (based on the concepts defined in the ontology) and checks for potential union and intersection axioms. If an appropriate match is found, our system generates the axioms as shown in Fig. 1. The first step is to extract the named entities from the text and perform entity linking, wherein each entity extracted from the text is assigned a type (a concept in the ontology). The entities were extracted using the SpaCy models for biomedical text processing[4] and the Metamap application[5] is used for recognizing those entities in the UMLS Metathesaurus[6]. Metathesaurus is an semantic network of biomedical entities taken from more than 200 vocabularies. It provides various definitions, taxonomic and non-taxonomic relations for every entity present in the network.

Some of the extracted entities from the text may not be associated with any of the concepts in the ontology. Entity mentions in the text are represented by $E = \{e_1, e_2, \ldots, e_n\}$ and the concepts in the ontology are represented by $C = \{c_1, c_2, \ldots, c_n\}$. All the concepts are considered as potential candidates for the entities to be linked. The pseudocode for entity linking is given in Algorithm 1.

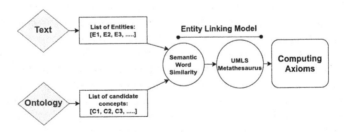

Fig. 1. Architecture for extracting union and intersection axioms from the text

---

[4] https://allenai.github.io/scispacy/.

[5] https://metamap.nlm.nih.gov/.

[6] https://www.nlm.nih.gov/research/umls/index.html.

Algorithm 1. Linking the entity mentions in the text to the concepts in the ontology

---

1: **for** $e_i \in entities = e_1, e_2, \ldots, e_n$ **do**
2:    **for** $c_j \in concepts = c_1, c_2, \ldots, c_m$ **do**
3:       $score_B \leftarrow cos_B(e_i, c_j)$ ▷ BioWordVec Model
4:       $score_C \leftarrow cos_C(e_i, c_j)$ ▷ Custom Word2Vec Model
5:       **if** $score_B \geq \alpha$ **AND** $score_C \geq \beta$ **then**
6:          **if** e_i **isDescendantOf** $c_j \in$ **UMLS then**
7:             $addPairToOntology(e_i, c_j)$
8:          **else**   ▷ α, β, γ are adjustable threshold parameters
9:             $L \leftarrow lowestCommonAncestor(e_i, c_j)$
10:            $M_e \leftarrow Metamap(e_i, L)$
11:            $M_c \leftarrow Metamap(c_j, L)$
12:            **if** $(M_e + M_c)/2 \geq \gamma$ **then**
13:               $addPairToOntology(e_i, c_j)$

Entity linking consists of three stages. Each pair of entity mention and concept (e_i, c_i) will go through all the three stages to determine if the entity mention e_i is an instance of the candidate concept c_i. In the first stage, the cosine distance of real-valued word embeddings of e_i are compared with c_i to determine if they have a qualitative semantic similarity. The comparison is made using the embeddings generated from BioWordVec[7] and a custom Word2Vec[8] model. The former model captures the contextual information around an entity from the unlabelled biomedical text using the MeSH vocabulary. The custom Word2Vec model is trained over only those biomedical text articles that contain the concepts in the given ontology. If the pair (e_i, c_i) satisfies the minimum threshold values (α, β from Algorithm 1), it moves to the next stage where we check whether e_i is an instance of c_i using UMLS Metathesaurus and Metamap (Figs. 2a and 2b). In *scenario-1*, if c_i is present in the UMLS tree, we check if e_i matches any of the descendants of c_i in the tree. Figure 2a shows that entity *Congenital Bacterial Pneumonia* is a descendant of the concept *Pneumonia*. In *scenario-2*, where e_i is not a direct descendant of c_i, we find the lowest common ancestor l_i of e_i and c_i. Figure 2b shows that the entity *Basal Pneumonia* and the concept *Infective Pneumonia* have a common ancestor *Respiratory Finding*. Using Metamap, we compare the number of semantic groups[9] the pairs (e_i, l_i) and (c_i, l_i) share. A semantic group is a broader group that a term (entity or concept in our case) can be a part of, according to Metamap. Further, we compare the UMLS generated context vectors of e_i, c_i and l_i (taken two at a time), using cosine measure. Based on these scores, we determine if e_i is an instance of c_i. The hyperparameter γ represents the neutralized score of these comparisons. The value of this hyperparameter is adjustable and can be set on the basis of experiments.

---

[7] https://github.com/ncbi-nlp/BioWordVec.
[8] https://code.google.com/archive/p/word2vec/.
[9] https://metamap.nlm.nih.gov/SemanticTypesAndGroups.shtml.

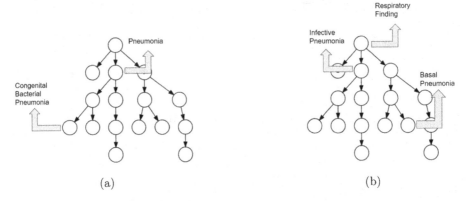

Fig. 2. (a) represents scenario-1 where entity e is a descendant of concept c and (b) represents scenario-2 where both Entity e and Concept c have a common ancestor L.

Finally, when a pair (e_i, c_i) is added in the ontology, e_i is also added as an instance of all the parent concepts of c_i. After repeating these three stages for each pair of e_i and c_i, we get a list of concepts with their corresponding sets of instances (entities). Using these instances, we compute union and intersection of the concepts based on the below formula

$$total\_sets = \binom{n}{1} + \binom{n}{2} + \binom{n}{3} + \binom{n}{4} + \binom{n}{5} + \binom{n}{6} \qquad (3)$$

where each $\binom{n}{i}$ represents sets of i concepts. Each of these sets is compared with every candidate concept to check for union and intersection axioms. For example, to obtain Axiom 1, the intersection of instances of *Astrocytoma* and *Oligodendroglioma* is compared with the instances of *Mixed Glioma*. If the latter is a subset of the former, we can add this axiom to the ontology. We have considered such combinations up to a size of 6. The size was determined using experiments by comparing the F1 scores of sets of different size.

3   Results and Discussion

We could not find any biomedical ontology that has union and intersection axioms along with the concepts that have instances for evaluating our model. Moreover, there is no dataset having such ontologies and the corresponding text corpora in the medical domain. We choose the Disease ontology[10] as it is rich in such axioms, but it lacks the concept-instance pairs. So we made an approximation here and preprocessed the ontology. We observed that the lowermost leaf-child concept could act as an instance of the directly connected parent class. Subsequently, it can be connected as an instance of all the subsequent parent classes in the hierarchy. This process is executed for all the leaf-nodes in the

---

[10] https://disease-ontology.org/.

ontology. We extracted 739 articles from PubMed Central[11] based on the concepts in the Disease Ontology. Within the ontology, there are a total of 10,085 intersection axioms and 323 union axioms. Based on the extracted articles and the Disease ontology, the F1 scores for the union axioms is 0.142, and for the intersection axioms, it is 0.1908.

While analyzing the results, we observed that many false positive axioms were generated, hence reducing the model's precision. One of the reasons is that many trivial union axioms were generated that contained many general classes and this increased the number of false positive axioms. Furthermore, there is the unavailability of a proper dataset consisting of a complete and rich ontology with the corresponding text corpora. Therefore, constructing a relevant dataset and defining baselines are some of the tasks of our future work. Furthermore, to improve the architecture, we are working on incorporating English language pattern heuristics where we can apply the syntactical rules to extract axioms from unstructured text robustly. We are also working on fine-tuned deep learning models to improve the contextual word embeddings for the target word. Based on our results, we plan to apply neural models like BERT [2] that use transformers to generate a language model with strong contextual relations between the words of the text.

References

1. Asim, M.N., Wasim, M., Khan, M.U.G., Mahmood, W., Abbasi, H.M.: A survey of ontology learning techniques and applications. In: Database (2018)
2. Devlin, J., Chang, M.W., Lee, K., Toutanova, K.: BERT: pre-training of deep bidirectional transformers for language understanding. In: Proceedings of the 2019 Conference of the NAACL) (2019)
3. Karadeniz, İ, Özgür, A.: Linking entities through an ontology using word embeddings and syntactic re-ranking. BMC Bioinform. **20**, 1–49 (2019)
4. Lehmann, J., Völker, J.: An Introduction to ontology learning. In: Perspectives on Ontology Learning, pp. ix–xvi. IOS Press (2014)
5. Wong, W., Liu, W., Bennamoun, M.: Ontology learning from text: a look back and into the future. ACM Comput. Surv. **44**, 1–36 (2012)
6. Yijia, Z., Chen, Q., Yang, Z., Lin, H., lu, Z.: Biowordvec, improving biomedical word embeddings with subword information and mesh. Sci. Data **6**, 1–9 (2019)

---

[11] https://www.ncbi.nlm.nih.gov/pmc.

PhD Symposium Track Papers

Implementing Informed Consent
with Knowledge Graphs

Anelia Kurteva[(⊠)]

Semantic Technology Institute (STI) Innsbruck, Department of Computer Science,
University of Innsbruck, Innsbruck, Austria
`anelia.kurteva@sti2.at`

Abstract. The GDPR legislation has brought to light one's rights and
has highlighted the importance of consent, which has caused a major shift
in how data processing and sharing are handled. Data sharing has been a
popular research topic for many years, however, a unified solution for the
transparent implementation of consent, in compliance with GDPR that
could be used as a standard, has not been presented yet. This research proposes a solution for implementing informed consent for sensor data sharing
in compliance with GDPR with semantic technology, namely knowledge
graphs. The main objectives are to model the life cycle of informed consent (i.e. the request, comprehension, decision and use of consent) with
knowledge graphs so that it is easily interpretable by machines, and to
graphically visualise it to individuals in order to raise legal awareness of
what it means to consent and the implications that follow.

Keywords: Knowledge graph · Knowledge graph visualisation ·
GDPR · Informed consent · Sensor data · Data sharing · Legal
comprehension

1 Introduction

The process of data sharing takes seconds and results in one's personal data being
accessed simultaneously by multiple independent entities for different purposes
without one even knowing (e.g. in smart cities). The General Data Protection
Regulation (GDPR)[1], which came into effect in 2018, aims to change that. GDPR
has introduced six lawful basis (Art. 6) that need to be met when dealing with
the data of European citizens. One of these basis is consent, which must be freely
given, specific, unambiguous and most of all informed (Art. 4 (11)). A common
understanding of what it means to consent and the implications of giving and
revoking it needs to be established between all entities involved in data sharing.

Semantic technology, namely knowledge graphs, have been gaining popularity in recent years due to their ability to transform data into information
and information into knowledge by creating meaningful relationships between

---

[1] https://eur-lex.europa.eu/eli/reg/2016/679/oj.

© Springer Nature Switzerland AG 2021
R. Verborgh et al. (Eds.): ESWC 2021 Satellite Events, LNCS 12739, pp. 155–164, 2021.
https://doi.org/10.1007/978-3-030-80418-3_28

entities [13,15]. In the context of implementing consent (i.e. modelling the life cycle of consent) in compliance with GDPR and raising one's legal awareness, knowledge graphs can support explainability and provide traceability and transparency [17]. Semantic technology is undoubtedly beneficial to machines, as shown in [7,13,28], but the benefits to individuals, especially non-experts in the case of consent comprehension need further exploration.

2   State of the Art

Semantic models such as ontologies, have been widely used through the years for modeling consent. For example, The Consent and Data Management Model (CDMM)[2], GConsent[3], Business Process Re-engineering and Functional Toolkit for GDPR Compliance (BPR4GDPR)[4], Data Privacy Vocabulary (DPV)[5], the SPECIAL Policy Log Vocabulary (SPLog)[6]. Despite most ontologies being open-access and fulfilling GDPR's requirements for informed consent, most were built for specific use case, have different maturity level and are somewhat limited, each in its own way. The GConsent ontology, for example, models GDPR knowledge, including consent, but does not model in detail the type of data consent is asked for [23]. In the case of data sharing in smart cities, the specific sensor from which data will be collected needs to be specified when consent is requested. Having such level of detail would be also beneficial when compliance checking is carried out. In comparison to GConsent, the CDMM ontology does not provide the same level of detail about consent but does offer classes to model the format in which consent was received (e.g. app based, audio, online form) [11].

The Data License Clearance Center (DALICC)[7] for license solicitation is an example of a semantic technology-based solution in the legal domain, from which both legal and non-legal experts benefit. With the help of a legal knowledge graph and the Open Rights Digital Language (ODRL)[8], licenses and their privacy policies are modeled in detail [24]. Similarly, the Scalable Policy-aware Linked Data Architecture For Privacy, Transparency and Compliance (SPECIAL-K) [17] framework focuses on modeling GDPR from a privacy policy perspective (i.e. models privacy policies and legal obligations) and consent is not the main focus. Other projects, which model consent and GDPR with semantic technologies are EnCoRe[9], ADvoCate [25], CampaNeo[10], smashHit[11] and the research in [16,19].

---

[2] https://openscience.adaptcentre.ie/ontologies/consent/docs/index-en.html.

[3] http://openscience.adaptcentre.ie/ontologies/GConsent/doc.

[4] https://www.bpr4gdpr.eu/wp-content/uploads/2019/06/D3.1-Compliance-Ontolog y-1.0.pdf.

[5] https://dpvcg.github.io/dpv/.

[6] https://ai.wu.ac.at/policies/policylog/.

[7] https://www.dalicc.net.

[8] https://www.w3.org/TR/odrl-model/.

[9] https://www.hpl.hp.com/breweb/encoreproject/index.html.

[10] https://projekte.ffg.at/projekt/3314668.

[11] https://www.smashhit.eu.

Standartisation of consent is a topic of interest and efforts in the field include Consent Receipt v1.1[12], the ISO/IEC 29184:2020[13] and the Transparency and Consent Framework (TCF)[14].

When dealing with informed consent the issue of comprehension relates to non-experts as well, as they are the main subjects of consent requests. Having this is mind, semantic technology should be used to not only enhance machines but also to empower people. A field with such focus is Linked Data visualisation. However, most of the work (e.g. [3,5,18,31]) focuses on Linked Data visualisation to experts and not specifically on informed consent visualisation for non-expert users. This topic is the focus of [9] and [10]. The CoRe User Interface (UI) [9], and its second iteration - Consent Request User Interface (CURE) [10] follow GDPR requirements for requesting informed consent and aim at raising one's awareness about consent with the help of graphical visualisations. The research in [9] and [10] showed that a graphical visualisation can improve one's comprehension of consent. However, the issue of information overload [14] is still present. Solutions with similar purpose (i.e. raising one's awareness about the implications of data sharing) are [1,26,30] and [12]. Consent should be given freely (Rec. 32), however, incentives can be used to attract one's attention. For example, gamification [27] can be used to raise consent awareness as it boosts curiosity and the motivation for participation of individuals [4,27].

3   Problem Statement and Contributions

Informed consent has a long history in the medical field, where standard procedures for obtaining it have already been established [20,21,32]. However, when it comes to fields such as technology, smart city and insurance, informed consent is still somewhat novel as no standard approaches and guidelines for its implementation have been set yet.

In smart cities, one's data is spread across different silos and can be used for different purposes by different entities simultaneously. Implementing consent should be done in a way that does not disrupt the data flow between those silos while being compliant with GDPR. For most individuals, the concepts of consent and smart city are still abstract [6]. Unless explicitly asked for permission, one might not be aware that their personal data is being collected. In most cases, the permission request are in the form of textual documents written in legalese. Presenting individuals, especially non-legal experts, with such documents can be intimidating, can cause information overload [14] and can lead to individuals giving consent without knowing their rights, understanding or even reading the presented data sharing policies [18]. The result is a *"culture of blind consent"* [2]. Further, it might be unclear what specific data is collected from one's vehicle while being in a smart city as data can be collected from both the vehicle itself and the surroundings (e.g. road speed detectors, street cameras).

---

[12] https://kantarainitiative.org/file-downloads/consent-receipt-specification-v1-1-0/.

[13] https://www.iso.org/standard/70331.html.

[14] https://iabeurope.eu/transparency-consent-framework/.

Existing semantic models for consent (see Sect. 2), have different maturity level, model consent and GDPR but do not model specific details about the data for which the consent was granted and the processing applied to it. In order to be reused for modelling the life cycle of consent in a smart city scenario, the existing ontologies need to be extended so that different domains such as transport, education, security, retail, energy etc., which are present in a smart city are modeled. It is yet unknown to what knowledge graphs can implement consent and what implications might arise in the event of consent revocation from both technical and legal standpoints. There is a need for a solution that equally considers the needs of both humans and machines when consent is implemented. A solution that provides a transparent view into the life cycle of one's consent and one's legal rights.

The main objective of this research is to provide a scalable knowledge graph-based solution for consent implementation in compliance with GDPR, which raises individual's legal awareness with the help of a graphical visualisations. The two main research questions that will be answered are:

- *How to implement informed consent with knowledge graphs in a way that supports its federation across multiple domains?*
- *Does a visualisation of a knowledge graph help improve one's comprehension of consent?*

Sub-questions that arise are: *How to explain privacy policies to individuals in an understandable way with the help of visualisations? How can incentives be used to raise one's legal awareness?*

The main contributions are: (i) a knowledge graph-based solution for implementing consent, which supports its synchronisation across multiple domains, (ii) an environment (i.e. a UI for consent management), which allows individuals to exercise their GDPR rights and (iii) raised legal awareness of individuals.

4   Methodology

The ontology development follows a top-down approach [22] thus general concepts from GDPR such as consent, data owner, data collector, data, purpose are defined first. This approach was selected due to having to collaborate with researchers with different backgrounds and points of view. The ontology needs to be both specific enough to model important information about compliance and general enough so that it could be reused for various use cases (e.g. transport, insurance) and seen as a potential standard model for consent. The creation of the legal knowledge graph follows the methodology of Fensel et al. [13]. Once the main ontology is defined it is extended with information that has been semantically annotated.

The visualisation of informed consent follows a methodology similar to the ones in [1,9,10]. The developments for this research are done is 3 main stages. Stage 1 - system architecture design, Stage 2 - specification of a semantic model for informed consent, Stage 3 - visualisation of the semantic model. Details about each stage are presented in Sect. 5.

5   Preliminary Results

Following the specified methodology in Sect. 4, this section presents the current developments.

5.1   System Architecture

This research is part of the smashHit[15] projects and will provide the main semantic data model (i.e. the smashHit Core ontology), based on which a tool for automatic contracting is built. The proposed semantic consent solution consists of (i) a consent UI that enables end-users to exercise their GDPR rights, (ii) a data checker responsible for validation of user's input, (iii) a legal knowledge graph that models and stores informed consent and (iv) a graph database, which has the role of a triple store. Requests for specific data to be shared are provided by an external database and are semantically annotated before being displayed on the UI.

5.2   Semantic Model for Informed Consent

The main semantic model[16] (Fig. 1) is based on requirements for informed consent as defined by the GDPR. The semantic model is currently being developed in collaboration with experts from the transport, law and insurance domains. The initial use case that the ontology models is sensor data sharing in a smart city, where data providers are asked to participate in a campaign (i.e. a request for sharing specific sensor data produced by one's vehicle for a specific purpose). For example, the campaign "Roads of Innsbruck" (Fig. 1) request individuals to share their sensor data (e.g. GPS coordinates) with a specific company for a specific amount of time. The main purposes of such campaign can be: to detect city areas with increased traffic or analysis of sensor data for personal vehicle maintenance (i.e. for accident prevention). Annotating and storing campaigns in a knowledge graph helps achieve transparency and traceability (e.g. one could trace in how many campaigns an individuals participate, who has access to the data etc.), which are amongst GDPR's key principles (Rec. 58).

The intial version of the ontology, developed with Protégé[17], focuses on modeling consent as a legal basis for data processing as defined by GDPR. The ontology reuses the concept of *"Consent"* from GConsent (See Footnote 3) and *"Agreeement"* from the Financial Industry Business Ontology (FIBO)[18]. Further, the class *"Data"* reuses the Semantic Sensor Network Ontology (SSN)[19]

---

[15] https://www.smashhit.eu.

[16] https://github.com/aneliamk/consent/raw/a8da0b3ae8f48f282f1006a68adea55c485
7bdc9/ontology/Consent_Sensor.owl.

[17] https://protege.stanford.edu.

[18] https://spec.edmcouncil.org/fibo/.

[19] https://www.w3.org/TR/vocab-ssn/.

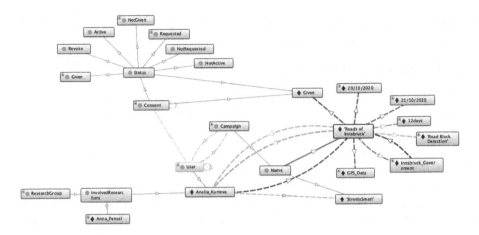

Fig. 1. Overview of the initial knowledge graph with instances

for modeling sensor data. The current version of the knowledge graph, which is stored in GraphDB[20], consists of 696 axioms, 166 classes, 42 object properties and 8 data properties.

5.3   Semantic Model Visualisation

The representation of the semantic model to end-users is made possible by having two visualisations - a graphical UI[21] for consent management (Fig. 2 and 3), implemented with Flutter[22], and a visualisation of the data sharing process itself after consent is given (Fig. 4 and 5), implemented with d3.js[23]. The UI's main aim is to allow individuals to exercise their GDPR rights (i.e. give, revoke, withdraw, modify consent), while the graphical visualisation (Fig. 4 and 5) is focused on raising one's awareness of what it means to consent.

The UI uses incentives, namely gamification [27], to create competition, which raises participation [4]. Participants collect points for each data type they share. The points can be then exchanges for vouchers and coupons (e.g. free car wash, discount on fuel). The consent and the data about it are stored in the legal knowledge graph (Fig. 2). The visualisation of the data sharing process (Fig. 4 and 5) follows Schneiderman's mantra [29] and has two levels of granularity - an overview of the process (Fig. 4) and a detailed time line view (Fig. 5). Individuals are able to interact directly with the graph by selecting specific data they wish to view, which according to [1] makes one feel more involved. The aim of this visualisation is to present how one's data is being used, by whom and for what

---

[20] https://graphdb.ontotext.com.
[21] https://github.com/aneliamk/CampaNeoUI.
[22] https://flutter.dev.
[23] https://d3js.org.

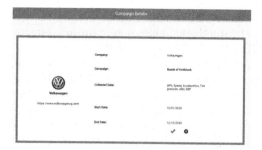

Fig. 2. Visualisation of the campaign "Roads of Innsbruck"

Fig. 3. Individuals can select which specific data to share and give consent.

purpose thus to raise one's awareness. The main challenges are to understand one's needs and to visualise the right data in the right way.

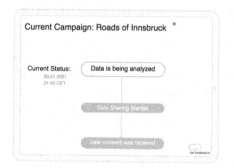

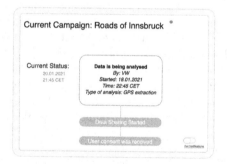

Fig. 4. Overview of a data flow

Fig. 5. Detailed overview of a data flow

6   Evaluation Plan

In order to understand how well the developed ontology models the consent life cycle in (e.g. in the case of a smart city) and how well it satisfies GDPR requirements, a set of competency questions will be (i) derived by legal experts and (ii) translated to SPARQL[24] queries. Existing ontologies such as GConsent (See Footnote 3), BPR4GDPR (See Footnote 4) and DPV (See Footnote 5) will also be evaluated with the same set of questions so that a comparison with the new model is possible. The results will be reviewed with experts from the legal, smart city and insurance domains. In later more mature stages, the truthfulness of the semantic model will be tested with ontology evaluation tools such as

---

[24] https://www.w3.org/TR/rdf-sparql-query/.

OntoManager[25]. The semantic model content and quality will be evaluated with the ODEval [8] method, which by using graph theory, helps detect inconsistencies and redundancies. Validation with SHACL[26] is planned as well.

The evaluation of the visualisations will be done with both legal and non-legal expert users. Similar to the evaluation of the CoRe [9] and CURE [10] UIs, the participants will be presented with questionnaires focused on evaluating one's comprehension of consent, and tasks focused on the usability of the UI. The consent comprehension survey will be in the form of a test consisting of questions such as: "What data did you share with company X?", "Can you name the purpose for giving consent for campaign X?". Further, when possible the "Think Aloud"[27] method will be used.

7   Conclusions and Lessons Learned

This paper presented the main research focus of the current thesis, the main research questions and early stage developments. Future developments include implementing the options to revoke and verify consent. The semantic model will be extended with concepts from DALICC (See Footnote 7) and will model processes such as data protection impact assessments (DPIAs)[28]. The legal rules of GDPR (e.g. rules about data usage) will be derived by following the Standard Data Protection Model (SDM)[29] and translated into machine-understandable rules with ODRL (See Footnote 8). The final step will be to integrate the consent solution within the automatic contracting tool of smashHit (See Footnote 11) and to ensure a smooth data flow between the knowledge graph and external components from the smashHit project that might use it.

Acknowledgements. This research is supported by the smashHit project funded under Horizon 2020 (grant 871477) and CampaNeo project funded by FFG (grant 873839). The main supervisor of this thesis is Assoc. Prof. Dr. Anna Fensel. I would like to thank Antonio Roa Valverde, Christof Bless, Lukas Dötlinger, Manuel Penz, Markus Reiter, Michael Kaltschmid, Petraq Nako, Stephanie Widauer, Sven Rasmusen for their support in the CampaNeo project.

References

1. Angulo, J., Fischer-Hübner, S., Pulls, T., Wästlund, E.: Usable transparency with the data track: a tool for visualizing data disclosures. In: Proceedings of the 33rd Annual ACM Conference Extended Abstracts on Human Factors in Computing Systems (2015)

---

[25] http://ontoware.org/projects/ontomanager.
[26] https://www.w3.org/TR/shacl/.
[27] https://www.nngroup.com/articles/thinking-aloud-the-1-usability-tool/.
[28] https://gdpr.eu/data-protection-impact-assessment-template/.
[29] https://www.datenschutzzentrum.de/uploads/sdm/SDM-Methodology_V2.0b.pdf.

2. Bechmann, A.: Non-informed consent cultures: privacy policies and app contracts on Facebook. J. Media Bus. Stud. **11**(1), 21–38 (2014). https://doi.org/10.1080/16522354.2014.11073574

3. Bikakis, N., Skourla, M., Papastefanatos, G.: rdf:SynopsViz - a framework for hierarchical linked data visual exploration and analysis. ArXiv abs/1408.3148 (2014)

4. Bretzke, H., Vassileva, J.: Motivating cooperation on peer to peer networks. In: Brusilovsky, P., Corbett, A., de Rosis, F. (eds.) UM 2003. LNCS (LNAI), vol. 2702, pp. 218–227. Springer, Heidelberg (2003). https://doi.org/10.1007/3-540-44963-9_30

5. Brunetti, J.M., Auer, S., García, R.: The linked data visualization model. In: Proceedings of the 2012th International Conference on Posters and Demonstrations Track, vol. 914. pp. 5–8. CEUR-WS.org (2012)

6. Cagáňová, D., Stareček, A., Horňáková, N., Hlásniková, P.: The analysis of the Slovak citizens' awareness about the smart city concept. Mob. Netw. Appl. **24**(6), 2050–2058 (2019). https://doi.org/10.1007/s11036-018-01210-6

7. Cardoso, J., Hepp, M., Lytras, M.: The Semantic Web: Real-World Applications from Industry. Springer, Heidelberg (2008). https://doi.org/10.1007/978-0-387-48531-7

8. Corcho, Ó., Gómez-Pérez, A., González-Cabero, R., Suárez-Figueroa, M.C.: ODEval: a tool for evaluating RDF(S), DAML+OIL, and OWL concept taxonomies. In: Bramer, M., Devedzic, V. (eds.) AIAI 2004. IIFIP, vol. 154, pp. 369–382. Springer, Boston, MA (2004). https://doi.org/10.1007/1-4020-8151-0_32

9. Drozd, O., Kirrane, S.: I agree: customize your personal data processing with the CoRe user interface. In: Gritzalis, S., Weippl, E.R., Katsikas, S.K., Anderst-Kotsis, G., Tjoa, A.M., Khalil, I. (eds.) TrustBus 2019. LNCS, vol. 11711, pp. 17–32. Springer, Cham (2019). https://doi.org/10.1007/978-3-030-27813-7_2

10. Drozd, O., Kirrane, S.: Privacy CURE: consent comprehension made easy. In: Hölbl, M., Rannenberg, K., Welzer, T. (eds.) SEC 2020. IAICT, vol. 580, pp. 124–139. Springer, Cham (2020). https://doi.org/10.1007/978-3-030-58201-2_9

11. Fatema, K., Hadziselimovic, E., Pandit, H.J., Debruyne, C., Lewis, D., O'Sullivan, D.: Compliance through informed consent: semantic based consent permission and data management model. In: PrivOn@ ISWC (2017)

12. Fensel, A., Tomic, S., Kumar, V., Stefanovic, M., Aleshin, S., Novikov, D.: SESAME-S: semantic smart home system for energy efficiency. Informatik-Spektrum **36**, 46–57 (2012). https://doi.org/10.1007/s00287-012-0665-9

13. Fensel, D., et al.: Knowledge Graphs: Methodology, Tools and Selected Use Cases. Springer, Cham (2020). https://doi.org/10.1007/978-3-030-37439-6

14. Gross, B.M.: The managing of organizations: the administrative struggle. Ann. Am. Acad. Polit. Soc. Sci. **360**(1), 197–198 (1965). https://doi.org/10.1177/000271626536000140

15. Hogan, A., et al.: Knowledge graphs. Commun. ACM **64**, 96–104 (2020)

16. Jaiman, V., Urovi, V.: A consent model for blockchain-based health data sharing platforms. IEEE Access **8**, 143734–143745 (2020). https://doi.org/10.1109/ACCESS.2020.3014565

17. Kirrane, S., Fernández, J.D., Bonatti, P., Milosevic, U., Polleres, A., Wenning, R.: The special-k personal data processing transparency and compliance platform. ArXiv abs/2001.09461 (2020)

18. Ma, X., et al.: Data visualization in the semantic web. In: Semantic Web Enabled Software Engineering (2015)

19. Mahindrakar, A., Joshi, K.P., et al.: Automating GDPR compliance using policy integrated blockchain. In: IEEE 6th International Conference on Big Data Security on Cloud (BigDataSecurity 2020) (2020)

20. Mallardi, V.: The origin of informed consent. Acta otorhinolaryngologica Italica: organo ufficiale della Società italiana di otorinolaringologia e chirurgia cervico-facciale **25**, 312–27 (2005)

21. Meisel, A., Kabnick, L.D.: Informed consent to medical treatment: an analysis of recent legislation. Univ. Pitt. Law Rev. **41**(3), 407–564 (1980). University of Pittsburgh. School of Law

22. Noy, N.: Ontology development 101: a guide to creating your first ontology. Technical report KSL-01-05 and SMI-2001-0880, Stanford Knowledge Systems Laboratory and Stanford Medical Informatics (2001)

23. Pandit, H.J., Debruyne, C., O'Sullivan, D., Lewis, D.: GConsent - a consent ontology based on the GDPR. In: Hitzler, P., et al. (eds.) ESWC 2019. LNCS, vol. 11503, pp. 270–282. Springer, Cham (2019). https://doi.org/10.1007/978-3-030-21348-0_18

24. Pellegrini, T., Mireles, V., Steyskal, S., Panasiuk, O., Fensel, A., Kirrane, S.: Automated rights clearance using semantic web technologies: the DALICC framework. In: Hoppe, T., Humm, B., Reibold, A. (eds.) Semantic Applications, pp. 203–218. Springer, Heidelberg (2018). https://doi.org/10.1007/978-3-662-55433-3_14

25. Rantos, K., Drosatos, G., Demertzis, K., Ilioudis, C., Papanikolaou, A., Kritsas, A.: ADvoCATE: a consent management platform for personal data processing in the IoT using blockchain technology. In: Lanet, J.-L., Toma, C. (eds.) SECITC 2018. LNCS, vol. 11359, pp. 300–313. Springer, Cham (2019). https://doi.org/10.1007/978-3-030-12942-2_23

26. Raschke, P., Küpper, A., Drozd, O., Kirrane, S.: Designing a GDPR-compliant and usable privacy dashboard. In: Hansen, M., Kosta, E., Nai-Fovino, I., Fischer-Hübner, S. (eds.) Privacy and Identity 2017. IAICT, vol. 526, pp. 221–236. Springer, Cham (2018). https://doi.org/10.1007/978-3-319-92925-5_14

27. Rodrigues, L., Toda, A., Oliveira, W., Palomino, P., Vassileva, J., Isotani, S.: Automating gamification personalization: to the user and beyond. ArXiv abs/2101.05718 (2021)

28. Sermet, Y., Demir, I.: A semantic web framework for automated smart assistants: Covid-19 case study. ArXiv abs/2007.00747 (2020)

29. Shneiderman, B.: The eyes have it: a task by data type taxonomy for information visualizations. In: Proceedings of IEEE Symposium on Visual Languages, pp. 336–343 (1996)

30. Simsek, U., et al.: A semantic approach towards implementing energy efficient lifestyles through behavioural change. In: Proceedings of the 12th International Conference on Semantic Systems, pp. 173–176 (2016)

31. Stuhr, M., Roman, D., Norheim, D.: LODWheel - Javascript-based visualization of RDF data. In: Proceedings of the 2nd International Workshop on Consuming Linked Data (COLD 2011). CEUR Workshop Proceedings, vol. 782, pp. 73–84 (2011)

32. Wolf, S., Clayton, E., Lawrenz, F.: The past, present, and future of informed consent in research and translational medicine. J. Law Med. Ethics **46**, 7–11 (2018)

Improving Decision Making Using Semantic Web Technologies

Tek Raj Chhetri[✉][iD]

Semantic Technology Institute (STI) Innsbruck, Department of Computer Science,
University of Innsbruck, Innsbruck, Austria
tekraj.chhetri@sti2.at

Abstract. With the rapid advance of technology, we are moving towards replacing humans in decision making–the employment of robotics and computerised systems for production and delivery and autonomous cars in the travel sector. The focus is placed on the use of techniques, such as machine learning and deep learning. However, despite advances in machine learning and deep learning, they are incapable of modelling the relationships that are present in the real world, which are necessary for making a decision. For example, automating sociotechnical systems requires an understanding of both human and technological aspects and how they influence one another. Using machine learning, we can not model the relationships of a sociotechnical systems. Semantic Web technologies, which is based on the concept of linked-data technology, can represent relationships in a more realistic way like in the real world, and be useful to make better decisions. The study looks at the use of Semantic Web technologies, namely ontologies and knowledge graphs to improve decision making process.

Keywords: Semantic Web technologies · Artificial Intelligence · Decision making

1 Motivation

More and more attention is being paid to the use of machine learning (ML) and deep learning (DL) algorithms these days for automated systems where machines are responsible for making decisions. *Decision making is defined as a mental process, which involves judging multiple options or alternatives, in order to select one, so as to best fulfil the aims or goals of the decision-maker* [9]. However, several studies have brought attention to problems such as the limited explainability, interpretability and potentially biased application of ML and DL [7,26,32,38]. The interpretability in ML focuses on designing inherently interpretable models, while the explainability tries to provide post hoc explanations for existing black-box models [32].

Semantic Web technologies, namely ontologies and knowledge graphs, are based on the concept of linked-data technology, can represent real world relationships, can also be used for knowledge building and can also provide reasoning, interoperability, data enrichment and handling data variety capabilities

© Springer Nature Switzerland AG 2021
R. Verborgh et al. (Eds.): ESWC 2021 Satellite Events, LNCS 12739, pp. 165–175, 2021.
https://doi.org/10.1007/978-3-030-80418-3_29

[3, 18, 25, 36, 37]. Furthermore, Semantic Web technologies can be used to supplement existing ML, and DL techniques by incorporating missing semantics, making ML more interpretable and explainable, and thereby increasing trustworthiness and accountability [16, 21, 22, 28, 34]. Panigutti et al. [28], and Lai et al. [21] have shown the explainability and interpretability in ML by using an ontology. The current need for interpretable and explainable ML models for transparency and trustworthiness in the automated decision and Semantic Web technologies 's potential to make ML interpretable, explainable is the first motivating factor.

The connectivity due to the Internet of Things (IoT) has led to a generation of an unprecedented amount of data, which according to the World Economic Forum[1] is a new asset in this modern time[2]. Everyone, particularly industries such as in manufacturing, is attempting to maximise profits and derive value from data. However, data consists of sensitive and personally identifiable information and depending on the use; the outcomes can be positive or negative impacting individuals and society as a whole, giving rise to the laws like European General Data Protection Regulation (GDPR)[3] [2]. GDPR provides the user or data owner control over their data, allowing them to specify whom they want to share their data, what they want to share, and what purpose they want to share their data. There exist different scalable and secure data-sharing solutions such as CCoDaMiC framework [13] and SPECIAL[4] but they all lack in the provision of solutions for consent creation, management and observation between two or more involved actors that aim to share Personally Identifiable Information (PII) data[5]. This has culminated in the H2020 project smashHit[6], which seeks to provide solutions to data-sharing problems while adhering to laws such as GDPR and enabling the potential of the data economy. The second motivation is the need for a unified data sharing solution capable of integrating existing fragmented data sharing landscapes, while being compliant with GDPR.

Since the realisation of the importance of fail-safe systems during World War II, there has been a plethora of research on failure prediction and predictive maintenance [14]. The goal of a number of research studies is to account for and capitalise on the changing computing landscape. Today, the importance of failure prediction and fail-safe systems is even more with the growing use of connected things in healthcare, industry and other mission-critical systems because depending on where the failure occurred, it can reduce productivity, increases downtime and even cost human lives. Most predictive maintenance studies are mostly data-driven and use contextless ML, or backbox DL techniques [43], and few are based on Semantic Web technologies like the studies by Ali

---

[1] https://www.weforum.org.

[2] http://www3.weforum.org/docs/WEF_ITTC_PersonalDataNewAsset_Report_2011.pdf.

[3] https://eur-lex.europa.eu/eli/reg/2016/679/oj.

[4] https://www.specialprivacy.eu/.

[5] smashHit Public Report D1.3 Public Innovation Concept March 2021.

[6] https://www.smashhit.eu.

et al. [4]. Furthermore, there is a high demand for predictive maintenance in manufacturing industries such as oil and gas as maintenance yields 15 to 60% of total manufacturing operating costs [47] and is projected to have a market value of USD 21.20 Billion by 2027[7], which is another motivating factor.

2   State-of-the-Art

The decision making domain is constantly being updated with new research findings with the ever-changing dynamics of society. There are different methodological approaches and works related to this research. In this section, I briefly outline existing studies related to this work.

2.1   Semantic Models in Decision Making

A large number of studies have shown the significance of ontologies in decision making [11,15,29,35,44]. Pease et al. [29] use an ontology and machine learning to determine whether it is more profitable to recycle or remanufacture a product. In contrast, Das et al. [11], and Spoladore et al. [35] use an ontology to support the designer in assembly variant design and domestic environments' reconfiguration. Similarly, Zhong et al. [44] use an ontology to help management decision making during the time of meteorological disasters, and D'Aniello et al. [15] offer a solution to decision support for smart city use case focused on semantic stream reasoning. Even though the above use cases differ, they demonstrate that Semantic Web technologies can be applied to a wide range of domains, which is noteworthy because our study aims to provide a solution covering a wide range of domains such as smart cities, insurance, and autonomous vehicles through smashHit (see footnote 6) project. The reason being we can use the learning from those studies. For example, D'Aniello et al. [15] makes use of SSNO[8] (Semantic Sensor Network Ontology) to enrich the sensor data and C-SPARQL[9] to filter, query, integrate data from the heterogenous source, which we can apply in our study as we also intend to cover smart city use case.

Knowledge graphs, similar to ontologies, could be used in decision making. Santos et al. [1] support clinical decision making using their clinical knowledge graph consisting of 16 million nodes and 220 million relationships while the works of Sun et al. [46], Zhou et al. [45], Wang et al. [40] are focused on improving recommendations based on the knowledge graph. Sun et al. [46] use a recurrent knowledge graph embedding (RKGE) that employs a novel recurrent network architecture to encode different paths via a batch of recurrent networks, as well as a pooling operation to determine which paths are more salient. Zhou et al. [45], on the other hand, used a fusion approach to bridge the semantic gap between natural language and external knowledge graphs with word-level enrichment, which is frequently overlooked in other studies. The other studies

---

[7] https://www.reportsanddata.com/report-detail/predictive-maintenance-market.

[8] https://www.w3.org/TR/vocab-ssn/.

[9] http://streamreasoning.org/resources/c-sparql.

by Nie et al. [24], Wang et al. [42], Wang et al. [41], Wan et al. [39], and Antanas et al. [5] focuses on knowledge graph reasoning to assist decision making using techniques such as graph neural networks, attention-based deep reinforcement learning framework and probabilistic logic-based reasoning. Logic-based reasoning is the reasoning performed using universally quantified logic rules [8]. The studies on using knowledge graphs for decision making similar to an ontology differ from our use case and cannot be directly applied. Sun et al. [46], for example, use a recurrent network and require a large amount of data. In the case of the automatic contracting tool (see Sect. 3.2), we do not have enough data to train, whereas in the case of predictive maintenance (see Sect. 3.2), the data does not have the required format, such as missing context. However, the approach taken by Zhou et al. [45] could serve as a starting point for our predictive maintenance use case, which could then be followed by Sun et al. [46] and Antanas et al. [5] for the automatic contracting tool use case.

2.2   Use Case Specific Studies

The studies by Ali et al. [4], Karray et al. [20] uses an ontology such as IMAMO (Industrial MAintenance Management Ontology) to provide a knowledge base for predictive maintenance decision making. Similarly, Z-BRE4K[10], a European Union H2020 project dedicated to improving predictive maintenance. The study Z-BRE4K (see footnote 10) uses three different ontologies SACMI, PHILIPS and GESTAMP[11] for their predictive maintenance use case to GESTAMP-Autotech[12], Philips[13], and Sacmi-CDS[14], demonstrating that no single implementation can cover all cases. Because our predictive maintenance use case differs from the existing one, these existing studies could not be applied completely, necessitating the search for new solutions.

Similar to the predictive maintenance case, the GDPR compliance studies like Mahindrakar et al. [23], and Jaiman et al. [19] and Davari et al. [12], as well as projects CampaNeo[15] and SPECIAL (see footnote 4), do not cover multiple scenarios such as smart cities, insurance, autonomous vehicles and broken consent chains due to transfer of consent ownership of the product or any other possible reason. Hence, the need to create a new solution. However, aforementioned studies can be taken as a base and existing ontologies such as PROV-O[16], GConsent[17], Data Protection Ontology[18] can be reused by extending them further.

---

[10] https://www.z-bre4k.eu.

[11] https://www.z-bre4k.eu/wp-content/uploads/2020/12/Z-BRE4K-semantic-modelling.pdf.

[12] http://www.gestamp.com/.

[13] https://www.philips.com/.

[14] http://www.sacmi.com/.

[15] https://projekte.ffg.at/projekt/3314668.

[16] https://www.w3.org/TR/prov-o/.

[17] http://openscience.adaptcentre.ie/ontologies/GConsent/docs/ontology.

[18] https://www.w3.org/community/dpvcg/wiki/Data_Protection_Ontology_by_Bartolini_et._al#Data_Protection_Ontology.

3   Problem Statement and Contributions

This section introduces our research question that will be focused on during the PhD and the expected contribution we aim to make while answering the research question.

3.1   Problem Statement and Research Question

The core of our research problem is how to improve machine-based automated decision making in a heterogeneous and distributed environment. Machine-based automated decision making in a heterogeneous and distributed environment refers to using a machine to decide in a distributed environment, such as smart cities, with complete or minimal human intervention. We believe that by combining multiple decision making approach; we can improve the automated decision making process. The aim is to combine multiple decision-making approaches, such as knowledge-driven, data-driven, model-driven [6]. The knowledge-driven approach is based on knowledge or experience, the data-driven approach is based on data and uses techniques like ML, and the model-driven approach is based on models such as algebraic models [17,30]. However, there exist several challenges with Semantic Web technologies, such as knowledge representation and processing at scale, integration with techniques like modern ML methods, and data complexity challenge, as highlighted by Bonatti et al. [10]. Further, challenges also exist with the integration of reasoning techniques, such as logic-based reasoning, embedding-based reasoning, which represents each entity as a vector and each relation as a matrix, and neural network-based reasoning techniques rely on neural network [8] and maintaining interoperability in a heterogeneous environment like IoT where there is a data flow from a variety of data sources [31]. The interoperability issue in distributed systems environment arises due to the heterogeneity of computing platforms, for example, IoT and the use of different standards and protocols [33]. The heterogeneity of computing platforms also introduces data heterogeneity and complexity issue, which hinders interoperability.

In light of our motivation and the open challenges, the research question is: *"To what extent we can leverage Semantic Web technologies to improve and automate decision making in a distributed and heterogeneous environment?"*. This research question can be further divided into following fine-grained research questions.

- **RQ1** - To what extent can we improve decision-making by combining a knowledge-driven approach with a data-driven approach where knowledge is represented using Semantic Web technologies in the form of knowledge graphs?
- **RQ2** - To what extent can we support the required decision while also dealing with complex interactions and maintaining the necessary scalability in dynamic and heterogeneous environments such as smart cities and manufacturing?

3.2 Contributions

The overall contribution would be to improve decision making by using Semantic Web technologies dealing with an assortment of challenges as presented in Sect. 3.1. Improving decision making would be realised through contributing to smashHit (see footnote 6) by developing an automatic contracting tool and KI-NET[19] with a prototype based on the predictive-maintenance use case. Details regarding how each use case contributes to the overall exhibit are outlined below.

Automatic Contracting Tool. The automatic contracting tool, a core of the smashHit (see footnote 6), will enable automatic data sharing between the data owner and data processor in compliance with GDPR. Figure 2a shows the high-level architecture of an automatic contracting tool. The automatic contracting tool will be in charge of making (or supporting) the following decisions: (i) whether data exchange should be permitted, (ii) performing verification to determine whether there is a breach of contract or a broken consent chain, and (iii) checking updated consent information to make a further decision, such as limiting data access to the data processor.

The Contracting engine of an automatic contracting tool, based on the consent stored in consent storage or GraphDB[20], generates a contract. A knowledge graph is used to represent both the consent and the generated contract. The Compliance engine then uses the contract to make the necessary decisions. The compliance engine performs the necessary checks for consent and contract, as well as the decision reasoning. The expected contribution would be to provide a decision making solution that is interpretable, interoperable, and scalable, thus answering *RQ1* and *RQ2*. Mahindrakar et al. [23], Panasiuk et al. [27], Jaiman et al. [19], Antanas et al. [5], Davari et al. [12], D'Aniello et al. [15], and project CampaNeo (see footnote 15) would be used as a foundation for an automatic contracting tool. Cloud computing platforms like Google Cloud[21], Amazon Web Service[22] would be used to support scalability.

Predictive Maintenance Prototype. The predictive maintenance prototype aims to improve the reliability and life-cycle of the machines used in the industry. The high-level architecture for the predictive maintenance prototype is depicted in Fig. 2b. The predictive maintenance prototype would assist in the following decisions: (i) determining when to perform maintenance, (ii) determining the type of action required, such as automatic or manual control action, and (iii) performing the appropriate automatic control action or selecting the best possible solution and presenting it to the user (or operator) in the case of manual control action. The studies by Zhou et al. [45], Sun et al. [46], Panigutti et al.

---

[19] https://scch.at/en/das-projects-details/ki-net.
[20] https://www.ontotext.com/products/graphdb/.
[21] https://cloud.google.com.
[22] https://aws.amazon.com.

[28], D'Aniello et al. [15], and Lai et al. [21], as well as the project Z-BRE4K (see footnote 10) would serve as a foundation for a predictive maintenance prototype.

The AI engine will learn the raw data using ML (or DL) techniques such as Long short-term memory (LSTM), which would then be used for automatic knowledge graph construction. The Semantic decision engine then uses the knowledge graph to perform the reasoning using advanced reasoning techniques such as reinforcement learning-based knowledge graph reasoning as demonstrated by Wang et al. [41] and finally making the decision. Similar to smash-Hit (see footnote 6), the expected contribution would be to provide an interpretable, interoperable, and scalable predictive maintenance decision making solution, thus answering *RQ1* and *RQ2*.

4   Research Methodology and Approach

The research methodology that will be followed is shown in Fig. 1. We begin with a review of the current state, followed by gathering information on the requirements of the project. Based on the gathered requirements, we design and validate the architecture of the system, which then will be implemented. Currently, we have conceptualised and validated system architecture. The remaining steps will be carried out as outlined in Fig. 1. Further, the details about the evaluation are discussed in Sect. 5.

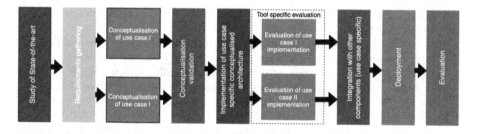

Fig. 1. Research methodology

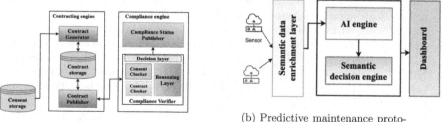

(a) Automatic contracting tool

(b) Predictive maintenance prototype

Fig. 2. High level architecture

5 Evaluation Plan

In this section, we describe the specifics of our evaluation plan. We intend to perform a two-stage evaluation, one before integrating and the other after integrating, as shown in Fig. 1. The purpose of this evaluation is to substantiate our claim to be able to improve decision making by employing Semantic Web technologies. The evaluation would be carried out using metrics such as accuracy, Precision at N (Prec@N), and the top-N Mean Reciprocal Rank (MRR), as in the studies of Sun et al. [46], and Wang et al. [42]. Furthermore, the approaches taken in studies by Mahindrakar et al. [23], and Jaiman et al. [19], and Davari et al. [12] would be taken into account when evaluating an automatic contracting tool. Non-functional requirements, such as performance and scalability, would be assessed using metrics such as throughput and response time.

Acknowledgements. This research has been supported by the European Union projects funded under Horizon 2020 research and innovation programme (smashHit (see footnote 6), grant agreement 871477 and Interreg Österreich-Bayern 2014–2020 programme project (KI-Net (see footnote 19), grant agreement AB 292). I want to express my gratitude to Assoc.-Prof. Dr. Anna Fensel for her support and insightful comments.

References

1. Clinical knowledge graph integrates proteomics data into clinical decision-making. bioRxiv (2020)
2. Regulation (eu) 2016/679 of the European parliamentand of the council of 27 April 2016 on the protectionof natural persons with regard to the processing of personal data and on the free movement of such data, andrepealing directive 95/46/ec (general data protectionregulation). Official Journal of the European Union, L119, May 2016. https://eur-lex.europa.eu/eli/reg/2016/679/oj
3. Akhtar, S.M., Nazir, M., Saleem, K., Haque, H.M.U., Hussain, I.: An ontology-driven IoT based healthcare formalism. Int. J. Adv. Comput. Sci. Appl. **11**(2), 479–486 (2020)
4. Ali, N., Hong, J.E.: Failure detection and prevention for cyber-physical systems using ontology-based knowledge base. Computers **7**(4), 68 (2018)
5. Antanas, L., et al.: Semantic and geometric reasoning for robotic grasping: a probabilistic logic approach. Auton. Robot. **43**(6), 1393–1418 (2018). https://doi.org/10.1007/s10514-018-9784-8
6. Antunes, F., Freire, M., Costa, J.P.: Semantic web tools and decision-making. In: Zaraté, P., Kersten, G.E., Hernández, J.E. (eds.) GDN 2014. LNBIP, vol. 180, pp. 270–277. Springer, Cham (2014). https://doi.org/10.1007/978-3-319-07179-4_31
7. Bellamy, R.K., et al.: Think your artificial intelligence software is fair? Think again. IEEE Softw. **36**(4), 76–80 (2019)
8. Bellomarini, L., Sallinger, E., Vahdati, S.: Chapter 6 reasoning in knowledge graphs: an embeddings spotlight. In: Janev, V., Graux, D., Jabeen, H., Sallinger, E. (eds.) Knowledge Graphs and Big Data Processing. LNCS, vol. 12072, pp. 87–101. Springer, Cham (2020). https://doi.org/10.1007/978-3-030-53199-7_6

9. Bohanec, M.: Decision making: a computer-science and information-technology viewpoint. Interdisc. Descrip. Complex Syst. Sci. J. **7**, 22–37 (2009)
10. Bonatti, P.A., Decker, S., Polleres, A., Presutti, V.: Knowledge graphs: new directions for knowledge representation on the semantic web (dagstuhl seminar 18371). In: Dagstuhl Reports vol. 8. Schloss Dagstuhl-Leibniz-Zentrum fuer Informatik (2019)
11. Das, S.K., Swain, A.K.: An ontology-based framework for decision support in assembly variant design. J. Comput. Inf. Sci. Eng. **21**(2), 021007 (2021)
12. Davari, M., Bertino, E.: Access control model extensions to support data privacy protection based on GDPR. In: IEEE International Conference on Big Data (Big Data), pp. 4017–4024 (2019). https://doi.org/10.1109/BigData47090.2019.9006455
13. Dehury, C.K., Srirama, S.N., Chhetri, T.R.: CCoDaMiC: a framework for coherent coordination of data migration and computation platforms. Futur. Gener. Comput. Syst. **109**, 1–16 (2020)
14. Dubrova, E.: Fault-Tolerant Design. Springer, New York (2013). https://doi.org/10.1007/978-1-4614-2113-9
15. D'Aniello, G., Gaeta, M., Orciuoli, F.: An approach based on semantic stream reasoning to support decision processes in smart cities. Telematics Inform. **35**(1), 68–81 (2018)
16. Futia, G., Melandri, A., Vetrò, A., Morando, F., De Martin, J.C.: Removing barriers to transparency: a case study on the use of semantic technologies to tackle procurement data inconsistency. In: Blomqvist, E., Maynard, D., Gangemi, A., Hoekstra, R., Hitzler, P., Hartig, O. (eds.) ESWC 2017. LNCS, vol. 10249, pp. 623–637. Springer, Cham (2017). https://doi.org/10.1007/978-3-319-58068-5_38
17. Hedberg, T., Barnard Feeney, A., Camelio, J.: Toward a diagnostic and prognostic method for knowledge-driven decision-making in smart manufacturing technologies. In: Madni, A.M., Boehm, B., Ghanem, R.G., Erwin, D., Wheaton, M.J. (eds.) Disciplinary Convergence in Systems Engineering Research, pp. 859–873. Springer, Cham (2018). https://doi.org/10.1007/978-3-319-62217-0_60
18. Horrocks, I., Giese, M., Kharlamov, E., Waaler, A.: Using semantic technology to tame the data variety challenge. IEEE Internet Comput. **20**(6), 62–66 (2016)
19. Jaiman, V., Urovi, V.: A consent model for blockchain-based health data sharing platforms. IEEE Access **8**, 143734–143745 (2020). https://doi.org/10.1109/ACCESS.2020.3014565
20. Karray, M.H., Chebel-Morello, B., Zerhouni, N.: A formal ontology for industrial maintenance. Appl. Ontol. **7**(3), 269–310 (2012)
21. Lai, P., Phan, N., Hu, H., Badeti, A., Newman, D., Dou, D.: Ontology-based interpretable machine learning for textual data. In: 2020 International Joint Conference on Neural Networks (IJCNN), pp. 1–10. IEEE (2020)
22. Lecue, F.: On the role of knowledge graphs in explainable AI. Semantic Web (Preprint), 1–11 (2019)
23. Mahindrakar, A., Joshi, K.P., et al.: Automating GDPR compliance using policy integrated blockchain. In: IEEE 6th International Conference on Big Data Security on Cloud (BigDataSecurity 2020) (2020). https://doi.org/10.1109/BigDataSecurity-HPSC-IDS49724.2020.00026
24. Nie, K., Zeng, K., Meng, Q.: Knowledge reasoning method for military decision support knowledge graph mixing rule and graph neural networks learning together. In: 2020 Chinese Automation Congress (CAC), pp. 4013–4018. IEEE (2020)
25. Noy, N., Gao, Y., Jain, A., Narayanan, A., Patterson, A., Taylor, J.: Industry-scale knowledge graphs: lessons and challenges. Queue **17**(2), 48–75 (2019)

26. Osoba, O.A., Welser, W., IV.: An intelligence in Our Image: The Risks of Bias and Errors in Artificial Intelligence. Rand Corporation (2017)

27. Panasiuk, O., Steyskal, S., Havur, G., Fensel, A., Kirrane, S.: Modeling and reasoning over data licenses. In: Gangemi, A., et al. (eds.) ESWC 2018. LNCS, vol. 11155, pp. 218–222. Springer, Cham (2018). https://doi.org/10.1007/978-3-319-98192-5_41

28. Panigutti, C., Perotti, A., Pedreschi, D.: Doctor XAI: an ontology-based approach to black-box sequential data classification explanations. In: Proceedings of the 2020 Conference On Fairness, Accountability, and Transparency, pp. 629–639 (2020)

29. Pease, S.G., et al.: An interoperable semantic service toolset with domain ontology for automated decision support in the end-of-life domain. Futur. Gener. Comput. Syst. **112**, 848–858 (2020)

30. Power, D.J., Sharda, R.: Model-driven decision support systems: concepts and research directions. Decis. Support Syst. **43**(3), 1044–1061 (2007)

31. Rahman, H., Hussain, M.I.: A comprehensive survey on semantic interoperability for internet of things: state-of-the-art and research challenges. Trans. Emerg. Telecommun. Technol. **31**(12), e3902 (2020)

32. Rudin, C.: Stop explaining black box machine learning models for high stakes decisions and use interpretable models instead. Nature Machine Intell. **1**(5), 206–215 (2019)

33. Samizadeh Nikoui, T., Rahmani, A.M., Balador, A., Haj Seyyed Javadi, H.: Internet of things architecture challenges: a systematic review. Int. J. Commun. Syst. **34**(4), e4678 (2021)

34. Sovrano, F., Vitali, F., Palmirani, M.: Modelling GDPR-compliant explanations for trustworthy AI. In: Kő, A., Francesconi, E., Kotsis, G., Tjoa, A.M., Khalil, I. (eds.) EGOVIS 2020. LNCS, vol. 12394, pp. 219–233. Springer, Cham (2020). https://doi.org/10.1007/978-3-030-58957-8_16

35. Spoladore, D., Sacco, M.: Semantic and dweller-based decision support system for the reconfiguration of domestic environments: Recaal. Electronics **7**(9), 179 (2018)

36. Tachmazidis, I., Davies, J., Batsakis, S., Antoniou, G., Duke, A., Stincic Clarke, S.: Hypercat RDF: semantic enrichment for IoT. In: Li, Y.-F., et al. (eds.) JIST 2016. LNCS, vol. 10055, pp. 273–286. Springer, Cham (2016). https://doi.org/10.1007/978-3-319-50112-3_21

37. Tao, M., Ota, K., Dong, M.: Ontology-based data semantic management and application in IoT-and cloud-enabled smart homes. Futur. Gener. Comput. Syst. **76**, 528–539 (2017)

38. Vasileva, M.I.: The dark side of machine learning algorithms: how and why they can leverage bias, and what can be done to pursue algorithmic fairness. In: Proceedings of the 26th ACM SIGKDD International Conference on Knowledge Discovery & Data Mining, pp. 3586–3587 (2020)

39. Wan, G., Pan, S., Gong, C., Zhou, C., Haffari, G.: Reasoning like human: hierarchical reinforcement learning for knowledge graph reasoning. In: International Joint Conference on Artificial Intelligence 2020, pp. 1926–1932. Association for the Advancement of Artificial Intelligence (AAAI) (2020)

40. Wang, H., Zhao, M., Xie, X., Li, W., Guo, M.: Knowledge graph convolutional networks for recommender systems. In: The World Wide Web Conference, pp. 3307–3313 (2019)

41. Wang, Q., Hao, Y., Cao, J.: ADRL: an attention-based deep reinforcement learning framework for knowledge graph reasoning. Knowl. Based Syst. **197**, 105910 (2020)

42. Wang, Z., Chen, T., Ren, J., Yu, W., Cheng, H., Lin, L.: Deep reasoning with knowledge graph for social relationship understanding. arXiv preprint arXiv:1807.00504 (2018)
43. Zhang, W., Yang, D., Wang, H.: Data-driven methods for predictive maintenance of industrial equipment: a survey. IEEE Syst. J. **13**(3), 2213–2227 (2019). https://doi.org/10.1109/JSYST.2019.2905565
44. Zhong, S., Fang, Z., Zhu, M., Huang, Q.: A geo-ontology-based approach to decision-making in emergency management of meteorological disasters. Nat. Hazards **89**(2), 531–554 (2017). https://doi.org/10.1007/s11069-017-2979-z
45. Zhou, K., Zhao, W.X., Bian, S., Zhou, Y., Wen, J.R., Yu, J.: Improving conversational recommender systems via knowledge graph based semantic fusion. In: Proceedings of the 26th ACM SIGKDD International Conference on Knowledge Discovery & Data Mining, pp. 1006–1014 (2020)
46. Zhu Sun, J.Y., Zhang, J., Bozzon, A., Huang, L.K., Xu, C.: Recurrent knowledge graph embedding for effective recommendation (2018)
47. Zonta, T., da Costa, C.A., da Rosa Righi, R., de Lima, M.J., da Trindade, E.S., Li, G.P.: Predictive maintenance in the industry 4.0: a systematic literature review. Comput. Ind. Eng. 106889 (2020)

Ontological Formalisation
of Mathematical Equations for Phenomic
Data Exploitation

Felipe Vargas-Rojas[1,2]([✉]) [ID]

[1] LEPSE, Université Montpellier, INRAE, Institut Agro, Montpellier, France
[2] MISTEA, Université Montpellier, INRAE, Institut Agro, Montpellier, France
luis-felipe.vargas-rojas@inrae.fr

Abstract. In recent years, plant phenomics community has adopted Semantic Web technologies in order to harmonise heterogeneous, multi-scale and multi-source datasets. Semantic Web provides inference services for representing logic relationships in an unambiguous, homogeneous and clean manner, which enhances data harmonisation. However, mathematical relationships involving numerical attributes are poorly formalised, despite the fact that they are supported for a theoretical and well-defined structure. For instance, whilst unit ontologies (e.g. UO, OM, QUDT) provide relationships and annotations to perform unit conversion, they are not effectively used for automating the integration of heterogeneous measurements. Here we propose an ontological framework for representing mathematical equations supporting the automatised use of inference services, metadata, domain ontologies, and the internal structure of mathematical equations. This approach is evaluated using two plant phenomics case studies involving the calculation of unit conversions and thermal time.

Keywords: Semantic Web · Plant phenomics · Ontological reasoning · Mathematical equations

1 Introduction

Plant Phenomics (PP) has produced massive datasets involving experiments performed in the field and controlled conditions, concerning hundreds of genotypes at different scales of organisation. These datasets are unprecedented resources for identifying and testing novel mechanisms and models [17]. Assembling and organising such datasets is not straightforward because of the heterogeneous, multi-scale and multi-source nature of data.

Supported by INRAE and #DigitAg. This work was supported by the French National Research Agency under the Investments for the Future Program, referred as ANR-16-CONV-0004

Category: Early Stage Ph.D. **Topic:** Deductive Reasoning, Neuro-symbolic reasoning, Inductive Reasoning.

Recently, the PHIS[1] [11] ontology-driven information system based on FAIR principles [18] has been proposed as a tool for managing phenomics data. PHIS allows expressing a number of relationships implicit in the data, like hierarchies, mappings and constraint values. However, some numerical relationships cannot be expressed using this mechanism neglecting a number of data often used in PP (observations and measurements). State-of-the-art in PP is populated by mathematical equations relating different plant and environmental traits in different scales, invoking arithmetic and series operations (summations, aggregations).

In this paper we propose an ontological framework for representing mathematical equations and exploiting inference services. Our main contributions are: (i) a model for representing mathematical equations, (ii) a reasoning-based mechanism to compute the equations, (iii) a module to automate unit conversion based on unit ontologies.

The paper is organised as follows. Section 2 discusses the related work describing mathematical equation representation in Semantic Web (SW) while Sect. 3 presents the problem and contributions. Sections 4 and 5 are the main part of the paper, presenting a preliminary methodology and evaluation plan. Finally, Sect. 6 presents the conclusions.

2   State of the Art

Although there is not an ontological framework that addresses directly the proposed features, a number methods allow computing mathematical expressions related to SW technologies.

- **Ontology-based information representation**: the expression is represented in some formal language but the machinery for evaluating is not associated
- **Ontological reasoning**: the expression is evaluated as part of the reasoning task
- **SPARQL extension**: an SPARQL [4] function facilitates the expression evaluation
- **Ontology-based delegated computing**: the expression is evaluated by an external tool and the necessary information is structured using ontologies

The following approaches are organised by the used method and reviewed taking into account these criteria: (i) how is the information represented, (ii) what is the expressive power for each approach, (iii) where is the computation executed, (iv) how are the inference services used.

2.1   Ontology-Based Information Representation

In these approaches the system contains annotated datasets, and occasionally information for describing some execution parameters. Hence, the information

---

[1] http://www.phis.inra.fr.

should be transferred to local scripts for handling the required transformations. As an example the Function Ontology [5] describes functions independently of the programming language, focusing on the function name and attributes information without semantic information about the internal computed mathematical model or the resulting value. A number of studies tackle the problem of representing units of measurement, providing means to describe units and to some extent model conversion between these units (e.g. unit ontologies UO [7] and OM [16]). However, non of these studies specify a concrete machinery to perform unit conversions [2].

In a recent study using two unit ontologies, OM [16] and QUDT [8], Martín-Recuerda et al. [10] evidence the challenges related to the use of metadata for computing unit conversion. Unit conversion is performed in QUDT by using the values of two data properties: *qudt:conversionMultiplier* and *qudt:conversionOffset*. The values of these properties determine how the magnitude of a quantity value can be converted to a base (or reference derived). Conversely, unit conversion in OM it is not straightforward since the conversion factor (or multiplier) and offsets are not available for all derived units. Consequently, it is necessary to navigate along the RDF graph to find an unit that has one or two of these properties to obtain the necessary conversion factors and offsets for a given unit. In this study the conversion is invoked within the query definition in SPARQL.

2.2   Ontological Reasoning

Ontological reasoning allows to define computations in terms of ontology concepts and assigning the resulting value to ontological properties.

In this line Bischof et al. [3] extended the inference services of RDFS allowing axioms about equations by adding the type "equation" to the TBOX. The expressive power of this proposal was limited to simple equations without considering aggregations or summations. In addition, the equations were embedded as strings without semantics inside the components. Besides the former problems, the incorporation of unit names into the properties instead of using unit ontologies (e.g. tempHighF, tempHighC), leads to an excessive proliferation of properties [13].

In another study, Parsia et Smith [13] introduced a method for unit conversions based on a new datatype system for quantities (e.g. "6 feet"^owl:quantity). They argued that axiomatising quantities leads to performance issues and contaminates the axiomatisation of the domain, whilst a new datatype will enable special syntax and semantic support for the worked out theory about quantities. This approach requires that conversions are calculated during insertion time, missing information about the original quantity form. This is also disconnected from the evolution of units ontologies, since the unit is imposed inside an string as a text and not as a linked resource.

2.3   SPARQL Extensions

SPARQL can be extended to perform calculations on top of the basic graph pattern (BGP) [6]. When a query is executed, all the data matching the pattern are loaded in memory for later operations, allowing operations like aggregation and SPARQL functions to be calculated based on these in-memory stored records. Although it is not possible to invoke inferences in these approaches, they offer a computation environment that could be exploited to evaluate the equations.

Hogan et al. [9] proposed a language aimed to integrate graph querying with analytical tasks supporting custom computations over the existing SPARQL infrastructure. The language increments the expressive power of SPARQL allowing *for loops* and variables to assign subgraphs. The proposed language is far from the mathematical notions and more related to SPARQL queries, and scripts are defined using the RDF structures. Nevertheless, it demonstrates that analytical tasks can be performed on a SPARQL extension.

2.4   Ontology-Based Delegated Computing

In these studies, computations are delegated to external tools such as Matlab, Python, SPSS, or R. This is a complementary approach to Ontology-based information representation adding semantic information about the external execution. For instance, Rijgersberg et al. [15] proposed the Ontology of Quantitative Research (OQR) for annotating scientific data, allowing people and machines to interpret and connect to real-world phenomena as well as metadata for automating invocation of numerical software. In this approach the computations follow a black-box model where is not possible to connect the internal structure with ontology concepts or inference services. Finally, the ontology is defined from scratch for an specific purpose.

Beck et al. [1] proposed an ontology for building simulations in agriculture systems modelling by including several web-based visual design tools where users can create a model and automatically generate the simulation code. Symbols, operators and variables are represented using a proposed ontology. This approach allows to represent the model structure, and to connect with the ontology concepts. Several inference services can be executed like subsumption and classification, but the computations remain delegated to the external software where the generated script will be executed.

3   Problem Statement and Contributions

The state of the art shows a lack of studies exploiting the inference services interconnected with a formalisation of mathematical equations. Despite the availability of several formal languages to represent mathematical formulas (MathML[2], OpenMath[3]), they are merely descriptive and not effectively integrated with the reasoning services. On the other hand, to the best of our knowledge, the few approaches addressing the integration of reasoning tasks do not consider units ontologies annotations neither the expressive power to deal with aggregations and summations (typical SPARQL operations).

---

[2] https://www.w3.org/Math/.
[3] https://www.openmath.org/.

Our contribution is to propose a framework using the SW stack for representing mathematical equations in terms of PP attributes. Here we will address: (i) how to easily represent mathematical equations independently on the execution engine, in a manner more compliant with symbolic mathematics than programming languages, (ii) how to link or define these equations using the ontology concepts and properties linked to public ontologies, (PO^4, CO^5, $AgrO^6$) instead of isolated meaningless variables (x, y, z). (iii) characterise the trade-off when equations are embedded within reasoning tasks, (iv) how to use unit ontologies in order to harmonise numerical data, (v) how to deal with nested equations.

For instance, assuming two environmental datasets (D1 and D2) with different schemes and the following equation:

$$sizeN = size(ex\!:\!dailyPrecipitation) \tag{1}$$

$$ex\!:\!avgMonthPrecipitacion = \frac{\sum(ex\!:\!dailyPrecipitation)}{sizeN} \tag{2}$$

Let us suppose that D1 has an attribute *ex:dailyPrecipitation* and that D2 uses another name convention like *ex2:dailyRaining*. Directly, D2 is not accepted by the equations, however we can state a rule to unify the two datasets through the inference services:

$$ex2\!:\!dailyRaining \quad rdfs\!:\!subPropertyOf \quad ex\!:\!dailyPrecipitation \tag{3}$$

Then, if during the calculation time the equation is interconnected with the reasoning task, the system can apply the computation to both datasets. In this regard, our contribution should also analyse the expected benefits, we present some examples:

1. Define equations close to mathematical structures instead of programming language expressions
2. Define equation variables using ontology terms
3. Apply same equations for heterogeneous datasets schemes using OWL/RDFS inference rules for mapping (owl:sameAs, rdf:subPropertyOf)
4. Offer up-to-date results avoiding proliferation of stored attributes (lazy evaluation)
5. Automate unit conversion harmonisation for heterogeneous observations

4   Research Methodology and Approach

The ontological framework development can be divided into different steps, each one addressing specific features and challenges.

The first step is about *mathematical equation representation*, in this step we will investigate alternatives to represent mathematical equations as shown

---

[4] http://obofoundry.org/ontology/po.

[5] https://www.cropontology.org/.

[6] http://obofoundry.org/ontology/agro.

in Sect. 2.1. In order to select the most appropriate model, the following criteria will be taken into account: (i) similarity with mathematical notation, (ii) expressive power, (iii) compatibility with RDF and OWL, Finally, if necessary, we should extend and adjust the provided functionalities to support the case study requirements.

The second step considers *revisiting unit ontologies*. As mentioned in Sect. 2.1, unit ontologies are a fundamental resource for exploiting numerical data. In this step, we will revisit unit ontologies in order to define which one among the publicly available is the more suitable to perform unit conversion.

The following step concerns the *reasoning implementation*. Several approaches were mentioned in Sect. 2.2 to perform reasoning coupled with computable expressions. In this step we will implement the code to embed equations within the inference engine. The following possibilities will be tested:

- **Modify a query rewriting algorithm:** given a user's query and a set of equations, rewrite the query to perform the calculations
- **Create a new literal data type:** a new data type such as *xsd:float* or *xsd:double* could be defined, e.g. *owl:equation*, then implement a machinery able to handle the data type
- **Extending SWRL rules:** this language to define rules can be extended to handle equations
- **A module extension of SPARQL:** create a module that recognises the equation and defines the calculations

In this step, we will face the computational boundaries of each approach and will test which of the former possibilities is more suited to exploit the inference services.

4.1 Case Studies

In order to prove the feasibility of the proposal, this research will focus in two concrete case studies from PP, each of them increases the complexity and the functionalities required to reach the task:

Perform Unit Conversions. The aim is to automate the unit conversion using a formal definition of formulas like:

$$1 \, \text{m}^2 = 10000 \, \text{cm}^2, 1 \, \text{cm}^2 = 1 \, \text{m}^2 \times 10^{-4} \tag{4}$$

As a result, the user could query the data asking in either centimetres or metres. Whilst this may seem trivial as simple equations allowing unit conversions are broadly known (e.g. cm^2 to m^2) and these are routine operations performed by users, they are often an important source of errors. This is particularly the case for complex unit conversions involving different concepts, units and dimensions, and when heterogeneous datasets should be harmonised (e.g. light units) [14]. For instance, combining data from a pyranometer (measuring global solar radiation (R_s)) and a quantum sensor (measuring photosynthetically active radiation

(PAR)) is not straightforward since both sensors measure different variables in different units. R_s is often expressed using multiple units (e.g. W m^{-2}, J cm^{-2} s^{-1}, MJ m^{-2} d^{-1}), and PAR data is usually provided in μmol m^{-2} s^{-1} thus requiring unit conversions and aggregation of data.

As an example, the conversion of 80 J cm^{-2} of solar radiation to μmol m^{-2} s^{-1} of PAR considering the time of 30 min (1800 s) involves a number of steps [14]:

First the conversion factor for solar radiation (kJ m^{-2} $time^{-1}$) to (W m^{-2}) is:

$$1\frac{kJ}{m^2 \cdot s} = 10^3 \frac{W}{m^2} \tag{5}$$

For a period of 30 min (1800 s):

$$\frac{80\ J}{cm^2 \cdot 1800\ s} \rightarrow \frac{10^{-3}\ kJ}{1\ J} \times \frac{1\ cm^2}{10^{-4}\ m^2} \times 10^3 \frac{W}{m^2} \rightarrow 444.4 \frac{W}{m^2} \tag{6}$$

Then the conversion factor for solar radiation (R_s in W m^{-2}) to PAR in μmol m^{-2} s^{-1} is:

$$1\frac{W}{m^2} = 2.02\frac{\mu mol}{m^2 \cdot s} \tag{7}$$

Finally:

$$444.4\frac{W}{m^2} \rightarrow 444.4 \times 2.02\frac{\mu mol}{m^2 \cdot s} \rightarrow 897.8\frac{\mu mol}{m^2 \cdot s} \tag{8}$$

Main challenges here are related to the specific designs of unit ontologies and the fact that each ontology individual can have distinct units.

Calculation of Thermal Time. Thermal time (i.e. growing degree units) is one of the common processes currently handled by biologists and agronomists which is used to normalise several temperature-dependent processes such as leaf-progression. It can be either calculated using a simple linear model and a species-specific base temperature parameter, a bilinear model with some optimum and minimum temperature parameters or even using a process-based bell-shaped model [12]. Its calculation requires then a number of steps and necessary meta-data (e.g. input temperatures, species, parameters, integration time, interval of calculation).

Thermal time using a species-dependent base temperature (T_0) and an observed temperature (T):

$$ThermalTime = T - T_0 \tag{9}$$

With some boundary conditions:

$$if\ T < T_0 \rightarrow T = T_0 \tag{10}$$

Thermal time using a species-dependent base, optimum and maximum temperatures (T_0, T_{opt}, T_{max})

$$if \ T > T_0 \leq T_{opt} \rightarrow ThermalTime = T - T_0 \tag{11}$$

$$if \ T > T_{opt} \leq T_{max} \rightarrow ThermalTime = T - T_{max} \tag{12}$$

With some boundary conditions:

$$if \ T < T_0 \rightarrow T = T_0 \tag{13}$$

$$if \ T > T_{max} \rightarrow T = T_{max} \tag{14}$$

The main challenges with thermal time calculation are related to the combination of if-then rules with equations, and the necessity to reuse the unit conversion module because the attributes are often in different units. Variable T_0 depends on the plant species that can be identified using ontologies to automatically assign T_0 values. As mentioned previously, the equations here should use concepts from domain ontologies instead of the generic variables used in the examples.

Figure 1 summarises the two case studies. On top, a model composed of different elements and below two specific models specifying the elements to be executed.

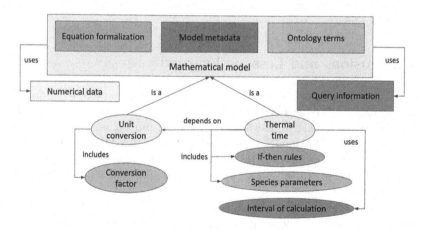

Fig. 1. Elements involved in each case study

5   Evaluation Plan

We will conduct some experiments to assess the efficacy of the framework for representing and computing the two case studies. For this aim, the experiments will require three main resources, (i) datasets, (ii) unit ontologies and (iii) a machine to perform computations. All the resources will be explained in this section.

In the unit conversion case study, two real-world datasets will be used. The first one contains plant measurements (leaf length and leaf width) annotated in different units. The second one contains weather measurements made by three different light sensors involving different light units and time granularities. The thermal time case study will use temperature data and plant annotations (e.g. events and species-specific factors). Datasets are annotated using the units of measurement ontology (UO).

For all the experiments data are stored in a GraphDB database and the experiments will be executed in an average machine with a Linux operating system, 16 GB RAM, and a processor of 1.8 GHz, 8-cores.

Assessing the equation representation. A qualitative evaluation comparing some representation methods will be proposed. This evaluation will consider criteria like the number of instructions necessary to express the case studies.

Assessing the unit conversion module. In this part we will evaluate the efficacy of the unit conversion module using the proposed case studies, and we will define the more appropriated ontology for unit conversion that does not affect the inference capabilities (e.g. such as ontology alignment).

Assessing the nested equation. The thermal time study case will be used to evaluate nested equations. Input data for the thermal time equation will be in different temperature units, thereby depending on the unit conversion module.

All the case studies will be evaluated considering the data volume and the equation complexity.

6   Conclusions and Lessons Learned

In this paper, we propose an ontological framework for representing and computing mathematical equations using Semantic Web technologies. In contrast to the state-of the art, this framework will offer an unified mechanism to represent common Plant Phenomics equations. By using this framework, we expect to have more linked models, more explainable equations, and a more effective use of unit ontologies. In this way, the neglected numerical relationships will be easier to express.

To assess the feasibility of the framework, the different experiments and case studies will evaluate specific computing boundaries. From these results, we will assess the performance of the model and the capability to express all the required functionalities. For each case study we will demonstrate that this representation facilitates the data exploitation and reduces the user's time-effort in favour of a simplified data retrieval process.

Although the case studies presented here belong to Plant Phenomics community (offering massive semantic datasets), the framework can be used for another domains dealing with numerical attributes and mathematical equations.

References

1. Beck, H., Morgan, K., Jung, Y., Grunwald, S., Kwon, H.y., Wu, J.: Ontology-based simulation in agricultural systems modeling. Agric. Syst. **103**(7), 463–477 (2010)
2. Bischof, S., Harth, A., Kämpgen, B., Polleres, A., Schneider, P.: Enriching integrated statistical open city data by combining equational knowledge and missing value imputation. J. Web Seman. **48**, 22–47 (2018)
3. Bischof, S., Polleres, A.: RDFS with attribute equations via SPARQL rewriting. In: Cimiano, P., Corcho, O., Presutti, V., Hollink, L., Rudolph, S. (eds.) ESWC 2013. LNCS, vol. 7882, pp. 335–350. Springer, Heidelberg (2013). https://doi.org/10.1007/978-3-642-38288-8_23
4. Consortium, W.W.W., et al.: Sparql 1.1 overview (2013)
5. De Meester, B., Dimou, A., Verborgh, R., Mannens, E.: An ontology to semantically declare and describe functions. In: Sack, H., Rizzo, G., Steinmetz, N., Mladenić, D., Auer, S., Lange, C. (eds.) ESWC 2016. LNCS, vol. 9989, pp. 46–49. Springer, Cham (2016). https://doi.org/10.1007/978-3-319-47602-5_10
6. DuCharme, B.: Learning SPARQL: Querying and Updating with SPARQL 1.1. O'Reilly Media, Inc., Sebastopol (2013)
7. Gkoutos, G.V., Schofield, P.N., Hoehndorf, R.: The units ontology: a tool for integrating units of measurement in science. Database **2012**, bas03 (2012)
8. Hodgson, R., Keller, P.J., Hodges, J., Spivak, J.: Qudt-quantities, units, dimensions and data types ontologies. USA Available http://qudt. org March 156 (2014)
9. Hogan, A., Reutter, J.L., Soto, A.: In-database graph analytics with recursive SPARQL. In: Pan, J.Z., Tamma, V., d'Amato, C., Janowicz, K., Fu, B., Polleres, A., Seneviratne, O., Kagal, L. (eds.) ISWC 2020. LNCS, vol. 12506, pp. 511–528. Springer, Cham (2020). https://doi.org/10.1007/978-3-030-62419-4_29
10. Martín-Recuerda, F., Walther, D., Eisinger, S., Moore, G., Andersen, P., Opdahl, P.-O., Hella, L.: Revisiting ontologies of units of measure for harmonising quantity values – a use case. In: Janowicz, K., et al. (eds.) ISWC 2020. LNCS, vol. 12507, pp. 551–567. Springer, Cham (2020). https://doi.org/10.1007/978-3-030-62466-8_34
11. Neveu, P., et al.: Dealing with multi-source and multi-scale information in plant phenomics: the ontology-driven phenotyping hybrid information system. New Phytol. **221**(1), 588–601 (2019)
12. Parent, B., Turc, O., Gibon, Y., Stitt, M., Tardieu, F.: Modelling temperature-compensated physiological rates, based on the co-ordination of responses to temperature of developmental processes. J. Exp. Bot. **61**(8), 2057–2069 (2010)
13. Parsia, B., Smith, M.: Quantities in Owl. Clark & Parsia LLC, Washington, DC (2008)
14. dos Reis, M.G., Ribeiro, A.: Conversion factors and general equations applied in agricultural and forest meteorology. Agrometeoros **27**(2), 227–258 (2020)
15. Rijgersberg, H., Top, J., Wielinga, B.: Towards conceptual representation and invocation of scientific computations. Int. J. Seman. Comput. **6**(04), 447–489 (2012)
16. Rijgersberg, H., Van Assem, M., Top, J.: Ontology of units of measure and related concepts. Semant. Web **4**(1), 3–13 (2013)
17. Tardieu, F., Cabrera-Bosquet, L., Pridmore, T., Bennett, M.: Plant phenomics, from sensors to knowledge. Curr. Biol. **27**(15), R770–R783 (2017)
18. Wilkinson, M.D., et al.: The FAIR guiding principles for scientific data management and stewardship. Sci. Data **3**(1), 1–9 (2016)

Identifying Events from Streams of RDF-Graphs Representing News and Social Media Messages

Marc Gallofré Ocaña$^{(\boxtimes)}$ (iD)

University of Bergen, Bergen, Norway
marc.gallofre@uib.no

Abstract. Identifying news events and relating current news to past events or already identified ones is an open challenge for news agencies. In this paper, I propose a study to identify events from semantic RDF graph representations of real-time and big data streams of news and pre-news. The proposed solution must provide acceptable accuracy over time and consider the requirements of incremental clustering, big data and real-time streams. To design a solution for identifying events, I want to study which clustering approaches are best for this purpose including methods for clustering RDF graphs using machine learning and "classical" algorithmic approaches. I also present three different evaluation approaches.

Keywords: Event detection · RDF · Graph similarity · Graph clustering · Semantic web

1 Introduction

Detecting and identifying news events is crucial for newsrooms business. Newsrooms compete between them in a demanding race to be the first one to publish news about events and fresh stories [31]. The vast amount of information that is continuously being published on the internet makes it significantly challenging for journalists to distill daily events [13]. For example, Twitter publishes more than 500 million tweets a day (i.e., an average of 5700 tweets per second) [21] and more than 10000 English news articles are published online every day worldwide [15]. Some news agencies have digitalized their newsrooms processes and employ software solutions to support journalistic work [6,9,12,22,26,28,30], like Reuters News Agency, which is using the *Reuters Tracer* [23] for detecting news from Twitter messages and automatizing news production processes.

In this paper, I present a study to address the question "How can events be identified from streams of published news and social media messages?". I want to explore the best solution to identify events from real-time streams of published

Supported by the News Angler project funded by the Norwegian Research Council's IKTPLUSS programme as project 275872.

R. Verborgh et al. (Eds.): ESWC 2021 Satellite Events, LNCS 12739, pp. 186–194, 2021.
https://doi.org/10.1007/978-3-030-80418-3_31

news and social media messages. Several approaches have tackled the identification of news events as an NLP problem [16, 32]. However, I have not found any work tackling the problem as a semantic problem and using semantic graphs representing the news content as input for identifying events. I hypothesize that capturing the semantic information of the stories would create representations that share similar structures for those stories belonging to the same event. One way of capturing and representing semantic information is using semantic web technologies, such as RDF and Linked Open Data (LOD), that facilitate external linking and data enrichment.

I decided to limit my solution to only using the RDF representations of the published news and social media messages because semantic representations (a) facilitate structural matching, (b) provide language neutrality and clear relations, and (c) the data is analyzed semantically once-and-for-all near the source. However, it makes my solution highly dependent on named entity linking (NEL) and relation extraction (RE) techniques in the lifting process [1] because the resulting representations may have less information as they are extracts and the lifting process can be imprecise due to the lack of precision of the underlying tools. Candidate solutions include machine learning and "classical" algorithmic approaches for clustering RDF graphs representing published news and social media messages.

The event identification solution must deal with live streams of published online news and social media messages. For each news item, these solutions must identify the event that the news item belongs to or if it represents a new event. However, events evolve and are unpredictable. Thus, these solutions must consider incremental clustering techniques, the requirements of real-time and big data streams, and provide acceptable performance over time.

To test the solution for identifying events, I have developed a platform that ingests real-time and big data streams of published online news (RSS feeds) and social media messages (Twitter), and lifts them into RDF graphs. Because there is no widely agreed-on gold standard, and because I want to evaluate the accuracy of the solution over time, I designed three different evaluation strategies using the Wikipedia Current Events Portal (WCEP)[1] as a reference data set of curated events.

The rest of the paper is structured as follows: Sect. 2 summarizes related work on semantic graphs clustering, Sect. 3 expands upon the research questions and contributions, Sect. 4 details the proposed approach, Sect. 5 describes the evaluation strategies, and Sect. 6 discusses the proposed study.

2 State of the Art

News events are defined in many different ways on a continuous scale from fine-grained actions like an action verb in a sentence [3] to happenings [20, 27]. Hence, I define news events as those stories that are part of the same happening, similar

---

[1] https://en.wikipedia.org/wiki/Portal:Current_events.

to the WCEP structure. For example, all stories regarding "The regional office of the leftist Unidas Podemos party in Cartagena, Murcia, is firebombed, damaging its exterior. WCEP - April 2, 2021" are part of the same event.

It is widely agreed that identifying the "5W" (*what, where, when, who* and *why*) is needed to frame a news event. Several approaches has tackled the identification of news events as an NLP problem [16,32] using linguistic pipelines [17,19], knowledge reasoning [7,18] and machine learning [10]. Only a few have considered using semantic data to disambiguate relations, concepts or named entities from text [3,17] or defining logic rules [7]. However, I have not found any work tackling the problem as a semantic problem and using semantic graphs representing the news content as input for identifying events.

Clustering and computing the similarity between heterogeneous RDF graphs are open challenges. Most of the solutions proposed use "classical" algorithmic approaches considering the graph structures for clustering them like computing the similarity of the instances [14], using entropy and term frequency (TF) scores on the predicates [8], using the full graph structure [24] and applying TF-IDF on the RDF serialization [2]. A few machine learning solutions have suggested the usage of graphs embeddings, for example, for criminal investigation [5], or actor participation in movies [4].

3   Problem Statement and Contributions

To address the question "How can events be identified from streams of published news and social media messages?", I formulated the following hypothesis:

Hypothesis: Events can be detected through the similarity between graphs generated from streams of news items.

Following the hypothesis, an RDF graph that represents published news or a social media message and contains information about the entities and relations involved in the story is part of an event. Therefore, given the context of my research, I decided to address the research question of "How to cluster streams of RDF graphs representing published news and social media messages in order to identify events?" by designing a solution that only considers the semantic representations to cluster those RDF graphs into events.

My solution is intended to work with real-time and big data volumes of news streams, and incrementally cluster news items into events. Thus, it requires minimal computational time, scale-out performance, and incremental clustering methods. Besides, the solution should provide acceptable results over time, because future world events are unpredictable and clustering techniques trained on past events may not remain optimal in the future.

The solution should take a timestamped sequence of graph representations and produce a timestamped stream of event graphs as output. There is no widely agreed-on gold standard for news events clustering which can be used as evaluation data set. However, some online archives of news classify their news into events such as the WCEP. These archives of events can be used as data sets and for validation purposes.

This research will contribute (a) a technique to identify events using only semantic graph representations that considers the requirements of real-time and big data, and provides acceptable accuracy over time, and (b) a method to evaluate similar problems using real data.

4 Research Methodology and Approach

I plan to follow an exploratory technology development process to answer my research question. With this empirical process, I want to explore and evaluate the best solution to cluster RDF graphs representing published news and social media messages into events. I am considering different clustering options including classical and machine learning techniques, and exploring the possible benefits and drawback of each. To test my solution, I developed a real-time and big data processing platform [11] that lifts social media messages and published news into RDF graphs, and I want to extend it with a pipeline (Fig. 1) for clustering events.

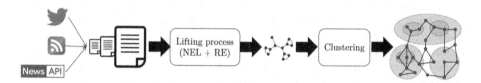

Fig. 1. Testing pipeline

The platform continuously harvests real-time streams of textual items from social media messages (viz., Twitter), published news from RSS feeds and online news agencies, and short news summaries from news aggregators (viz., News-API[2]). It lifts the streams of text into RDF semantic graphs using NEL and RE techniques [1] and represents them following the *news item* ontology described in [25]. The lifting process outputs a stream of semantic graphs representing the published news and social media messages. Then, the clustering solution should ingest the stream of semantic graphs and output RDF graphs representing the clusters of events following the *event item* ontology described in [25]. For each incoming news item, the clustering solution must consider the news items stored in a knowledge base and the already identified events. Besides, this solution must consider different pruning techniques to reduce the number of candidate news items considered for clustering. These pruning techniques can consider, for example, the time windows (e.g., one day period) and only those news items that share the same entities or actors.

---

[2] https://newsapi.org.

To evaluate the clustering solution, I consider different set-ups to determine the best technique to cluster news events and validate the results and the performance of each technique. The different set-ups are also designed to fine-tune the parameters of the clustering solution and optimize the pruning techniques. I evaluate my solution with real data streams instead of a curated data set to facilitate the evaluation of the results over time. However, it is challenging to interpret the results of the experiment because there is no reference data set. For that reason, I use data from the WCEP as a reference. The WCEP is an open-collaborative online portal of daily events that represent events of international interest from reliable sources, and links them to larger events, background articles from Wikinews and topics in Wikipedia[3]. I can extract events from WCEP to create a data set for evaluating my solution or use the published events as a reference to compare them with the events identified by the pipeline.

5   Evaluation Plan

To evaluate the results of my experiment with real data, I use the WCEP as reference data set together with the streamed data produced by the pipeline. The WCEP is a clean human-curated ground-truth repository, from which I can extract a data set of *true event texts* and use them as baseline or gold-standard. Then, I propose three strategies for evaluating the clustering solution:

- Auto-lift each true event text from the WCEP into a *true event graph* using the developed pipeline and try to match true event graph with *candidate event graphs* generated from the stream of published news and social media messages (*candidate event text*) using the clustering technique. To match true and candidate event graphs, I can use the timestamps to manually check them.
- Auto-summarize the textual items behind each candidate event graph into a candidate event text and match true and candidate event texts. To match the true and candidate events text, I can use techniques such as bag-of-words and TF-IDF. Then, I can manually assess each match.
- A combination of the two previous methods. First, I auto-lift each true event text and compute the similarity between true and candidate event graphs using the clustering technique to match them. Then, I extract a random sample of the graphs that have high similarity scores. From this sample, I auto-summarize both the true and candidate text and compare them using bag-of-words and TF-IDF. This comparison can also help me to evaluate the optimal similarity threshold.

These proposed strategies can be executed following two different approaches that consider the timestamp of the data used for evaluating the clustering solution:

---

[3] https://en.wikipedia.org/wiki/Wikipedia:How_the_Current_events_page_works.

- "A priori": by knowing the real current events, I want to detect them using past data (e.g., the stream of published news and social media messages from the previous two months). I run the clustering technique over the past data and generate event graphs. Then, I can check the event graphs using their timestamps and validate if they correspond to real events that have already happened.
- "A posteriori": by validating if the real-time detected events correspond to real events that are currently happening or are going to happen. I run the experiment in real-time for one or two months and constantly monitor if the identified events correspond to real events.

6   Conclusions and Lessons Learned

This study contributes towards the design of a method and techniques that exclusively use RDF graph representations to cluster big data streams of real-time news and social media messages into events. It considers the time performance, scale-out, and incremental clustering as requirements. Besides, the objective is to provide a method to detect events with acceptable results over time. Therefore, I plan to validate the method with current news and social media messages items instead of data sets from past data.

Because my solution is based on semantic graph representations of news items, it relies on the quality of the news items representations that depend on the NEL and RE process. This approach requires less data than using full texts, minimizing the data transmission and the subsequent energy cost. It also reduces the possible text ambiguities, that can affect the performance of natural language techniques, by using linked open data and semantic vocabularies. On the other hand, semantic graphs may contain less information than the news text, making it challenging to cluster the news items.

Machine learning techniques have been positioned as state-of-the-art solutions, outperforming the more "classical" algorithmic approaches. However, they have a high dependency on the training materials and it is challenging to provide good performance on those new cases that have not been considered in the training data sets. For that reason, I want to validate my results with live data instead of a training/validation gold standard and I do not discard the classical approaches. Besides, I consider the possibility to use the WCEP to create a baseline data set that can be used for validating events. In any case, both machine learning and "classical" approaches have to be tuned to optimize the hyper-parameters, clustering features and pruning techniques. To optimize these parameters, I plan to run in parallel multiple versions of the same experiment with different set-ups to test the different parameters.

Validating the clustering method with the WCEP and publishing the data streams make the results easy to reproduce and replicate elsewhere. It is also possible to use a group of expert users to provide a qualitative validation of the detected events. However, the evaluation with expert users may be influenced by the user interface and experience, which makes the qualitative validation more challenging.

Further work includes exploring techniques to find networks of events or connections between them such as Event2vect [29].

Acknowledgements. Thesis supervised by Prof. Andreas L. Opdahl and co-supervised by Bjørnar Tessem.

References

1. Al-Moslmi, T., Gallofré Ocaña, M.: Lifting news into a journalistic knowledge platform. In: Proceedings of the CIKM 2020 Workshops. Galway, Ireland (2020)
2. Ali, M., Mohamed, Y.: A method for clustering unlabeled BIM objects using entropy and TF-IDF with RDF encoding. Adv. Eng. Inform. **33**, 154–163 (2017). https://doi.org/10.1016/j.aei.2017.06.005
3. Araki, J., Mitamura, T.: Open-domain event detection using distant supervision. In: Proceedings of the 27th International Conference on Computational Linguistics, pp. 878–891. Association for Computational Linguistics, Santa Fe, New Mexico, USA, August 2018. https://www.aclweb.org/anthology/C18-1075
4. Bai, Y., Ding, H., Bian, S., Chen, T., Sun, Y., Wang, W.: SimGNN: a neural network approach to fast graph similarity computation (2020)
5. Bellandi, V., Ceravolo, P., Maghool, S., Siccardi, S.: Graph Embeddings in Criminal Investigation: Extending the Scope of Enquiry Protocols, pp. 64–71. Association for Computing Machinery, New York (2020). https://doi.org/10.1145/3415958.3433102
6. Castells, P., et al.: Neptuno: Semantic Web Technologies for a Digital Newspaper Archive. In: Bussler, C.J., Davies, J., Fensel, D., Studer, R. (eds.) ESWS 2004. LNCS, vol. 3053, pp. 445–458. Springer, Heidelberg (2004). https://doi.org/10.1007/978-3-540-25956-5_31
7. Dami, S., Barforoush, A.A., Shirazi, H.: News events prediction using Markov logic networks. J. Inf. Sci. **44**(1), 91–109 (2018). https://doi.org/10.1177/0165551516673285
8. Eddamiri, S., Zemmouri, E.M., Benghabrit, A.: An improved RDF data clustering algorithm. In: The Second International Conference on Intelligent Computing in Data Science (ICDS2018). vol. 148, pp. 208–217 (2019). https://doi.org/10.1016/j.procs.2019.01.038
9. Fernández, N., Fuentes, D., Sánchez, L., Fisteus, J.A.: The news ontology: design and applications. Exp. Syst. Appl. **37**(12), 8694–8704 (2010). https://doi.org/10.1016/j.eswa.2010.06.055
10. Florence, R., Nogueira, B., Marcacini, R.: Constrained hierarchical clustering for news events. In: Proceedings of the 21st International Database Engineering & Applications Symposium (IDEAS 2017), pp. 49–56. Association for Computing Machinery, New York (2017). https://doi.org/10.1145/3105831.3105859
11. Gallofré Ocaña, M., Nyre, L., Opdahl, A.L., Tessem, B., Trattner, C., Veres, C.: Towards a big data platform for news angles. In: 4th Norwegian Big Data Symposium (NOBIDS 2018), pp. 17–29 (2018). http://ceur-ws.org/Vol-2316/paper1.pdf
12. Gallofré Ocaña, M., Opdahl, A.L.: Challenges and opportunities for journalistic knowledge platforms. In: Proceedings of the CIKM 2020 Workshops. Galway, Ireland (2020)

13. Germann, U., Liepins, R., Barzdins, G., Gosko, D., Miranda, S., Nogueira, D.: The SUMMA platform: a scalable infrastructure for multi-lingual multi-media monitoring. In: Proceedings of ACL, System Demonstrations, pp. 99–104, July 2018. https://doi.org/10.18653/v1/P18-4017

14. Grimnes, G.A.A., Edwards, P., Preece, A.: Instance based clustering of semantic web resources. In: Bechhofer, S., Hauswirth, M., Hoffmann, J., Koubarakis, M. (eds.) ESWC 2008. LNCS, vol. 5021, pp. 303–317. Springer, Heidelberg (2008). https://doi.org/10.1007/978-3-540-68234-9_24

15. Hamborg, F., Meuschke, N., Gipp, B.: Bias-aware news analysis using matrix-based news aggregation. Int. J. Digit. Lib. **21**(2), 129–147 (2020)

16. Hogenboom, F., Frasincar, F., Kaymak, U., de Jong, F., Caron, E.: A survey of event extraction methods from text for decision support systems. Decis. Supp. Syst. **85**, 12–22 (2016). https://doi.org/10.1016/j.dss.2016.02.006

17. Huang, L., et al.: Liberal event extraction and event schema induction. In: Proceedings of the 54th Annual Meeting of the Association for Computational Linguistics (vol. 1: Long Papers), pp. 258–268 (2016)

18. Hunter, A., Summerton, R.: Merging news reports that describe events. Data Knowl. Eng. **59**(1), 1–24 (2006). https://doi.org/10.1016/j.datak.2005.06.005

19. Jackoway, A., Samet, H., Sankaranarayanan, J.: Identification of live news events using twitter. In: Proceedings of the 3rd ACM SIGSPATIAL International Workshop on Location-Based Social Networks (LBSN2011), pp. 25–32. Association for Computing Machinery, New York (2011). https://doi.org/10.1145/2063212.2063224

20. Jin, P., Mu, L., Zheng, L., Zhao, J., Yue, L.: News feature extraction for events on social network platforms. In: International World Wide Web Conferences Steering Committee (WWW 2017) Companion, pp. 69–78. Republic and Canton of Geneva, CHE (2017). https://doi.org/10.1145/3041021.3054151

21. Krikorian, R.: New tweets per second record, and how! (Aug 2013), https://blog.twitter.com/engineering/en_us/a/2013/new-tweets-per-second-record-and-how.html

22. Leban, G., Fortuna, B., Brank, J., Grobelnik, M.: Event registry: Learning about world events from news. In: Proceedings of the 23rd International Conference on World Wide Web (WWW 2014) Companion, pp. 107–110. Association for Computing Machinery (2014). https://doi.org/10.1145/2567948.2577024

23. Liu, X., Nourbakhsh, A., Li, Q., Shah, S., Martin, R., Duprey, J.: Reuters tracer: toward automated news production using large scale social media data. In: 2017 IEEE International Conference on Big Data (Big Data), pp. 1483–1493 (2017). https://doi.org/10.1109/BigData.2017.8258082

24. Maedche, A., Zacharias, V.: Clustering ontology-based metadata in the semantic web. In: Elomaa, T., Mannila, H., Toivonen, H. (eds.) PKDD 2002. LNCS, vol. 2431, pp. 348–360. Springer, Heidelberg (2002). https://doi.org/10.1007/3-540-45681-3_29

25. Opdahl, A.L., Tessem, B.: Ontologies for finding journalistic angles. Softw. Syst. Model. **20**, 1–17 (2020)

26. Raimond, Y., Scott, T., Oliver, S., Sinclair, P., Smethurst, M.: Use of semantic web technologies on the BBC web sites. In: Wood, D. (ed.) Linking Enterprise Data, pp. 263–283. Springer, Boston (2010). https://doi.org/10.1007/978-1-4419-7665-9_13

27. Ribeiro, S., Ferret, O., Tannier, X.: Unsupervised event clustering and aggregation from newswire and web articles. In: Proceedings of the 2017 EMNLP Workshop: Natural Language Processing meets Journalism, pp. 62–67. Association for Computational Linguistics, Copenhagen, Denmark, September 2017. https://doi.org/10.18653/v1/W17-4211

28. Rudnik, C., Ehrhart, T., Ferret, O., Teyssou, D., Troncy, R., Tannier, X.: Searching news articles using an event knowledge graph leveraged by wikidata. In: Companion Proceedings of The 2019 World Wide Web Conference, pp. 1232–1239 (2019). https://doi.org/10.1145/3308560.3316761

29. Setty, V., Hose, K.: Event2vec: Neural embeddings for news events. In: The 41st International ACM SIGIR Conference on Research & Development in Information Retrieval (SIGIR 2018), pp. 1013–1016. Association for Computing Machinery, New York (2018). https://doi.org/10.1145/3209978.3210136

30. Vossen, P., et al.: Newsreader: Using knowledge resources in a cross-lingual reading machine to generate more knowledge from massive streams of news. Special Issue Knowledge-Based Systems, Elsevier **110**, 60–85 (2016). https://doi.org/10.1016/j.knosys.2016.07.013

31. Vázquez Herrero, J., Direito-Rebollal, S., Rodríguez, A.S., García, X.: Journalistic Metamorphosis: Media Transformation in the Digital Age. Springer International Publishing (2020). https://doi.org/10.1007/978-3-030-36315-4

32. Xiang, W., Wang, B.: A survey of event extraction from text. IEEE Access **7**, 173111–173137 (2019). https://doi.org/10.1109/ACCESS.2019.2956831

Towards Visually Intelligent Agents (VIA): A Hybrid Approach

Agnese Chiatti[✉][iD]

Knowledge Media Institute, The Open University,
Walton Hall, Milton Keynes MK7 6AA, UK
agnese.chiatti@open.ac.uk

Abstract. Service robots can undertake tasks that are impractical or even dangerous for us - e.g., industrial welding, space exploration, and others. To carry out these tasks reliably, however, they need Visual Intelligence capabilities at least comparable to those of humans. Despite the technological advances enabled by Deep Learning (DL) methods, Machine Visual Intelligence is still vastly inferior to Human Visual Intelligence. Methods which augment DL with Semantic Web technologies, on the other hand, have shown promising results. In the lack of concrete guidelines on which knowledge properties and reasoning capabilities to leverage within this new class of hybrid methods, this PhD work provides a reference framework of epistemic requirements for the development of Visually Intelligent Agents (VIA). Moreover, the proposed framework is used to derive a novel hybrid reasoning architecture, to address real-world robotic scenarios which require Visual Intelligence.

Keywords: Hybrid AI · Visual Intelligence · Service robotics

1 Introduction and Motivation

With the fast-paced advancement of the Artificial Intelligence (AI) and Robotics fields, there is an increasing potential to resort to *service robots* (or *robot assistants*) to help with daily tasks, especially in scenarios where it is unsafe or impractical for us to intervene - e.g., under extreme weather conditions or when social distance needs to be maintained. However, succeeding in the real world is a challenge because it requires robots to make sense of the high-volume and diverse data collected through their perceptual sensors [2]. From the entry point of vision, in particular, the problem then becomes one of enabling robots to correctly interpret the stimuli of their vision system, with the support of background knowledge sources, a capability also known as *Visual Intelligence* [8]. The first prerequisite to building *Visually Intelligent Agents (VIA)* is the ability to robustly *recognise* the different *objects* occupying the robot's environment. Let us consider the case of HanS, the Health and Safety (H&S) robot inspector at the Knowledge Media Institute (KMi) [4]. HanS is expected to monitor the Lab in search of potentially dangerous situations, such as fire hazards. Imagine

© Springer Nature Switzerland AG 2021
R. Verborgh et al. (Eds.): ESWC 2021 Satellite Events, LNCS 12739, pp. 195–206, 2021.
https://doi.org/10.1007/978-3-030-80418-3_32

that Hans was observing a flammable object (e.g., a paper cup) left on top of a portable heater. To conclude that it is in the presence of a potential fire hazard, the robot first needs to detect the cup and the heater. However, HanS also needs access to many other reasoning capabilities and knowledge components: it needs to know that paper cups are flammable, and that portable heaters can produce heat. It also needs spatial reasoning capabilities, to infer that the cup is touching the heater, and so forth.

Currently, the predominant approach to tackling visual reasoning tasks is applying methods which are based on Machine Learning (ML). In particular, the state-of-the-art performance is defined by the latest approaches based on Deep Learning (DL) [20,22]. Despite their popularity, these methods have received many critiques due to their brittleness and lack of transparency [24,26,28]. These limitations are particularly evident when compared against the excellence of the human vision system [15,19]. Indeed, we can learn rich object representations very rapidly, even from minimal observations, and adapt these representations to reflect changes in the environment. To compensate for the limitations of ML-based methods, a more recent trend among AI researchers has been to combine ML with knowledge-based reasoning, thus adopting a *hybrid approach* [1,13]. Concurrently, thanks to efforts in the Semantic Web and Knowledge Engineering communities, an increasing number of large-scale resources encoding linguistical, encyclopaedical and common-sense knowledge have been made available [30]. Thus, a promising research direction is capitalising on these knowledge resources to develop hybrid reasoning architectures. A question remains, however, on what type of knowledge resources and reasoning capabilities should be leveraged within hybrid methods [11].

Based on these premises, the first objective of this PhD research is identifying a set of *epistemic requirements*, i.e., a set of capabilities and knowledge properties, required for service robots to exhibit Visual Intelligence. Another objective is mapping these epistemic ingredients to the knowledge properties available within state-of-the-art Knowledge Bases (KB), to evaluate to which extent they can support VIA. Together, the produced requirement analysis and coverage study provide a framework for the development of VIA which is fit for use, as well as a research agenda to build improved knowledge representations for robotic applications. Moreover, the error analysis informs our hypotheses on which epistemic requirements to prioritise, in the real-world use-case of monitoring H&S in the office. Specifically, our intermediate results [8,9] indicate that knowledge of the typical size of objects and of their typical spatial locations are key factors contributing to Visual Intelligence. Thus, in this work, a hybrid architecture is proposed, which leverages both types of reasoners.

This paper is structured as follows. Section 2 reviews the state of the art in autonomous reasoning for Visual Intelligence. The research questions informing this work are presented in Sect. 3. Section 4 describes the methodological rationale followed to tackle each of these questions. Additionally, the proposed experimental design plan is discussed in Sect. 5. The proposal concludes with overviewing the current research progress as well as the next relevant activities.

2   Summary of Literature Review

Machine Learning methods (and the Deep Learning paradigm in particular) have expedited the improvement on several Computer Vision benchmarks [14,18,22]. Deep Neural Networks (NNs), however, come with their limitations. These models (i) are notoriously data-hungry, (ii) assume to operate in a closed world [23], and (iii) extract representational patterns through successive iterations over raw data [20]. The latter trait can drastically reduce the start-up costs of feature engineering. However, it also complicates tasks such as explaining results and integrating explicit knowledge statements in the pipeline [24,28]. Considering the limitations of state-of-the-art visual reasoning methods based on ML, hybrid approaches to visual reasoning, i.e., methods which combine ML with knowledge-based components, have been recently proposed [1,13]. In DL setups, in particular, knowledge-based reasoning can be integrated at four different levels of the NN [1]: (i) in **pre-processing**, to augment the training examples [23], (ii) within the **intermediate layers** [10], (iii) as part of the **architectural topology** or **optimisation function** [16,25,29], and (iv) in the **post-processing** stages, to validate the NN predictions [33]. Compared to the other classes of hybrid methods, a post-hoc approach offers the advantage of modularity, i.e., it is agnostic to the specific ML architecture used. Additionally, this approach increases the transparency of results, because it allows to decouple the ML predictions from the knowledge-based predictions and, thus, to evaluate how the different architectural components contribute to the overall performance. This characteristic is an important pre-condition to identifying the strengths, weaknesses and complementarities of each module, so that a more seamless integration is ensured and potentially conflicting outcomes between the different ML-based and knowledge-based predictors are handled effectively. For instance, on the one hand, applying off-the-shelf DL-based methods typically allows faster inference at test time than querying various knowledge sources [19]. On the other hand, the integration of large-scale knowledge bases allows a more transparent control of which knowledge properties and features contribute to the reasoning process. Thus, a hybrid system is expected to capitalise on the best of both worlds. Nonetheless, the literature lacks a systematic study of which ML-based and knowledge-based components are to be leveraged in hybrid systems. Specifically, this PhD work is focused on approaching this open problem from the angle of improving the Visual Intelligence of robots to support real-world application scenarios.

With the evolution of Semantic Web technologies, many large-scale knowledge resources have become available, which can be integrated within hybrid frameworks, such as the knowledge representations surveyed in [21,27,30,31]. However, because several different types of background knowledge and reasoning capabilities are needed for robots to exhibit Visual Intelligence, choosing which knowledge resources and reasoning components to prioritise within hybrid architectures remains an open problem [11]. In [8] we have analyzed the types of classification errors emerging during robot monitoring activities, after applying state-of-the-art ML methods. Our error analysis indicated that two epistemic components, in particular, have the potential to significantly improve the robot's capability to recognise objects: (i) the ability to compare objects by size, (ii) qualitative spatial reasoning capabilities. Indeed, the intermediate results of this PhD work [9] show that a novel hybrid system where knowledge of the typical size of objects is integrated in post-processing can significantly augment object recognition pipelines which are purely based on ML. With respect to the implementation of spatial reasoning capabilities, we propose a novel framework for qualitative spatial reasoning, which extends the work in [5,12]. Differently from existing approaches, the proposed approach provides a mapping between formal representations of space in AI and the types of commonsense spatial representations used in everyday language [3]. As such, the proposed representational framework can be used to extract commonsense Qualitative Spatial Relations (QSR) from large-scale KBs which encode spatial knowledge [21,30,31]. Crucially, the proposed mapping can be fully implemented with state-of-the-art Geographic Information System (GIS) technologies.

Overall, the results obtained from evaluating the two proposed reasoners will inform the implementation of a meta-reasoning architecture, which can exploit the complementary strengths of the ML-based and knowledge-based reasoners.

3   Problem Statement and Contributions

The main objective of this doctoral research is to study ways to improve the Visual Intelligence of service robots when making sense of complex, real-world environments. Based on evidence from the literature, the overarching hypothesis is that: *A hybrid approach (ML-based and knowledge-based) can improve a robot's performance on tasks that require Visual Intelligence (e.g., sensemaking), compared to approaches which rely solely on Machine Learning techniques.*

This hypothesis also raises a series of research questions. First, **RQ1:** *what are epistemic requirements, i.e., the set of required knowledge components and reasoning capabilities, of developing Visually Intelligent Agents?* Second, **RQ2:** *which epistemic requirements are the most important ones, in the considered use-case scenario?* Specifically, the intermediate results achieved while tackling RQ2 have indicated that two epistemic requirements, in particular, have the potential to significantly enhance HanS' Visual Intelligence: (i) the capability to reason on the physical size of objects, and (ii) the capability to reason about the spatial relations between objects. Therefore, the further inquiry will focus not only on *the extent to which the state-of-the-art Knowledge Bases support VIA* **(RQ3)**, but also on *the extent to which existing resources can be repurposed to support size and spatial reasoning* **(RQ4)**. Hence, another related question is about *the extent to which a concrete architecture which effectively leverages both types of reasoners can be developed* **(RQ5)**.

4   Research Methodology

To address RQ1, requirements are gathered both through a top-down approach, i.e., based on seminal frameworks describing the human visual cognition, and

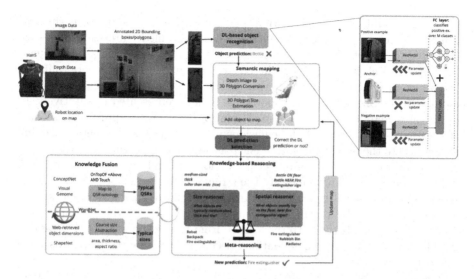

Fig. 1. The proposed hybrid architecture which leverages size and spatial reasoning. In this instance, hybrid reasoning is applied to the case of object recognition tasks.

from the bottom-up, i.e., based on the errors emerged from a real-world application scenario. The incentive of taking inspiration from the Human Visual Intelligence is motivated by the brittleness of current approaches to Machine Visual Intelligence. In addition to cognitively-inspired requirements, however, concrete requirements gather from error analysis are included as well. As such, the error analysis also provides a way to asses the relative impact of each requirement (RQ2). Moreover, the identified epistemic requirements can be used to assess the coverage of each required knowledge component that is provided with the state-of-the-art KBs.

The results from RQ2 and RQ3 inform the selection of which reasoners and external KBs to include in a concrete hybrid architecture for VIA, also exemplified in Fig. 1. The proposed architecture integrates auxiliary knowledge in post-processing, i.e., after generating the ML-based predictions. The object recognition pipeline exemplified in Fig. 1 relies on the state-of-the-art multi-branch Network of [34]. In this setup, the NN is optimised to learn a feature space where similar objects lie closer than dissimilar objects. Training triplets consist of an anchor image, a positive (similar) example to the anchor, as well as a negative (dissimilar) example. At inference time, for each observed object, a ranking of object predictions is produced, based on similarity matching against the learned image embeddings. A few-shot metric learning approach was chosen as ML baseline to keep the required training examples to a minimum, while also ensuring that objects unseen at training time can still be classified at test time, by matching the learned representations against a reference image set. Nevertheless, the hybrid approach proposed in this work is general and any ML-based methods which provides the bounding boxes and predicted categories for the observed objects can modularly interface with it. The Knowledge Base supporting this reasoning architecture will include: (i) a novel coarse-grained representation of size abstracted from lower-level size features, as further illustrated in [9], (ii) Qualitative Spatial Relations (QSR) gathered from a combination of general-purpose KBs, which are repurposed automatically through a dedicated knowledge fusion module (RQ4). Size and spatial knowledge is here represented qualitatively, to ensure the scalability of the proposed solution to broader application scenarios. A crucial component of the envisioned architecture is the meta-reasoning module, where the outcomes of different reasoners are opportunely leveraged, to converge towards a final set of object predictions. Therefore, a detailed ablation study will be carried out to identify the strengths and weaknesses of each component contributing to the overall performance. Indeed, the background knowledge available may be incomplete or unreliable. Similarly, the ML algorithm will be biased towards the patterns learned from the distribution of the training set. Thus, conflicting recommendations need to be leveraged, in an ensemble approach.

It is also worth noting that, although this PhD work is focused on implementing an architecture which combines size and spatial reasoning with ML, the proposed hybrid architecture is general, i.e., any other cognitive reasoner identified in [8] can be plugged in. Thus, in Fig. 1, we use the broad term "Knowledge-based Reasoning" to refer to the process validating the knowledge properties extracted from the robot's observations against knowledge priors gathered from external resources. The size and spatial reasoner are only two instances of this general approach.

Another requirement to test the utility of the proposed architecture (RQ5) is defining a predetermined set of evaluation tasks that entail Visual Intelligence capabilities. These tasks are derived from the use-case scenario of H&S monitoring in the office. Namely, to anticipate the emergence of H&S threats through Vision, a robot will need to: (i) robustly recognise a set of known objects in a target environment (i.e., the task of *object recognition*), (ii) update its learning models and knowledge base, when exposed to new object classes (i.e., the task of *incremental object learning*), (iii) react based on the interpreted state of the environment - e.g., notify the designated fire wardens in case of a fire (i.e., *decision-making tasks*). An evaluation plan for each of these tasks is provided in the next Section.

5   Evaluation Plan

KB Evaluation. Based on the epistemic requirements identified through RQ1, in [8], we have constructed a matrix where columns correspond to the identified knowledge requirements and rows indicate the state-of-the-art KBs reviewed in Sect. 2.3. The level of coverage of the required knowledge properties provided with each KB was then assessed on a qualitative scale.

Object Recognition. The state-of-the-art ML methods presented in [34] were taken as baseline to conduct preliminary trials during the robot's patrolling rounds. A qualitative error analysis has been conducted on the basis of these preliminary data collection and trials, as further illustrated in [8]. Specifically, each classification error was recorded on a Boolean matrix, to mark the epistemic requirements which would have helped: (i) identifying the ground truth class, or (ii) ruling out the incorrect class. Then, in [9], the reference ML baselines were quantitatively evaluated on a larger dataset, to measure the performance effects of integrating knowledge of the typical size of objects. Performance was here evaluated based on: the P,R and F1 of the top-1 predictions; the standard ranking quality metrics P@5, Mean Normalised Discounted Cumulative Gain (Mean nDCG@5) and hit ratio. Specifically, the P, R and F1 were aggregated class-wise before and after weighing the averages by class support, i.e., the number of instances within each class, to account for the natural class imbalance in the dataset (e.g., fire extinguishers occur more often than printers, on the robot's scouting route). In these experiments, all object classes have been treated as known, i.e., introduced since training time. The same experimental setup will be replicated to test the introduction of the spatial reasoning module. Moreover, further tests will be conducted to evaluate the computational overhead introduced by the post-hoc reasoning steps, by tracking the processing times of each tested hybrid solution. Additional metrics to measure the inter-agreement (e.g., MCC and Cohen's Kappa) between the different ML-based and knowledge-based classifiers will be also considered, to inform the implementation of the meta-reasoning module.

Incremental Object Learning. To test the scalability of the proposed hybrid framework to novel objects, i.e., unseen at training time, the first step has been to reproduce the experimental setup of the selected ML baselines [34]. In this setup, two ML-based methods are applied: (i) K-net, trained to overfit on a set of known objects, (ii) N-net, conceived to generalise to novel objects. Indeed, the dataset introduced in [34] in the context of the 2017 Amazon Robotic Challenge includes a combination of known objects, i.e., seen since training time, and novel objects, i.e., introduced only at test time. A preliminary ablation study on this datasets has allowed us to test performance in the presence of novel object classes. Because images in the Amazon dataset [34] only depict one object at a time, this dataset is not suitable for evaluating the performance of the spatial reasoner. Nonetheless, different splits of robot's dataset collected at the prior step will be tested, where only a subset of objects is treated as known.

Decision-Making. The objective of this phase is evaluating the robot's ability to reliably assess the state of risk of the environment it is monitoring. To this aim, a set of Health & Safety risk assessment scenarios will be defined: e.g., notifying fire wardens that a pile of paper was let on top of a portable heater or that the path of an emergency exit is not correctly signalled. In this phase, H&S experts at the Open University will be involved through a focus group discussion, to converge towards a small set of use-case scenarios which the experts consider as useful and worth implementing. Then, for each scenario, the robot's performance will be evaluated based on: (i) the accuracy of the assessments (compared to the expert's indicated risk), (ii) the time elapsed before completing each assessment.

6 Summary of Intermediate Results

This Section summarises the current progress in tackling the research questions guiding this PhD research. Thus, in what follows, intermediate results are organised by research question.

RQ1: *what are the epistemic requirements of developing VIA?* In [8], we identified a set of top-down epistemic ingredients. Specifically, the requirement of learning as model building is transversal to all the other ingredients and entails: (i) defining concept representations and taxonomies which can be adequately expanded as new concepts are learned, as well as (ii) causal reasoning capabilities. The remaining top-down ingredients are: (iii) Intuitive Physics, (iv) compositionality, (v) Generic 2D views, (vi) Motion Vision, and (vii) fast perception. Thanks to a bottom-up analysis of object recognition errors emerging in a real-world robotic scenario, I have also completed the former set of requirements with (viii) the Machine Reading capability.

RQ2: *which epistemic requirements are the most important ones, in the considered use-case scenario?* The error analysis conducted in [8], also summarised in Fig. 2, indicates that the majority of ML misclassifications could have been in principle avoided, with access to: (i) knowledge of the typical size of objects and the capability to compare objects by size, which falls under the Intuitive Physics component; (ii) knowledge of the typical Qualitative Spatial Relations (QSR) between objects, as well as spatial reasoning capabilities, which are part of the epistemic requirement of compositionality. Our most recent empirical findings also confirmed that size reasoning can significantly augment the object recognition performance of state-of-the-art ML solutions. On the KMi dataset (Table 1), the tested hybrid solution which integrates all the proposed size features (front surface area, thickness and Aspect Ratio) ensured to improve the unweighted and weighted F1 scores by **6%** and **5%**, compared to ML baselines. The quality of the top-5 results in the ranking also improved as a result of introducing these knowledge priors. Notably, in the case of the Amazon dataset, i.e., in the presence of known and novel objects, and of two ML algorithms of complementary efficacy, the introduced size reasoner provided a rationale to dynamically choose which ML algorithm to apply in each case. As highlighted in Table 2, the top-1 accuracy increased by **9.5%** in this scenario.

RQ3: *to what extent do the state-of-the-art Knowledge Bases support VIA?* In [8], we selected a set of KBs for review and assessed their coverage of the knowledge properties required for VIA. None of the reviewed KBs covers the identified knowledge requirements in full. The two most impactful knowledge attributes exposed by the bottom-up analysis (the object relative sizes and QSR) are covered only for a limited set of objects. Particularly striking is the lack of comprehensive knowledge representations which describe the typical motion trajectories of objects, e.g., as static or moving. Nonetheless, this coverage study

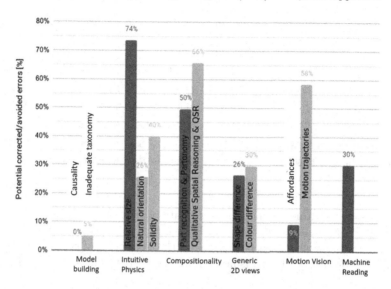

Fig. 2. From [8]: percentage of cases where a specific component of Visual Intelligence would help correcting or avoiding the classification error.

highlighted that most of the reviewed KBs are complementary to one another, with respect to the types of provided knowledge properties. Thus, a promising research direction is combining different external KBs to capitalise on synergistic effects.

RQ4: *to what extent the state-of-the-art Knowledge Bases be repurposed, to support size and spatial reasoning?* The positive performance results highlighted in Tables 1 and 2 were achieved thanks to automatically generating a catalogue of qualitative size descriptions from raw size measurements gathered from a combination of ShapeNet [6], Amazon and manual collection. Moreover, in [7], we have proposed a knowledge representation framework to map the commonsense and linguistic spatial predicates provided with state-of-the-art KBs to both:

Table 1. Evaluation results (in percentages), on the KMi test set.

Method	Top-1 unweigh.			Top-1 weigh.			Top-5 unweigh.		
	P	R	F1	P	R	F1	P@5	nDCG@5	HR
N-net [34]	34.0	**40.1**	31.0	61.5	45.2	47.2	33.1	36.0	63.0
K-net [34]	39.0	39.9	34.0	68.0	47.9	50.4	38.5	40.7	65.1
Hybrid (area)	39.6	39.5	35.5	65.5	50.3	51.6	41.0	43.1	68.0
Hybrid (area+flat/non-flat)	41.0	39.3	35.7	65.8	50.1	52.1	40.5	42.8	65.8
Hybrid (area+thickness)	44.5	38.9	38.6	65.0	**51.4**	53.9	**41.8**	**44.1**	**68.5**
Hybrid (area+flat/non-flat+AR)	42.9	38.8	36.6	68.9	49.1	52.9	39.9	42.0	66.3
Hybrid (area+thickness+AR)	**47.2**	39.1	**40.0**	**69.1**	**51.4**	**55.4**	41.6	43.9	68.4

Table 2. Evaluation results (in percentages), on the test set of [34].

Method	Top-1 accuracy			Top-5 unweighted		
	Known	Novel	Mixed	P@5	nDCG@5	HR
N-net [34]	56.8	**82.1**	64.6	61.9	62.7	72.6
K-net [34]	**99.7**	29.5	78.1	73.7	75.0	82.4
Hybrid (area)	94.7	71.7	**87.6**	**82.6**	**84.1**	**89.7**
Hybrid (area+flat/non-flat)	94.5	71.7	87.5	82.5	84.0	**89.7**
Hybrid (area+thickness)	81.7	39.3	68.7	64.6	65.8	70.1

(i) the spatial operators available within state-of-the-art spatial databases, and (ii) formal AI statements expressed in First Order Logic (FOL). The next step will be applying the proposed framework to the extraction of spatial priors from general-purpose KBs such as Visual Genome [17], SpatialSense [32], and others.

7   Conclusions and Lessons Learned

Before we delegate complex tasks to robots, we need to ensure that they can reliably make sense of their environment. This PhD work proposes a framework of epistemic requirements for the development of Visually Intelligent Agents (VIA), i.e., robots which exhibit improved visual sensemaking capabilities. In particular, the main hypothesis underlying this work is that adopting a hybrid approach, which combines Machine Learning with Semantic Web technologies, has the potential to significantly improve the performance of service robots on tasks that require Visual Intelligence. To test this hypothesis, a system is devised which integrates ML with two types of knowledge-based reasoners: (i) a reasoner which can take object sizes into account, and (ii) a qualitative spatial reasoner. The utility of this hybrid system is evaluated in the context of real-world robotic scenarios. At the time of this writing, the epistemic framework for VIA has already been defined and used to verify the level of support to the development of VIA which is provided with state-of-the-art Knowledge Bases [8]. Moreover, the intermediate results of this work show that a hybrid reasoner which integrates knowledge of the typical object sizes can significantly outperform object recognition methods based on ML. Nonetheless, the evaluation of the proposed framework is still incomplete, specifically with respect to testing: (i) the effects of integrating the spatial reasoning module presented in [7], (ii) the possibility to leverage both reasoners to reconcile potentially conflicting outcomes, (iii) the scalability to novel objects, as well as (iv) the level of support to concrete decision-making tasks which require Visual Intelligence.

Acknowledgements. I would like to thank my supervisors, Prof. Enrico Motta and Dr. Enrico Daga, for their continuous support and guidance throughout this PhD project. It is also thanks to them if I have found out about the ESWC PhD symposium.

References

1. Aditya, S., Yang, Y., Baral, C.: Integrating knowledge and reasoning in image understanding. In: Proceedings of IJCAI 2019, pp. 6252–6259 (2019)
2. Alatise, M.B., Hancke, G.P.: A review on challenges of autonomous mobile robot and sensor fusion methods. IEEE Access **8**, 39830–39846 (2020)
3. Landau, B., Jackendoff, R.: "What" and "where" in spatial language and spatial cognition. Behav. Brain Sci. **16**, 217–265 (1993)
4. Bastianelli, E., Bardaro, G., Tiddi, I., Motta, E.: Meet HanS, the heath & safety autonomous inspector. In: Proceedings of the International Semantic Web Conference (ISWC), Poster&Demo Track (2018)
5. Borrmann, A., Rank, E.: Query support for BIMs using semantic and spatial conditions. In: Handbook of Research on Building Information Modeling and Construction Informatics: Concepts and Technologies (2010)
6. Chang, A.X., et al.: ShapeNet: an information-rich 3d model repository. arXiv preprint arXiv:1512.03012 (2015)
7. Chiatti, A., Bardaro, G., Motta, E., Daga, E.: Commonsense spatial reasoning for visually intelligent agents. arXiv preprint arXiv:2104.00387 (2021)
8. Chiatti, A., Motta, E., Daga, E.: Towards a framework for visual intelligence in service robotics: epistemic requirements and gap analysis. In: Proceedings of KR 2020- Special session on KR & Robotics, pp. 905–916. IJCAI (2020)
9. Chiatti, A., Motta, E., Daga, E., Bardaro, G.: Fit to measure: reasoning about sizes for robust object recognition. In: To appear in Proceedings of the AAAI2021 Spring Symposium on Combining Machine Learning and Knowledge Engineering (AAAI-MAKE 2021) (2021)
10. Daruna, A., Liu, W., Kira, Z., Chetnova, S.: RoboCSE: robot common sense embedding. In: Proceedings of ICRA, pp. 9777–9783. IEEE (2019)
11. Daruna, A.A., et al.: SiRoK: situated robot knowledge-understanding the balance between situated knowledge and variability. In: 2018 AAAI Spring Symposium Series (2018)
12. Deeken, H., Wiemann, T., Hertzberg, J.: Grounding semantic maps in spatial databases. Robot. Auton. Syst. **105**, 146–165 (2018)
13. Gouidis, F., Vassiliades, A., Patkos, T., Argyros, A., Bassiliades, N., Plexousakis, D.: A review on intelligent object perception methods combining knowledge-based reasoning and machine learning. arXiv:1912.11861 [cs], March 2020
14. He, K., Zhang, X., Ren, S., Sun, J.: Deep residual learning for image recognition. In: Proceedings of CVPR, pp. 770–778 (2016)
15. Hoffman, D.D.: Visual Intelligence: How We Create What We See. WW Norton & Company, New York (2000)
16. van Krieken, E., Acar, E., van Harmelen, F.: Analyzing differentiable fuzzy implications. In: Proceedings of KR 2020, pp. 893–903 (2020)
17. Krishna, R., Zhu, Y., Groth, O., Johnson, J., et al.: Visual genome: connecting language and vision using crowdsourced dense image annotations. Int. J. Comput. Vision **123**(1), 32–73 (2017)
18. Krizhevsky, A., Sutskever, I., Hinton, G.E.: ImageNet classification with deep convolutional neural networks. Commun. ACM **60**(6), 84–90 (2017)
19. Lake, B.M., Ullman, T.D., Tenenbaum, J.B., Gershman, S.J.: Building machines that learn and think like people. Behav. Brain Sci. **40** (2017)
20. LeCun, Y., Bengio, Y., Hinton, G.: Deep learning. Nature **521**(7553)(2015)

21. Liu, D., Bober, M., Kittler, J.: Visual semantic information pursuit: a survey. IEEE Trans. Pattern Anal. Mach. Intell. (2019)

22. Liu, L., et al.: Deep learning for generic object detection: a survey. Int. J. Comput. Vis. **128**(2), 261–318 (2020)

23. Mancini, M., Karaoguz, H., Ricci, E., Jensfelt, P., Caputo, B.: Knowledge is never enough: towards web aided deep open world recognition. In: IEEE ICRA, p. 9543, May 2019

24. Marcus, G.: Deep learning: a critical appraisal. arXiv preprint arXiv:1801.00631 (2018)

25. Marino, K., Salakhutdinov, R., Gupta, A.: The more you know: using knowledge graphs for image classification. In: Proceedings of IEEE CVPR, pp. 20–28, July 2017

26. Parisi, G.I., Kemker, R., Part, J.L., Kanan, C., Wermter, S.: Continual lifelong learning with neural networks: a review. Neural Netw. **113**, 54–71 (2019)

27. Paulius, D., Sun, Y.: A survey of knowledge representation in service robotics. Robot. Auton. Syst. **118**, 13–30 (2019)

28. Pearl, J.: Theoretical impediments to machine learning with seven sparks from the causal revolution. In: Proceedings of WSDM 2018, p. 3. ACM, February 2018

29. Serafini, L., Garcez, A.D.: Logic tensor networks: deep learning and logical reasoning from data and knowledge. arXiv:1606.04422 [cs], July 2016

30. Storks, S., Gao, Q., Chai, J.Y.: Recent advances in natural language inference: a survey of benchmarks, resources, and approaches. arXiv preprint arXiv:1904.01172 (2019)

31. Wu, Q., Teney, D., Wang, P., Shen, C., Dick, A., van den Hengel, A.: Visual question answering: a survey of methods and datasets. Comput. Vis. Image Underst. **163**, 21–40 (2017)

32. Yang, K., Russakovsky, O., Deng, J.: Spatialsense: an adversarially crowdsourced benchmark for spatial relation recognition. In: Proceedings of the IEEE/CVF International Conference on Computer Vision, pp. 2051–2060 (2019)

33. Young, J., Kunze, L., Basile, V., Cabrio, E., Hawes, N., Caputo, B.: Semantic web-mining and deep vision for lifelong object discovery. In: Proceedings of ICRA, pp. 2774–2779. IEEE (2017)

34. Zeng, A., et al.: Robotic pick-and-place of novel objects in clutter with multi-affordance grasping and cross-domain image matching. In: 2018 IEEE ICRA, pp. 1–8. IEEE (2018)

Using Knowledge Graphs for Machine Learning in Smart Home Forecasters

Roderick van der Weerdt$^{(\boxtimes)}$ (iD)

Vrije Universiteit Amsterdam, Amsterdam, The Netherlands
r.p.vander.weerdt@vu.nl

Abstract. Internet of Things (IoT) brings together heterogeneous data from smart devices in smart homes. Smart devices operate within different platforms, but ontologies can be used to create a common middle ground that allows communications between these smart devices outside of those platforms. The data communicated by the smart devices can be used to train the prediction algorithms used in forecasters. This research will first focus on the creation of a mapping to transform IoT data into a knowledge graph than can be used in the common middle ground and investigate the effect of using that IoT knowledge graph data as input for prediction algorithms. Experiments to determine the impact of incorporating other related information in the training of the prediction algorithms will be performed by using external datasources that can be linked to the knowledge graph and by using federated learning over IoT data from other smart homes. Initial results on the transformation mapping of IoT data to an ontology is presented.

Keywords: Internet of Things · Ontology · Data mapping · Smart home · Forecasting · Machine learning · Federated learning

1 Introduction

Smart devices are on the rise, ranging from dishwashers and televisions to lamps and curtains. We define smart devices as physical objects that are able to communicate, have a unique identifier, with (at least) basic computing power and that may have a sensor [11]. The collection of smart devices and the technologies needed to make them operate is called Internet of Things (IoT). Many different technical platforms are available that allow interactions between devices, but connecting devices functioning on different platforms is often not possible [6], either due to proprietary software, vendor locking, or other implementation choices.

To solve this problem, multiple ontologies [2,3,7,17] have been created to serve as a common middle ground, with the goal of creating interoperability between smart devices. They do this by not simply creating another platform, but by connecting the separate platforms used by all different devices. Devices still operate within their original platform with the common middle ground

© Springer Nature Switzerland AG 2021
R. Verborgh et al. (Eds.): ESWC 2021 Satellite Events, LNCS 12739, pp. 207–217, 2021.
https://doi.org/10.1007/978-3-030-80418-3_33

allowing communications between the devices by translating the communications to and from their original platforms, whatever they may be, using the central ontology. Our research is done in the context of SAREF (as described in Sect. 2.1) but it is extendable to other ontologies.

Being able to map the smart device data structure into the ontology and then populate it with the smart device data itself creates one knowledge graph that can be used to make a forecaster with combined data from different devices. Using information from related devices has been shown to improve the forecast results of prediction algorithms [16]. Data aggregated from multiple smart home devices will be heterogeneous [13], as it includes different modalities, timescales and data originating from different types of devices (e.g. temperature measurements, camera images or the amount of apples left in the refrigerator). Most machine learning (ML) models are trained on raw data, which is also the case for prediction algorithms used in IoT [9]. Using those models means we would lose the information about the relations between the devices, because we can not use the heterogeneous IoT data as input [19].

The main goal of this research is to investigate the impact of using heterogeneous data from smart devices represented as a knowledge graph to train prediction algorithms used for forecasting in IoT. Before the prediction algorithms can be trained on IoT data, this data first needs to be transformed into the RDF data of a knowledge graph because RDF is capable of handling the heterogeneity of the data.

1.1 Internet of Things

Interoperability through ontologies and learning over knowledge graphs has been done before, the challenges in this research come from applying it to the IoT domain. The two main issues that we address are: distributed knowledge and privacy sensitive data.

Distributed knowledge: The goal of the common middle ground is to connect all the smart devices in a smart home, but for a forecaster the data from other smart homes is also useful. Because the data is privacy sensitive it can not be directly shared between different smart homes. Federated learning allows for the sharing of ML model parameters instead of data [10]. These parameters are used to let the other models learn from each other, sharing knowledge about the model and not about the data. Our research will include experiments that use federated learning to increase the learning possibilities of the prediction algorithms.

Privacy sensitive data: IoT data from smart devices contains privacy sensitive information about the behaviour of the device's user [6]. For the first experiments we will use open data or refrain from sharing the user data (keep it local in the smart homes environment), but when we use data of multiple users, federated learning will allow us the use of the knowledge in the data without have to share the data itself.

1.2   Interconnect Project

The Interconnect project is a collaboration between 50 partners from 11 European countries with the goal to create "interoperable solutions connecting smart homes, buildings and grids"[1]. One of the pilots part of this project consists of 200 smart homes (apartments with smart devices) that will be built and installed in the Netherlands. Experiments proposed as part of this research will be performed in this setting.

2   State of the Art

The next section will present work related to our research, starting with the ontology that we will use to represent IoT data, the SAREF ontology. The Sects. 2.2 through 2.5 present related work on: the transformation process from raw data to knowledge graph data, different ML models that can be used as forecasters, how the knowledge graph can be used directly for the training of ML models and the last subsection describes federated learning and how it relates to IoT and this research.

2.1   SAREF

The Smart Applications REFerence ontology (SAREF) was created for the specific purpose of interoperability between IoT devices from different manufacturers [3]. Figure 1 shows the relations between the main classes used in the ontology. The `saref:Device` class is the central class used in every mapping while the other classes are optional depending on the case under consideration. For example the `saref:Measurement` and `saref:UnitOfMeasure` classes are relevant whenever an observation is mapped, but not when a command to a device is mapped.

SAREF contains some subclasses and instances related to IoT data, such as for example the `saref:Property` subclasses: `saref:Light`, `saref:Motion` and `saref:Temperature`. However more subclasses and instances should be added if needed. To that end SAREF was created to be extendable, allowing for new subclasses or instances to be added or re-used from other ontologies (such as OM-1.8 for units of measurements [14]).

2.2   Creating the Mapping

Creating a mapping to transform the output of the smart home devices into a knowledge graph will allow us to include heterogeneous data and combine data from all smart devices.

Creating this mapping can be done by hand by creating a seperate template for each individual device in RDF (as detailed in Sect. 6) or it can be done by creating specific mapping rules using a RDF mapping language (RML) [4].

---

[1] https://interconnectproject.eu/.

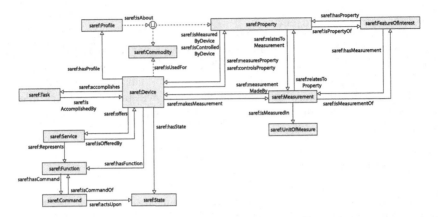

Fig. 1. Overview of the SAREF ontology. (Image taken from: https://saref.etsi.org/core/v3.1.1/#Figure_1)

Multiple RMLs have been developed varying in complexity, with the less complex languages being more restricted to the information that is available in the original dataset and the more complex, transformation oriented RDF languages such as D2RML [1], allowing for more elaborate manipulations as, for example, joining data from separate rows.

2.3 Prediction Algorithms in IoT

Prediction algorithms are used in smart homes to predict the value of a specific measurement in the future based on its previous measurements and other types of relevant measurements [20]. An example of a prediction algorithm in a smart home is a forecaster that predicts the future temperature of a room based on the current temperature of the room, the temperature of different rooms in the same house and the brightness of the sun on specific walls among other factors [16]. Other possible predictions include category and occurrence time forecasting of daily activity of occupants [21] and energy usage [12].

Multiple forecasters have been created before using machine learning models such as: forward stepwise linear resolution [16], multi-layer perceptron [12], convolutional neural network [21] among other methods.

ML models training data is commonly expected to be raw data (such as the pixels from an image) or a representation of that data (such as vector embeddings representing words). This is also the case with the models presented here, the next section presents methods to transform the knowledge graph without losing its information.

2.4 Learning over Knowledge Graphs

Heterogeneous data is a problem if you want to use it as training data for a ML model [19]. Using a knowledge graph to model that data makes it usable, since it is not heterogeneous anymore, now it is one knowledge graph that can be used as input. Not many models are able to train directly over knowledge graphs, but there are methods to transform a knowledge graph into data that is accepted by most ML models.

A knowledge graph can be restructured into a table by adding a row for every node-edge-node set in the graph. However, this transformation loses information about the node neighbourhoods around nodes by simplifying to one to one relations.

Graph Neural Networks (GNN) make a knowledge graph processable by creating embedding representations for each node in the graph. Embeddings are vector representations of points in a high dimensional space (vector space). An example of a GGN is Node2vec [5], it trains a model to create embeddings for similar representations, based on neighbouring nodes and the "role" of the node in the graph, placing them closer together in the vector space. The role of a node is based on its position in relation to other nodes (e.g. is it a central node or is it a leaf node). The embeddings can then be used as input for other ML models, because embeddings are strings of numbers, which is a very common input for ML models [9]. Node2vec was used in [8] where a knowledge graph of stock market listed companies was used to create embeddings. The embeddings representing the companies were used to predict the stock price of these companies based on previous results of the company itself and the results of similar companies (because those were the companies closest to it in the vector space).

More elaborate GNNs such as Heterogeneous GNN (HetGNN) [23] consist of multiple models connected end-to-end, allowing for multi-modal data to be embedded by models tailored to the specific kind of data (such as CNNs for images and par2vec for text) before bringing those embeddings together again into one embedding for each node. Zhang et al. demonstrate in their paper how the embeddings can consequently be used with generic ML models for a variety of tasks, such as link prediction, node classification and clustering.

A prediction algorithm for a forecaster could use the embeddings created with a GNN to train a ML model to make predictions based on a set of embeddings. For example, a set of embeddings representing all the measurements made in the previous twelve hours as input and predicted energy consumption in the next twelve hours as output.

2.5   Federated Learning

In federated learning the ML model is trained locally at each data location on the available data, creating a local model. At certain points during the training the parameters of the local models are sent to a central location were they are averaged to create the global model. The parameters from the global are then send back to the local models which continue training with these parameters [10].

The consensus approach does not use a global model, instead the parameters of one smart device hop to the next smart device and the hopped parameters are used to update the local model of the second smart device. Over a number of communication rounds each device is visited, while the local models are also still trained on the local data [15].

With federated learning we can experiment with larger knowledge bases, using information from other smart homes without having to access the data.

3 Problem Statement and Contributions

The main research question of this work is: *Can we improve the accuracy of prediction algorithms by integrating heterogeneous IoT and Smart energy data and background knowledge?* This research question is broken up into the following subquestions:

RQ1: *Is SAREF an appropriate ontology to model heterogeneous IoT data?* We want to represent as much of the heterogeneous smart device data as possible therefore we want to use a knowledge graph that includes the structure of the data (the ontology) and the data itself (instances in the ontology). We validate SAREF to determine if it is the appropriate ontology to represent all the available information from the smart devices.

RQ2: *Which prediction algorithms are best suited for training on the IoT data knowledge graph?* There are multiple ML models usable as predictions algorithms, but for the forecaster we need to determine which is the best to be used for IoT with a knowledge graph as training data.

RQ3: *Can we improve the accuracy of forecasters by learning over a heterogeneous set of diverse knowledge?* A main advantage of knowledge graphs is that they are linkable with other knowledge graphs, adding more related (for example: outside) data should produce better forecasters.

RQ4: *Can we maintain the accuracy of forecasters with federated learning (over other smart homes)?* In RQ3 we include data from other households in order to increase the data available for training the prediction algorithms, but in practice due to privacy requirements, we can not include the data from other homes directly. Federated learning allows the data from other homes to remain private while making part of their model available to be included in the training of models in other homes. We can formalize this RQ as: given a knowledge graph KG of triples with time bound information, and learning agents that own and see only (overlapping) subsets of this knowledge graph $KG_i \subseteq KG$. How can we define a federated learning approach that best predicts target triples (not available in the KG) without agents exchanging information about the triples they see.

3.1 Contributions

The contributions of the research to the state of the art are the following:

- Validation of the SAREF ontology in a realistic and large scale smart home setting.
- A comparison of ML solutions that can train on knowledge graph data.

- A GNN approach that works in an IoT federated learning setting.
- An evaluation of the mapping and forecaster using the ML solutions in a real world case, using the Dutch pilot of the Interconnect project.

4   Research Methodology and Approach

The approach to answering these research questions is detailed in this section for each research question.

RQ1: Before a model can be trained for a forecaster the first step will be the creation of a dataset. To the best of our knowledge there is no IoT data knowledge graph available so it will have to be created by transforming IoT data available in another format to RDF. Non-RDF dataset are available, such as the dataset from [22]. An initial mapping for this transformation has already been performed by hand and is reported on in Sect. 6. A more generic mapping using RML will be created that is reusable to allow for all the different smart devices data to be transformed. The creation of this mapping allows for the validation of the SAREF ontology, if it able to represent all the data from the smart devices.

RQ2: The second challenge is to create a new forecaster that uses the IoT data knowledge graph as input to train a prediction algorithm. GNN models will be implemented to create predictions based on the data in the IoT data knowledge graph. The resulting forecaster will be tested in a practical setting, as an extended version of the experiment performed in [18], to research the tradeoff between computational resources and accuracy.

This forecasting system will initially be a specific forecaster focusing only on temperature. A second version could be a more general purpose forecaster that is able to collect all the measurements from a smart home and make predictions about what those measurements would look like in the future. This more general purpose forecaster is a more interesting forecaster as it would be able to make the most use of the data collected, using it to make predictions of all the different measurement types.

RQ3: Other datasets with information that is informative for the prediction will also be transformed to RDF to expand the knowledge graph with more information. This can concern datasets about weather forecasts[2], historical weather data[3], information from neighbours or something similar. When the extra data is added to the knowledge graph the prediction algorithm can train a second model with the new knowledge graph to determine the effect the extra data has on the accuracy of the forecaster.

RQ4: We investigate this RQ by using federated learning to collect more information from other smart homes, without directly sharing the data of the smart homes. The Dutch pilot of the Interconnect project with 200 smart

---

[2] https://data.buienradar.nl/2.0/feed/json.
[3] http://projects.knmi.nl/klimatologie/uurgegevens/selectie.cgi.

homes will be launched in 2022. Federated learning will allow the forecasters in those smart homes to train their ML models on the data from neighbouring homes.

5   Evaluation Plan

The evaluations of the results from the methods described in the previous two sections to answer the research questions will be described next.

RQ1: The two implementations described in Sect. 6 and [18] describe how the data from a smart home can be mapped to a knowledge graph, showing that an ontology is capable of mapping relevant data available in a smart home, sufficiently to accomplish a scenario using multiple devices. To provide a more robust answer it will be tested thoroughly in combination with the prediction algorithms used in the other RQs. Competency questions will be defined to determine if the knowledge graph is able to contain all the available information.

RQ2: The IoT data knowledge graph that will be created for RQ1 will be used as input to train state of the art predictors. The prediction task will be to predict the temperature measurement values for the next twelve hours based on the available knowledge of the previous twelve hours. The real values of the temperature measurement values for the next twelve hours will be used as a gold standard for the prediction algorithms to be tested against. Using this gold standard to train multiple prediction algorithm allows us to evaluate the accuracy and efficiency of each model while using the same knowledge graph.

RQ3: Two forecasters will be trained, one on the knowledge graph as used in RQ2 and one on the new extended knowledge graph. The same gold standard created for RQ2 will be used to calculate the accuracy of the new model. A significance test will then be used to show if the accuracy of model trained on the extended knowledge graph significantly differs from the accuracy of the model trained only on the "original" knowledge graph.

RQ4: Two models will be used for the evaluation of RQ4. One model trained using a prediction algorithm that uses federated learning to include data from neighboring houses. And a second model that is again trained with the "original" knowledge graph from RQ2. Applying a significance test on the resulting accuracy of both models will provide a clear answer to the research question.

6   Intermediate Results

To create an initial dataset of RDF data, a mapping for the output of nine different smart devices was created by hand [18]. These mappings were created in collaboration with domain experts knowledgeable about the devices and experts knowledgeable about the SAREF ontology.

To answer RQ1 an experiment with SAREF in a practical setting was created that used the Knowledge Engine [18]. The Knowledge Engine is a custom built interoperability framework, built by a partner from the Interconnect project, that allows multiple smart devices to communicate using RDF data. This was achieved by adding to every smart device a smart connector, a single board computer with a script capable of communicating directly with "its" smart device in whatever format it was programmed. It sends the data in RDF to the other smart connectors, which in turn interprets it and send it to their smart device in the formats that it accepts.

We set up an experiment that recreated a scenario from a smart home setting. One smart connector was connected to a thermometer, one smart connector was connected to a smart thermostat and one smart connector was connected to a smart heater. Through this communication the smart thermometer was able to send its current temperature measurement, which was received by the smart thermostat that compared it to an internal setting (controlled with buttons) and based on this either send a `saref:OnState` or `saref:OffState` to the smart heater. All of these messages were possible to express using SAREF.

7   Conclusions

This research plan shows how we intend to answer the research question: *Can we improve the accuracy of prediction algorithms by integrating heterogeneous IoT and Smart energy data and background knowledge?*

After this first year of research the first research question has been partially answered by the two implementations of SAREF described in [18], showing how an ontology can be used to create a knowledge graph of IoT data. But more research will have to determine whether a knowledge graph can hold all the information required for the prediction algorithms that will be used for the other research questions.

When this research is completed it will introduce a new way of combining the information from connected IoT devices, resulting in more accurate forecasters and leading to more efficient smart homes.

Acknowledgements. This work is part of the Interconnect project (interconnectproject.eu/) which has received funding from the European Union's Horizon 2020 research and innovation program under grant agreement No. 857237.

I would like to thank Victor de Boer, Laura Daniele, Frank van Harmelen, Ronald Siebes and Steffen Staab for their guidance and feedback.

References

1. Chortaras, A., Stamou, G.: Mapping diverse data to RDF in practice. In: Vrandečić, D., et al. (eds.) ISWC 2018. LNCS, vol. 11136, pp. 441–457. Springer, Cham (2018). https://doi.org/10.1007/978-3-030-00671-6_26
2. Compton, M., et al.: The SSN ontology of the W3C semantic sensor network incubator group. J. Web Semant. **17**, 25–32 (2012)

3. Daniele, L., den Hartog, F., Roes, J.: Created in close interaction with the industry: the smart appliances REFerence (SAREF) ontology. In: Cuel, R., Young, R. (eds.) FOMI 2015. LNBIP, vol. 225, pp. 100–112. Springer, Cham (2015). https://doi.org/10.1007/978-3-319-21545-7_9

4. Dimou, A., Vander Sande, M., Colpaert, P., Verborgh, R., Mannens, E., Van de Walle, R.: RML: a generic language for integrated RDF mappings of heterogeneous data. In: Ldow (2014)

5. Grover, A., Leskovec, J.: node2vec: scalable feature learning for networks. In: Proceedings of the 22nd ACM SIGKDD International Conference on Knowledge Discovery and Data Mining, pp. 855–864 (2016)

6. Hsu, C.L., Lin, J.C.C.: An empirical examination of consumer adoption of Internet of Things services: network externalities and concern for information privacy perspectives. Comput. Hum. Behav. **62**, 516–527 (2016)

7. Janowicz, K., Haller, A., Cox, S.J., Le Phuoc, D., Lefrançois, M.: SOSA: a lightweight ontology for sensors, observations, samples, and actuators. J. Web Semant. **56**, 1–10 (2019)

8. Long, J., Chen, Z., He, W., Wu, T., Ren, J.: An integrated framework of deep learning and knowledge graph for prediction of stock price trend: an application in Chinese stock exchange market. Appl. Soft Comput. **91**, 106205 (2020)

9. Mahdavinejad, M.S., Rezvan, M., Barekatain, M., Adibi, P., Barnaghi, P., Sheth, A.P.: Machine learning for internet of things data analysis: a survey. Digit. Commun. Netwo. **4**(3), 161–175 (2018)

10. McMahan, B., Moore, E., Ramage, D., Hampson, S., Aguera y Arcas, B.: Communication-efficient learning of deep networks from decentralized data. In: Artificial Intelligence and Statistics, pp. 1273–1282. PMLR (2017)

11. Miorandi, D., Sicari, S., De Pellegrini, F., Chlamtac, I.: Internet of Things: vision, applications and research challenges. Ad Hoc Netw. **10**(7), 1497–1516 (2012)

12. Nawaz, A., et al.: An intelligent integrated approach for efficient demand side management with forecaster and advanced metering infrastructure frameworks in smart grid. IEEE Access **8**, 132551–132581 (2020)

13. Qin, Y., Sheng, Q.Z., Falkner, N.J., Dustdar, S., Wang, H., Vasilakos, A.V.: When things matter: a survey on data-centric Internet of Things. J. Netw. Comput. Appl. **64**, 137–153 (2016)

14. Rijgersberg, H., van Assem, M., Top, J.: Ontology of units of measure and related concepts. Semant. Web **4**(1), 3–13 (2013)

15. Savazzi, S., Nicoli, M., Rampa, V.: Federated learning with cooperating devices: a consensus approach for massive IoT networks. IEEE Internet Things J. **7**(5), 4641–4654 (2020)

16. Spencer, B., Al-Obeidat, F.: Temperature forecasts with stable accuracy in a smart home. Procedia Comput. Sci. **83**, 726–733 (2016)

17. W3C: Web of Things (WoT) Thing Description (2020). https://www.w3.org/TR/2020/REC-wot-thing-description-20200409/

18. van der Weerdt, R., de Boer, V., Daniele, L., Nouwt, B.: Validating SAREF in a smart home environment. Metadata Semant. Res. **1355**, 35–46 (2021). https://doi.org/10.1007/978-3-030-71903-6_4

19. Wilcke, X., Bloem, P., De Boer, V.: The knowledge graph as the default data model for learning on heterogeneous knowledge. Data Sci. **1**(1–2), 39–57 (2017)

20. Wu, S., et al.: Survey on prediction algorithms in smart homes. IEEE Internet Things J. **4**(3), 636–644 (2017)

21. Yang, H., Gong, S., Liu, Y., Lin, Z., Qu, Y.: A multi-task learning model for daily activity forecast in smart home. Sensors **20**(7), 1933 (2020)

22. Zamora-Martínez, F., Romeu, P., Botella-Rocamora, P., Pardo, J.: On-line learning of indoor temperature forecasting models towards energy efficiency. Energy Build. **83**, 162–172 (2014)
23. Zhang, C., Song, D., Huang, C., Swami, A., Chawla, N.V.: Heterogeneous graph neural network. In: Proceedings of the 25th ACM SIGKDD International Conference on Knowledge Discovery & Data Mining, pp. 793–803 (2019)

Stigmergic Multi-Agent Systems in the Semantic Web of Things

Daniel Schraudner[(✉)] [ID]

Chair of Technical Information Systems, Friedrich-Alexander-University
Erlangen-Nürnberg, Nuremberg, Germany
`daniel.schraudner@fau.de`

Abstract. Intelligent, autonomous agents are still not available in the
Semantic Web at large scale today. Also the fields of Semantic Web and
Multi-Agent Systems are not working together very closely although they
could profit much from each other. Existing approaches merely use the
Web as a transport layer and are not properly aligned to the architectural
style of the Web. The Internet of Things, which would be very useful for
agents to act upon Things in the real world, on the other side is very fragmented and not easily inter-operable. The Web of Things has emerged
as an approach to use the (Semantic) Web as an application layer for
Things. It is still unclear however, how agents on the WoT should look
like. We propose that the Semantic Web is a suitable integration layer,
both for agents and Things. We investigate how a Multi-Agent System
in the Semantic Web of Things can be build by utilizing simple reflex
agents and the communication paradigm of stigmergy. We map Things
and artifacts to Web resources that are managed by a Web server and
provide affordances to agents through hypermedia.

Keywords: Multi-Agent Systems · Web of Things · Simple reflex
agents · Stigmergy · Rest · Hypermedia

1 Introduction

In their groundbreaking Scientific American article in 2001 Berners-Lee et al.
[3] proposed their vision of the Semantic Web. From this very beginning on
intelligent agents were an integral part of this vision basically being responsible
for doing all the work thus unleashing the "real power" of the Semantic Web.

Six years after this initial proposal Hendler [13] began to ask "Where are all
the intelligent agents?". He was not the only one to ask this to the present day
[7,8]. The reality we have to face is that a lot of work has been done on the
technical foundations of the Semantic Web but the agent side has been scarcely
considered.

This work was funded by the German Federal Ministry of Education and
Researchthrough the MOSAIK project (grant no. 01IS18070A).

R. Verborgh et al. (Eds.): ESWC 2021 Satellite Events, LNCS 12739, pp. 218–229, 2021.
https://doi.org/10.1007/978-3-030-80418-3_34

At the same time a whole research field with its own community and knowledge about intelligent agents exists: The field of Multi-Agent Systems. However today there is not much collaboration between the Semantic Web and Multi-Agent System communities even though the Semantic Web could profit greatly from the insights of Multi-Agent Systems and vice versa – an insight that already was acknowledged in 2002 [10] and still is today [7].

In fact, there have been approaches to build Multi-Agent Systems with Web technologies in the past. However these approaches almost always are built upon RPC-styled architectures like SOAP or the WS-* specifications. Those Multi-Agent Systems use the Web merely as a communication layer to transport messages but not as an application layer to host the agents and their environment [6].

We presume that using the Web as an actual application layer would be beneficial for Multi-Agent Systems. One method to achieve this is to use the architectural style of Representational State Transfer (REST) consequently for the whole system (including the agents). REST has proven useful for building the Web as it is today, though we expect that it will also be useful for building a Multi-Agent System that is directly embedded into the (Semantic) Web.

Agents that cannot only interact with information resources on the Web but also with non-information resources in the real world would be even more beneficial for the Semantic Web.

The advent and popularization of the Internet of Things (IoT) made it possible to communicate with physical things. A lot of devices have and are accessible through IP addresses today. However the IoT is very fragmented and a lot of vendor-specific walled gardens exist [5], i.e. things can only be used for the applications and in combination with the things that have been intended by their manufacturers.

What the IoT brought us is a uniform communication layer for the internet and physical things (namely TCP/IP) but we are still missing a uniform application layer which would help to overcome the closed platforms in the IoT, enable devices to be inter-operable with each other and users to create the applications they want.

The (Semantic) Web can be this uniform application layer (it already is for most of the things we do in the internet today, in fact). The proposal of the Web of Things (WoT) by the World Wide Web Consortium has been the first step towards this direction. Naturally most of the work regarding the WoT has gone into describing things and their interactions. It is still an open questions how the Web agents (i.e. the clients) that are going to use the things are going to look like.

We think that the three research fields Semantic Web, Multi-Agent Systems and the Web of Things have many overlappings but also that their communities could profit much from more interaction among them. With this work we want to show an approach to bridge the gaps between the three fields by investigating how a Multi-agent System can be build into the Semantic Web of Things based on simple agents that coordinate in a stigmergic, self-organizing way by exploiting the native application structure of the Web (which can be characterized by the REST constraints).

2   State of the Art

2.1   Multi-Agent Systems

Intelligent agents have been a basic building block of Artificial Intelligence for a long time. Agents can be conceived as entities receiving percepts from their environment and performing actions upon their environment [25]. Multiple autonomous intelligent agents coordinating to reach a common goal form a Multi-Agent System (MAS).

In recent times, not only the agents but also their environment has become a focus of interest. The commonly accepted agent and artifacts meta-model (A&A) [21] considers the environment as first-class citizen. The A&A meta-model thus partitions entities in the system in proactive agents and reactive artifacts which make up the environment for the agents.

Agent-Oriented Programming and BDI Agents. Agent-Oriented Programming (AOP) is a programming paradigm first introduced by Shoham [27] which is centered around intelligent software agents. AOP frameworks have since then been a popular method for building Multi-Agent Systems.

For programming the agents the Belief-Desire-Intention (BDI) model [22] is the quasi-standard. BDI refers to the three main components each agent is built of where

- **Beliefs** represent the current state of knowledge the agent beliefs to be true
- **Desires** are the overall goal the agents tries to reach and
- **Intentions** are desires that the agent has committed to at the moment.

The most prominent AOP framework incorporating the BDI model is JaCaMo [4]. JaCaMo in fact is a combination of three different systems:

- **Jason**: A dedicated language for specifying agents' beliefs, desires and intentions based on AgentSpeak
- **Cartago** for programming artifacts in the environment compliant to the A&A meta-model
- **Moise** for creation and management of agent organizations (allowing to give a higher-level structure to the agents)

It has been used extensively to build many different kinds of Multi-Agents Systems [24,24,29,31].

JaCaMo by default uses the *Centralized* infrastructure which means that all agents and artifacts run on the same host and cannot communicate with the outside world (an inherent requirement for any Web-based application). Amaral et al. [1] propose a REST-based abstraction to access JaCaMo entities through the Web. However they state the limitedness of their approach as the MAS cannot work as a client on the Web, i.e. the agents can be only manipulated from the outside but cannot themselves manipulate something outside of their system through the Web.

Semantic Web Services and FIPA. There have been approaches to build Multi-Agent Systems on the Web by using the RPC-style Semantic Web Services and service-oriented architectures [11,14]. The Foundation for Intelligent Physical Agents (FIPA) has also released standards [20] to enable communication and interaction between several Multi-Agent Systems. The FIPA standard allows to use HTTP – a Web protocol – for passing messages between agents. JADE is an implementation of FIPA [2] that is also usable in conjunction with JaCaMo (by choosing the *Jade* infrastructure) thereby allowing JaCaMo Agents to communicate through the Web.

The problem with those two approaches is that even though they are using Web protocols, they utilize the Web only as a communication layer and HTTP only as a mechanism for passing messages. They are not properly aligned with the REST architectural style which is the foundation for the application layer of the Web. Applications that are not aligned with REST suffer from several disadvantages like limited scalability, tight coupling, caching, etc.) [7].

Hypermedia Agents. There also have been approaches to build Multi-Agent Systems that are more conformant with the architectural style of the application layer of the Web. Most of those systems [12,19], however, do not rely on hypermedia at all and thus are not truly RESTful.

Hypermedia agents on the other side are a more recent approach to build Web-based Multi-Agent Systems. The idea is to discover other entities (agents, artifacts) and how to interact with them during run time using hyperlinks and forms. This approach conforms to the *Hypermedia as the Engine of Application State* (HATEOAS) constraint of REST and helps systems to a better scalability and evolvability [6]. However those approaches seem to focus heavily on the HATEOAS constraint neglecting other important architectural constraints of web applications, e.g. the client-server principle (there is no clear separation between client and server on the application level as agents are allowed to communicate with artifacts as well as with other agents) and statelessness (communication between two BDI agents is not stateless in general).

Rule-Based Systems and Simple Reflex Agents. Rule-based systems are systems that can process information in such a way that they can create new knowledge by applying rules to the already existing knowledge base, i.e. they are capable of reasoning. An example for a rule-based systems grounded on formal logic would be the programming language Prolog.

Rules have already been used in conjunction with Linked Data: Käfer and Harth [15] showed that they can use rules specified in Notation3 (a super set of the Turtle RDF serialization) for specifying the execution of reading and writing Linked Data with operational semantics grounded on Abstract State Machines.

Rule-based systems like this can be used to easily implement simple reflex agents. Simple reflex agents are, according to Russel and Norvig [25], the simplest form of agents that can be build. However those simple rule based agents would still be capable of doing a lot of useful things on the Web. Even more promising is the interplay of many simple reflex agent which can lead to a self-organizing emergent behaviour and as such be very efficient.

Stigmergy. Stigmergy is a communication paradigm that allows agents to only communicate with their environment, not with each other. It is inspired by the behaviour of social insects. By using Stigmergy simple beings like termites are capable of coordinating to show a complex behaviour.

Stigmergy has been used successfully in many Multi-Agent Systems [9,23,30] to foster self-organizing and emergent behaviour but it has never consequently been applied to build a Multi-Agent System in the Web, as we do.

2.2   Web of Things

The term *Web of Things* describing the idea to use the Web as an application layer for the Internet of Things has been around for quite a long time [32]. But only since 2014, when the W3C Web of Things Interest Group has been started, the idea was getting more concrete. The Web of Things as of today comprises the five building blocks *Architecture, Thing Descriptions, Scripting API, Binding Templates* and *Security and Privacy Guidelines* with the first two being official W3C recommendations, the other three being work in progress. In the following we will focus on the Architecture [16] and Things Descriptions [17] as these are the most relevant parts for our work.

Architecture. The Architecture of the Web of Things differentiates between Web Things that are described by standardized metadata and Consumers that consume these descriptions and interact with the Things based on these descriptions. Things can be physical or virtual entities and also can be abstractions of other Things. Things should link to other Things that are relevant for them and can use additional semantics by typing those links. Intermediaries can act as proxy for Things and thereby augmenting them or mixing up different Things. As Intermediaries are described by the same metadata as Things, they can be indistinguishable from Things [16].

Consumers are enabled to interact with Things through interaction affordances. There exists three types of interaction affordances:

- **Property Affordances:** Allow consumers to read or right a specific part of the internal state of a thing
- **Interaction Affordances:** Allow consumers to invoke a function of the Thing that may not have an instant effect on the state of the Thing but may manipulate the state eventually
- **Event Affordances:** Allow consumers to subscribe to events that are broadcasted by the Thing

The affordances also include hypermedia controls (i.e. hyperlinks and forms) and protocol bindings (e.g. for HTTP, COAP and MQTT) to specify how exactly to interact with the Thing [17].

Thing Descriptions. Thing Descriptions describe the standardized metadata for Things. They consist of a JSON-LD document of a given structure that must be available on a Web server (not necessarily on the Thing itself). Thing descriptions can be seen as entry points to Things for Web clients (similar to the index.html file for classical web sites). They define the different affordances a Thing has, how to use them (links, forms, protocols and data scheme) and can contain additional information. As JSON-LD is a Linked-Data-enabled format the semantics can be specified using RDF.

3   Problem Statement and Research Questions

Our problem statement is two-fold:

On the one side we observe that, even though being an integral part of the initial proposal, there are still not many intelligent, autonomous agents in the Semantic Web. These agents would without question be helpful and enable people to do more practical things using the Semantic Web [3].

On the other side, a lot of real world Things have access to the internet these days but they are not accessed via a uniform application layer and are not inter-operable with each other. We should enable agents on the Web (both intelligent, autonomous agents and classical user agents like Web browsers) to interact with these Things in a uniform and predictable way. This means there should be a standard method for agents to get and derive enough information to make informed decisions when interacting with the Thing enabling the agents to reach their goals.

We propose that the Semantic Web and its technologies are a well-suited integration mechanism for Web Agents, Multi-Agents Systems and the Web of Things. However, we suppose that is not sufficient to just build interfaces between existing Multi-Agent Systems frameworks and the Semantic Web or the Internet of Things platforms and the Semantic Web respectively. Both fields should be integrated tightly into the application architecture of the Semantic Web to be more useful.

From this statement we have derived the following two research questions:

RQ 1: How can Multi-Agent Systems in the Semantic Web solve a given problem as fast as a classical Multi-Agent implementation while strictly adhering to the REST constraints?

RQ 2: What extensions to WoT Thing Descriptions and what constraints for the design of WoT Thing Descriptions help Multi-Agent Systems in the Semantic Web to solve a given problem faster?

For the problem mentioned in these questions please refer to Sect. 5.

Our main contribution will be the investigation of methods of how to build a Multi-Agent System in the Semantic Web that is properly aligned with its application layer that can make use of real-world Things as artifacts and achieve global goals efficiently.

4   Research Methodology and Approach

4.1   Methodology

Our research methodology is based on building prototypes of Multi-Agent Systems using real-world Things in the Semantic Web and evaluating their performance either using simulations, real-world scenarios or a combination of both (see Sect. 5).

4.2   Approaches

Artifacts and Things as Web Resources. The A&A meta-model partitions Multi-Agent Systems in proactive entities – the agents following their goals – and reactive entities – artifacts that passively provide functions for the agents. In our approach we model agents as clients and artifacts as web resources managed by a Web server.

Agents can interact with artifacts by sending HTTP requests to the Web server responsible for the URI that has been assigned to an artifact. Agents can only get the current state of the artifact and thus perceive their environment using a HTTP GET request and they can manipulate the state of the artifact and thus act on their environment using the unsafe HTTP requests (PUT, POST, DELETE, etc.). The only way agents can observe other agents is indirectly through the modifications those agents made to the environment.

The concept of an artifact is very similar to Things in the WoT, i.e. we just treat Things as artifacts that can be manipulated by agents through their different affordances. However, there should be a uniform description for both, information resource artifacts that just provide a digital service and Thing artifacts that act on the real world, possibly based on WoT Thing Descriptions.

Aligning Stigmergy and REST. We use stigmergy to ease the communication between agents and align it to the architectural style of Web applications. Forcing the agents to coordinate by writing messages to their environment for other agents to pick them up helps to establish the separation of concerns between client and server that is one constraint of REST. Agents only act as clients and artifacts as servers; communication always happens between client and server and is initiated by the client[1].

---

[1] It is important here to stress that the REST constraints are only referring to the application layer. Of course one can on a technical level always differentiate between client and server. A publish–subscribe architecture e.g. has no clear separation between client and server on the application level but every IP packet on a lower layer has a source ("client") and a destination ("server").

Stigmergy also is beneficial for fulfilling the other constraints of REST like statelessness and cacheability (artifacts always communicate their global resource state; agent-agent communication is dependent on the context), HATEOAS (artifacts provide hyperlinks and forms, agents can change the links of an artifact to give hints to other agents), etc.

To enable the agents to not only read Linked Data from their environment but also be able to write Linked Data to it, the Web servers that manage the artifacts should conform to the Linked Data Platform standard [28].

Self-organization Through Stigmergy. Using stigmergy means that all agents in our Multi-Agent System can share information with each other asynchronously through their environment. This opens up the possibility to use many simple agents that each each contribute only a small part to fulfill the global goal but show a self-organizing, emergent behaviour by coordinating themselves through their environment, i.e. by leaving information in their environment which can be helpful for other agents – as opposed to more sophisticated but also complicated agents like e.g. BDI agents that need to coordinate by communicating directly with each other. We thus try to make our agents as simple as possible by using rule-based systems and simple reflex agents to implement the agents behaviour.

Hypermedia Affordances and Decentralized Planning. Affordances can be seen as an offer from an artifact to an agent to perform an action. In our systems affordances are represented by hypermedia links and forms which means that agents do not need to know the artifacts and their possible actions a priori (e.g. by hard coding or out-of-band communication) but can discover them at run time. This mechanism helps to cope with a dynamic environment that is changing all the time (like it is often the case in real world applications). This view is also consistent with the affordance concept implemented in the WoT Thing Descriptions.

In order for agents to take the right decision about which affordances to use to reach their goal, the affordances will need a description about their preconditions and about the effects they have to their artifact (or other artifacts that are influenced by this artifact).

When we have these descriptions we can have agents that are responsible for decentralized planning in their environment. They can do decentralized planning by matching pre- and postconditions of affordances and composing those affordances if they match thus providing shortcuts to other agents in a stigmergic way. We assume that this form of planning is very flexible and can easily adapt to a changing environment.

5   Evaluation Plan

We have two scenarios to evaluate the prototypes we build. The first scenario is a hypothetical manufacturing scenario based on real-world Industry 4.0 facility[2], the second one is a smart home scenario.

5.1   Modular Smartphone Manufacturing

The first evaluation scenario is motivated by the common requirement for modern shop floors to be flexible enough to produce very small batches of customized products down to lot size one. In our scenario the product is a modular smartphone that can be configured by the customer to a very large extend (e.g., processor, memory size, display, SIM card slots, etc.). Parts are processed by different stations and transported between them using autonomously guided vehicles. Both, stations and vehicles can be addressed using IP in combination with different application protocols (e.g. MQTT).

The goal of the system we build is to control this shop floor in a decentralized fashion, i.e. using multiple collaborating agents, as efficiently as possible. We can measure the efficiency of the system e.g. by measuring the average time to completion for each smartphone order. The system should be resilient against disturbances from the environment, i.e. it should be able to handle sudden machine breakdown, bursts of different orders etc. Disturbances like these can be easily introduced into the simulation and the performance of the system can be compared to other classical approaches (e.g. having a central instance computing a global optimum).

5.2   Smart Home

Smart homes are typical use cases for Internet of Things devices. Those devices usually communicate wirelessly on the physical layer and only with applications provided by their manufacturer on the application level.

A very popular standard for wireless communication with Things is *Bluetooth Low Energy* (BLE). The actual communication with BLE devices happens on a very low level, i.e. writing and reading bytes to and from different characteristics. Nevertheless we can map this communication to HTTP and describe those devices and their behaviour using Thing Descriptions.

As there are plenty of cheap BLE devices available on the market especially in the smart home domain we want to examine how easy it is to program our agents to build useful mashups of those devices and how efficiently the agents can control them.

Here the performance of our system could be evaluated by comparing the reaction time of our system for a specified task (a simple example would be "Turning on a light, when the temperature rises over a threshold") to an existing vendor-specific solution.

---

[2] https://www.arena2036.de/en/.

6   Preliminary Results

We already have successfully shown that it is possible to use simple reflex agents in a Semantic Web environment to drive a simple manufacturing use case by using stigmergy [26].

7   Conclusion

The goal of our thesis is to contribute to integrating the fields of Multi-Agent Systems, Internet of Things and the Semantic Web. We do this by developing a Multi-Agent System comprising simple reflex agents that are tightly integrated into the application layer of the Semantic Web by using the communication paradigm of stigmergy. Things from the Internet of Things shall also be integrated into this system as artifacts by using tools from the Web of Things. Artifacts advertise their affordances and their effects to agents through hypermedia enabling the agents how to take autonomous decisions and eventually do useful things on the Web and in the real world.

References

1. Amaral, C.J., Hübner, J.F., Kampik, T.: Towards jacamo-rest: a resource-oriented abstraction for managing multi-agent systems. arXiv preprint arXiv:2006.05619 (2020)
2. Bellifemine, F., Poggi, A., Rimassa, G.: Jade-a FIPA-compliant agent framework. In: Proceedings of PAAM, vol. 99, p. 33. London (1999)
3. Berners-Lee, T., Hendler, J., Lassila, O.: The semantic web. Sci. Am. **284**(5), 34–43 (2001)
4. Boissier, O., Bordini, R.H., Hübner, J.F., Ricci, A., Santi, A.: Multi-agent oriented programming with JaCaMo. Sci. Comput. Program. **78**(6), 747–761 (2013)
5. Bröring, A., et al..: Enabling IoT ecosystems through platform interoperability. IEEE Softw. **34**(1), 54–61 (2017)
6. Ciortea, A., Boissier, O., Ricci, A.: Engineering world-wide multi-agent systems with hypermedia. In: Weyns, D., Mascardi, V., Ricci, A. (eds.) EMAS 2018. LNCS (LNAI), vol. 11375, pp. 285–301. Springer, Cham (2019). https://doi.org/10.1007/978-3-030-25693-7_15
7. Ciortea, A., Mayer, S., Gandon, F., Boissier, O., Ricci, A., Zimmermann, A.: A decade in hindsight: the missing bridge between multi-agent systems and the world wide web. In: Proceedings of the International Conference on Autonomous Agents and Multiagent Systems (2019)
8. Dikenelli, O., Alatlı, O., Erdur, R.C.: Where Are all the semantic web agents: establishing links between agent and linked data web through environment abstraction. In: Weyns, D., Michel, F. (eds.) E4MAS 2014. LNCS (LNAI), vol. 9068, pp. 41–51. Springer, Cham (2015). https://doi.org/10.1007/978-3-319-23850-0_3
9. Dorigo, M., Bonabeau, E., Theraulaz, G.: Ant algorithms and stigmergy. Fut. Gen. Comput. Syst. **16**(8), 851–871 (2000)

10. Gandon, F.: Distributed artificial intelligence and knowledge management: ontologies and multi-agent systems for a corporate semantic web. Ph.D. thesis, Université Nice Sophia Antipolis (2002)
11. Gibbins, N., Harris, S., Shadbolt, N.: Agent-based semantic web services. In: Proceedings of the 12th International Conference on World Wide Web, pp. 710–717 (2003)
12. Gouaïch, A., Bergeret, M.: Rest-a: an agent virtual machine based on rest framework. In: Advances in Practical Applications of Agents and Multiagent Systems, pp. 103–112. Springer (2010). https://doi.org/10.1007/978-3-642-12384-9_13
13. Hendler, J.: Where are all the intelligent agents? IEEE Ann. Hist. Comput. **22**(03), 2–3 (2007)
14. Huhns, M.N.: Agents as web services. IEEE Internet Comput. **6**(4), 93–95 (2002)
15. Käfer, T., Harth, A.: Rule-based programming of user agents for linked data. In: LDOW@ WWW (2018)
16. Kajimoto, K., Toumura, K., Matsukura, R., Kawaguchi, T., Lagally, M., Kovatsch, M.: Web of things (wot) architecture. In: W3C Recommendation, W3C, April 2020. https://www.w3.org/TR/2020/REC-wot-architecture-20200409/
17. Kovatsch, M., McCool, M., Käbisch, S., Kamiya, T., Charpenay, V.: Web of things (wot) thing description. In: W3C Recommendation, W3C, April 2020. https://www.w3.org/TR/2020/REC-wot-thing-description-20200409/
18. Martins, R., Meneguzzi, F.: A smart home model using JaCaM framework. In: 2014 12th IEEE International Conference on Industrial Informatics (INDIN), pp. 94–99. IEEE (2014)
19. Mitrović, D., Ivanović, M., Budimac, Z., Vidaković, M.: Radigost: interoperable web-based multi-agent platform. J. Syst. Softw. **90**, 167–178 (2014)
20. O'Brien, P.D., Nicol, R.C.: FIPA-towards a standard for software agents. BT Technol. J. **16**(3), 51–59 (1998)
21. Omicini, A., Ricci, A., Viroli, M.: Artifacts in the a&a meta-model for multi-agent systems. Auton. Agents Multi-agent Syst. **17**(3), 432–456 (2008)
22. Rao, A.S., Georgeff, M.P., et al.: BDI agents: from theory to practice. ICMAS. **95**, 312–319 (1995)
23. Ricci, A., Omicini, A., Viroli, M., Gardelli, L., Oliva, E.: Cognitive Stigmergy: towards a framework based on agents and artifacts. In: Weyns, D., Parunak, H.V.D., Michel, F. (eds.) E4MAS 2006. LNCS (LNAI), vol. 4389, pp. 124–140. Springer, Heidelberg (2007). https://doi.org/10.1007/978-3-540-71103-2_7
24. Roloff, M.L., Stemmer, M.R., Hübner, J.F., Schmitt, R., Pfeifer, T., Hüttemann, G.: A multi-agent system for the production control of printed circuit boards using JaCaMo and prometheus aeolus. In: 2014 12th IEEE International Conference on Industrial Informatics (INDIN), pp. 236–241. IEEE (2014)
25. Russell, S.J., Norvig, P.: Artificial Intelligence: A Modern Approach, 2nd Edn. Prentice Hall (2002). ISBN: 0137903952
26. Schraudner, D., Charpenay, V.: An HTTP/RDF-based agent infrastructure for manufacturing Using stigmergy. In: Harth, A., et al. (eds.) ESWC 2020. LNCS, vol. 12124, pp. 197–202. Springer, Cham (2020). https://doi.org/10.1007/978-3-030-62327-2_34
27. Shoham, Y.: Agent-oriented programming. Artif. Intell. **60**(1), 51–92 (1993)
28. Speicher, S., Arwe, J., Malhotra, A.: Linked data platform 1.0. W3C Recommendation, February 26 (2015)

29. Toledo, C.M., Bordini, R.H., Chiotti, O., Galli, M.R.: Developing a knowledge management multi-agent system using *JaCaMo*. In: Dennis, L., Boissier, O., Bordini, R.H. (eds.) ProMAS 2011. LNCS (LNAI), vol. 7217, pp. 41–57. Springer, Heidelberg (2012). https://doi.org/10.1007/978-3-642-31915-0_3
30. Valckenaers, P., Kollingbaum, M., Van Brussel, H., et al.: Multi-agent coordination and control using stigmergy. Comput. Ind. **53**(1), 75–96 (2004)
31. Van Haare Heijmeijer, A., Vaz Alves, G., et al.: Development of a middleware between sumo simulation tool and jacamo framework (2018)
32. Wilde, E.: Putting things to rest. UC Berkeley: School of Information (2002). https://escholarship.org/uc/item/1786t1dm

Towards an Ontology for Propaganda Detection in News Articles

Kyle Hamilton[(⊠)] [iD]

Technological University Dublin, Dublin, Ireland
`kyle.i.hamilton@mytudublin.ie`

Abstract. The proliferation of mis/disinformation in the media has had a profound impact on social discourse and politics in the United States. Some argue that democracy itself is threatened by the lies, chicanery, and flimflam - in short, propaganda - emanating from the highest pulpits, podiums, and soapboxes in the land. Propaganda differs from mis/disinformation in that it need not be false, but instead, it relies on rhetorical devices which aim to manipulate the audience into a particular belief or behavior. While falsehoods can be debunked, albeit with disputable efficacy, beliefs are harder to cut through. The detection of "Fake News" has received a lot of attention recently with some impressive results, however, propaganda detection remains challenging. This proposal aims to further the research into propaganda detection by constructing an ontology with this specific goal in mind, while drawing from multiple disciplines within Computer Science and the Social Sciences.

Keywords: Propaganda · Semantic Web · Knowledge extraction · Ontology · Argument Mining

1 Introduction

In 1936, Clyde Miller, founder and CEO of the Institute For Propaganda Analysis, received a grant from philanthropist Edward A. Filene who was "afraid that America was becoming the victim of propaganda, that Americans had lost their capacity to think things through" [18]. In May, 2021, the defence for US Capitol rioter Anthony Antonio, put forward the argument that Mr. Antonio was suffering from "Foxitis" - a condition brought on by watching excessive amounts of FOX NEWS in the six months prior to the insurrection. Former FOX NEWS political editor Chris Stirewalt put it this way: "Having worked in cable news for more than a decade after a wonderfully misspent youth in newspapers, I can tell you the result: a nation of news consumers both overfed and malnourished. Americans gorge themselves daily on empty informational calories, indulging their sugar fixes of self-affirming half-truths and even outright lies" [27].

This publication has emanated from research supported in part by a grant from Science Foundation Ireland under Grant number 18/CRT/6183. For the purpose of Open Access, the author has applied a CC BY public copyright licence to any Author Accepted Manuscript version arising from this submission.

R. Verborgh et al. (Eds.): ESWC 2021 Satellite Events, LNCS 12739, pp. 230–241, 2021.
https://doi.org/10.1007/978-3-030-80418-3_35

There is agreement among scholars that in combating mis/disinformation and propaganda, solutions will have to be multi-pronged. Tumber & Waistford identify three levels at which to combat the threats posed: individual, group, and systemic/structural [1]. Media literacy education resides at the center of the individual level. But the media landscape today is many orders of magnitude more complex than it was in Miller's time. This is evidenced not only by the sheer speed and volume of information flowing into the public sphere, but also by the many modes by which it flows, from television and radio, to social networks public and private, each of which is competing for the undivided attention of information consumers. And this will only become more complex in the future, as deep fakes are beginning to make their debut, while ubiquitous virtual reality is only around the corner, opening the door for information delivery via a multi-sensory experience [32].

But even though technology may advance exponentially, the fundamental human condition, basic psychological needs and desires have not changed that dramatically throughout history. The study of rhetoric has been nurtured over thousands of years, the results of which still explain much of human communication to this day. The use of rhetoric as a way to describe propaganda has been widely accepted. "The propagandist will attempt to control information flow and manage a certain public's opinion by shaping perceptions through strategies of informative communication" [18].

2   State of the Art

For the purposes of this work, any information which is intended to influence beliefs or modify behaviors in order to further an agenda, will be considered propaganda. Often, this type of information is of questionable veracity, but this is not a requirement. The use of logical fallacies and/or emotional appeals are the hallmarks of propagandist messaging. However, to qualify as *not* propaganda the arguments must be both valid and sound, or in other words, the premises must be true. Automatic detection of dis/misinformation, sometimes referred to as "fake news"[1], has received a lot of attention in recent years. Section 2.1 highlights the State of the Art (SOTA) in this field. Section 2.2 highlights relevant work in the field of Argument Mining as it relates to identifying the more elusive characteristics of propaganda such as implicit arguments and rhetorical figures. Cabrio & Villata describe Argument Mining as a combination of Natural Language Processing (NLP) and Knowledge Representation & Reasoning (KRR) [4]. An overview of these topics is presented in Sect. 2.3, and in particular, in the area of ontology engineering for the propaganda domain. Finally, Sect. 2.4 points to SOTA for the automatic extraction of knowledge (triples) from text.

2.1   Dis/Misinformation Identification

Style Based. These techniques take into consideration the linguistic content of the news piece. The premise being, that the writing style of a fake news item

---

[1] The label "Fake News" requires explanation beyond the scope of this paper - for more information see Wardle & Derakhshan [31].

differs from a true one. The theory is that fake news items tend to appeal to emotions and be generally more sensationalist. These nuances can be picked up from the text using NLP [2,34].

Content/Knowledge Based. This is an approach which relies on fact checking against a large knowledge base, usually one which is publicly available, for example Wikipedia. This data is represented as a Knowledge Graph (KG) in the form of SOP (subject, object, predicate) triples. At a high level, such triples are extracted from the news item in question, and checked against the KG. This is typically posed as a link prediction problem. The challenge with content based approaches is that KGs are often incomplete, especially when it comes to recent events [3,5,20].

Network Based. Utilizing social context, how false information propagates through the network, who is spreading the false information, and how the spreaders connect with each other, is used to understand the patterns of false information through network theory. Here the challenge lies in the dependency on the social context which is only available after the news item has propagated through the network, thus early detection, a crucial component of the solution, is difficult [22,26,33].

Human-in-the-Loop. To leverage both human insight and computational efficiency, hybrid approaches have been developed. In the "wisdom-of-the-crowd" approach [8,12,21,25,28,29], no one individual has to score a news item correctly. If enough independent scores are averaged, this results in an unbiased estimator of the correct score of the item. Another hybrid technique involves the identification of "checkworthy content" automatically [10], for manual review.

2.2   Argument Mining

In *Five Years of Argument Mining: a Data-driven Analysis* [4], Cabrio and Villata discuss current approaches to Argument Mining, ranging from SVM (Support Vector Machine) to RNN (Recurrent Neural Networks), and NB (Naive Bayes) among others. They list disinformation detection among the applications of Argument Mining, but they point out that more work is required to improve the performance of these systems. None of the techniques surveyed used Semantic Web techniques. Moreover, the majority of the work on propaganda detection is done at the document level, or even more coarsely, at the source level. There are drawbacks to such coarse classifications. For example, a news source can be generally propagandist, but that doesn't mean that all documents produced or published by that source are necessarily so. In fact, a technique of propaganda is to disseminate legitimate information in order to build trust, thus making it easier to manipulate the reader at a later stage. Another downside of the above approaches, is the lack of explain-ability as to exactly which fragments of a doc-ument are deemed propagandist and why. Hence it's important to aim to detect propaganda techniques at a more granular level.

In 2019, De San Martino et al. [7] created and released the PTC data set for the detection of 18 propaganda techniques in News articles, and invited the AI community to compete in the challenge of detecting said techniques at a granular level at SEMEVAL 2020 [14]. The competition consists of two tasks: the first task is to identify spans of text containing propaganda techniques, and the second task is a multilabel classification to identify the specific technique used, such as *name calling*, or *loaded language*. Looking at the leader-board[2] results, this is a difficult task rarely exceeding F1 scores above 0.5, leaving ample opportunity for further research. All of the top ranking approaches are based on deep learning.

A natural fit for detecting propaganda techniques such as faulty logic is to borrow from the field of Argument Mining. If logical arguments can be modelled using graphical representations [30] it may be worth exploring whether graphical representations (ontologies) can be used to model logical validity, for example by using description logic such as OWL. Indeed, in their survey of ontological modeling of rhetorical concepts for Argument Mining, Mitrovic et al. [15], list "political discourse analysis" as a potential application.

Related to Argument Mining, is the identification of rhetorical figures. Lawrence & Reed state that "in much the same way that argumentation schemes capture common patterns of reasoning, rhetorical figures capture common patterns of speech" [13]. They point to the above mentioned task in SEMEVAL 2020 focusing on the detection of rhetorical figures (propaganda techniques) in news articles as a case in point. In addition to such rhetorical figures, Moens points out, "a lot of content is not expressed explicitly but resides in the mind of communicator and audience. This content includes common sense and world knowledge, domain knowledge and knowledge of the broader context in which the discourse functions (e.g., political or cultural context)" [17]. When it comes to propaganda, such "hidden" messaging is commonplace. Here, augmenting a labeled news corpus with external knowledge such as DBpedia seems promising.

2.3 Ontology Engineering

A closely related topic to propaganda techniques is that of rhetorical figures. Mitrovicć et al. survey ontological modeling covering two main topics: *RetFig - Ontology of Rhetorical Figures for Serbian* [16], and the *Lassoing Rhetoric project* [19]. The authors list political discourse analysis, and argument/intent analysis as possible areas of application, and "hope that further analysis of rhetorical figures will reveal a deeper understanding of the cognitive aspects that underlie the impact of persuasive communication." Harris et al. [9] developed a cognitive ontology of rhetorical figures using OWL, *RhetFig*, and discuss some lessons learned when creating such ontologies. They started with a top-down approach, tried working middle-out, and eventually settled on a bottom

---

[2] https://propaganda.qcri.org/semeval2020-task11/leaderboard.php.

-up approach as the most fruitful. Based on their experience they propose creating mini ontologies for specific rhetorical figures. The authors refer to the work of Douglas Walton on argumentation schemes and "envision a convergence of our research with Walton's line." Clearly there are overlaps in the area of ontology design for rhetorical figures and Argument Mining, which are ripe for further exploration for the purposes of propaganda detection.

2.4   Automatic Knowledge Extraction from Text

Extracting structured knowledge from text is a research area onto itself, and a detailed literature review is beyond the scope of this paper. However, as it is an important component of the overall pipeline some attention is warranted. Three main areas of NLP are relevant to this work: NER (Named Entity Recognition, EL (Entity Linking), and RE (Relation Extraction). SOTA in NER and EL achieve F1 scores in the mid-nineties, while RE is more challenging. A list of SOTA in NLP can be found on Sebastian Ruder's website [23].

3   Problem Statement and Contributions

Propaganda and disinformation in the media is a serious problem and has been the subject of research in multiple disciplines. Propaganda is particularly tricky because the techniques used can be difficult to detect computationally. Consider the following examples of recent news headlines:

1. *Medical Examiner: Drugs, Heart Disease Contributed To George Floyd's Death.*
2. *Medical examiner says heart disease, drugs contributed to but didn't cause George Floyd's death.*

In example 1, a hasty reader might infer a causal effect of drugs and heart disease in the death of George Floyd. Given the context surrounding this event, and the source of the article, this may very well have been the intent of the publisher. It is difficult to flag this headline as disinformation since the information presented is indeed factual. A common technique of the propagandist is to tell the truth, but not the whole truth. So a mechanism is needed to recognize this omission. Applying Walton's system for argument schemes [30], these two headlines might look something like Fig. 1. Representing the text in a graphical manner such as this, opens the door for the use of logical inference.

Currently, most of the work in automating the detection of propaganda and disinformation has focused on NLP and network analysis. While some efforts have been made to utilize Semantic Web techniques for fact-checking, the application of reasoning to this task is an opportunity for further research. A contribution of this work is the development of an ontology for the media ecosystem with the explicit purpose of detecting propaganda techniques and rhetorical devices in the news. The identification of relevant devices in the current social context

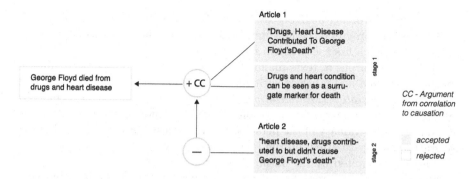

Fig. 1. Argument Diagram representing the example headlines from Sect. 3. In stage 1, the premises are accepted, and therefore the conclusion would also be accepted. Only in stage 2 the second article undercuts the first one, and ultimately the conclusion is correctly classified as false.

comes from the development of a context mapping and vocabulary from literature in the social sciences. This ontology can then be used to build a knowledge base from news articles. Data represented this way can be utilized in both deep learning architectures, as well as reasoning.

3.1   Research Question and Hypothesis

RQ: Based on the vocabulary and mapping developed from the literature in the social sciences, how effective can Description Logics such as OWL be at modeling propaganda?

H1: By utilizing techniques from Semantic Web and Argument Mining, and a theoretical foundation from the social sciences, the accuracy, and interpretabilty of propaganda detection can be improved over existing deep learning methods.

4   Research Methodology and Approach

An ontology suitable for describing propaganda techniques and rhetorical devices, as well as a pipeline for ingesting new data and model training will be constructed. Current propaganda detection solutions exhibit precision and recall scores below a useful threshold and lack interpretability. In other words, there is no mechanism for explaining "why" a technique was identified as propagandist beyond the label itself. They do not take into consideration the behavioral dynamics of the audience, or the social context. Mapping this context from a social science perspective in order to better understand the audience, i.e. the demand side of mis/disinformation and propaganda, is an important aspect of the methodology which will help inform and evaluate the relevance of the ontology. Specifically, this effort will help identify the relevant propaganda techniques in a continually evolving media ecosystem and social context. See Fig. 3. As this is still a work-in-progress, the first iteration of the design will utilize an existing data set, one which fits the problem most closely.

PTC [6] is a corpus of texts manually annotated by six professional annotators (both unitized and labeled) with 18 propaganda techniques such as *Loaded Language, Exaggeration/Minimization*, and *Flag-Waving* among others. The training and the development partitions of PTC include 446 articles from 48 news outlets. A dictionary of the persuasion techniques is provided, and descriptive statistics are visualized, on the PTC authors' website[3].

This data is limited by the nature of the problem itself, namely the rapidly evolving social context and the emergence of new stories. It is expected that the rhetoric will likewise evolve over time, therefore continuous monitoring of the landscape and data updating is planned. Figure 2 illustrates the proposed pipeline, the development of which will be undertaken in an iterative manner, and evaluated according to the plan in the next section.

The methodology described involves a lot of manual labor, and the input of domain experts. While this may not be the most efficient process, it is often more sophisticated and offers more valuable insight than a purely numerical approach.

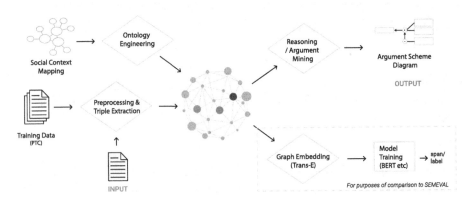

Fig. 2. Proposed pipeline components

5   Evaluation Plan

As this is early stage research, it is anticipated that the evaluation plan may change as the research progresses and additional related work comes to light. A comprehensive literature review is yet to be conducted, and in the spirit of reuse, several ontology projects in the related area of rhetorical figures and argumentation are yet to be reviewed. These include *The Rhetorical Figure Ontology Project* [11], *Computational Rhetoric Project* at the University of Waterloo, organized

---

[3] https://www.tanbih.org/.

around a comprehensive OWL based ontology of rhetorical figures, *RhetFig*[4]; the work of Mitrovic et al. [15] on *Ontological representations of rhetorical figures*, and possibly others yet to be discovered.

Ultimately the criteria for evaluating the proposed ontology is how useful it will be for the propaganda detection task, how generalizeable it will be to similar or related tasks, and if it will enable interpretability of the results for a general audience. The plan for evaluation of the ontology is currently based on the *NeOn methodological guidelines* [24].

Frame of Reference (baseline): Since this is a new ontology, what constitutes a gold-standard in this case is unclear, but again, this is early stages, and such a gold-standard may yet emerge from a more thorough understanding of ontology engineering. In the meantime, the following frames of reference can be utilized:

1. *Data-driven* - This is a measure of coverage based on the corpus. Currently, this is the PTC corpus as described earlier.
2. *Assessment-by-humans* - Experts in behavioral/social sciences will be recruited to augment the data-driven approach in determining domain coverage. Experts in ontology engineering will be recruited to help assess semantic quality and reasoning capability.

Evaluation Goals:

1. *Domain coverage* - This is an iterative process where the ontology will be compared with the proposed social context mapping and vocabulary.
2. *Quality of modeling* - Reasoner software to be determined. Human assessments of syntactic, structural, and semantic quality may also be employed.
3. *Suitability to application/task* - This will be determined by the quality of the results from the overall software pipeline, based on precision/recall of the identified propaganda techniques, as well as the ability to answer the "competency questions" (yet to be defined).

6 Conclusions and Limitations

The ability to identify propaganda and disinformation could help businesses and policy makers implement better long term business models and practices. It can also be utilized in the development of media literacy projects such as the BBC's *Evidence Toolkit*. The addition of a suitable ontology and social context mapping for detecting propaganda techniques can help further research in this area, and more broadly in the identification of rhetorical figures in unstructured text.

Currently, this work is focused only on (English) text, while propaganda can be spread using images (i.e. *Instagram*), and audio/visual media (i.e. *Youtube*).

Acknowledgements. Sponsored by Science Foundation Ireland.

---

[4] https://artsresearch.uwaterloo.ca/chiastic/display/.

A   Figures

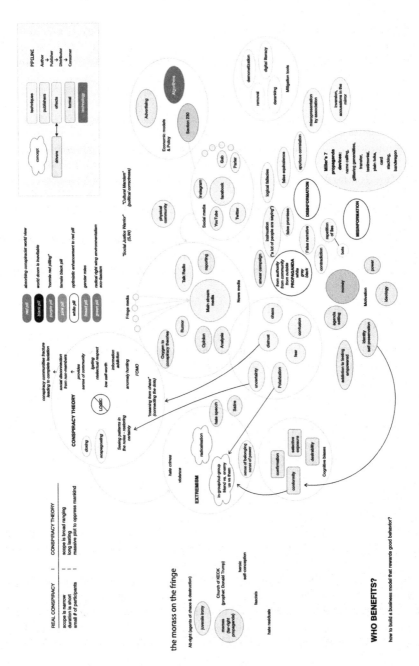

Fig. 3. Propaganda and disinformation ecosystem - WORK IN PROGRESS.

References

1. The Routledge companion to media disinformation and populism. Routledge media and cultural studies companions. Routledge (2021)
2. Bond, G.D., et al.: 'lyin'ted','crooked hillary', and 'deceptive donald': language of lies in the 2016 US presidential debates. Appl. Cogn. Psychol. **31**(6), 668–677 (2017)
3. Bordes, A., Usunier, N., Garcia-Duran, A., Weston, J., Yakhnenko, O.: Translating embeddings for modeling multi-relational data. In: Burges, C.J.C., Bottou, L., Welling, M., Ghahramani, Z., Weinberger, K.Q. (eds.) Advances in Neural Information Processing Systems. vol. 26, pp. 2787–2795. Curran Associates, Inc., (2013). https://proceedings.neurips.cc/paper/2013/file/1cecc7a77928ca8133 fa24680a88d2f9-Paper.pdf
4. Cabrio, E., Villata, S.: Five years of argument mining: a data-driven analysis. In: Proceedings of the Twenty-Seventh International Joint Conference on Artificial Intelligence, pp. 5427–5433. International Joint Conferences on Artificial Intelligence Organization (2018). https://doi.org/10.24963/ijcai.2018/766, https://www.ijcai.org/proceedings/2018/766
5. Ciampaglia, G.L., Shiralkar, P., Rocha, L.M., Bollen, J., Menczer, F., Flammini, A.: Computational fact checking from knowledge networks. PLoS One **10**(6), 15 (2015). https://doi.org/10.1371/journal.pone.0128193
6. Da San Martino, G., Yu, S., Barr'on-Cede no, A., Petrov, R., Nakov, P.: Fine-grained analysis of propaganda in news articles. In: Proceedings of the 2019 Conference on Empirical Methods in Natural Language Processing and 9th International Joint Conference on Natural Language Processing, EMNLP-IJCNLP 2019, Hong Kong, China. EMNLP-IJCNLP 2019 (2019)
7. Da San Martino, G., Yu, S., Barrón-Cedeño, A., Petrov, R., Nakov, P.: Fine-grained analysis of propaganda in news article. In: Proceedings of the 2019 Conference on Empirical Methods in Natural Language Processing and the 9th International Joint Conference on Natural Language Processing (EMNLP-IJCNLP), pp. 5635–5645. Association for Computational Linguistics (2019). https://doi.org/10.18653/v1/ D19-1565, https://www.aclweb.org/anthology/D19-1565
8. Dang, D.T., Nguyen, N.T., Hwang, D.: Multi-step consensus: an effective approach for determining consensus in large collectives. Cybern. Syst. **50**(2), 208–229 (2019). https://doi.org/10.1080/01969722.2019.1565117
9. Harris, R.A., et al.: A cognitive ontology of rhetorical figures (2017)
10. Hassan, N., Arslan, F., Li, C., Tremayne, M.: Toward automated fact-checking: detecting check-worthy factual claims by claimbuster. In: 23rd ACM SIGKDD International Conference on Knowledge Discovery and Data Mining, pp. 1803–1812. ACM (2017)
11. Kelly, A.R., Abbott, N.A., Harris, R.A., DiMarco, C., Cheriton, D.R.: Toward an ontology of rhetorical figures. In: Proceedings of the 28th ACM International Conference on Design of Communication. SIGDOC 2010, pp. 123–130. Association for Computing Machinery (2010). https://doi.org/10.1145/1878450.1878471
12. Kim, J., Tabibian, B., Oh, A., Schölkopf, B., Gomez-Rodriguez, M.: Leveraging the crowd to detect and reduce the spread of fake news and misinformation. In: Proceedings of the Eleventh ACM International Conference on Web Search and Data Mining - WSDM 2018, pp. 324–332. ACM Press (2018). https://doi.org/10. 1145/3159652.3159734, http://dl.acm.org/citation.cfm?doid=3159652.3159734

13. Lawrence, J., Reed, C.: Argument mining: a survey. Comput. Linguist. **45**(4), 765–818 (2020). https://doi.org/10.1162/coli_a_00364
14. Martino, G.D.S., Barrón-Cedeño, A., Wachsmuth, H., Petrov, R., Nakov, P.: Semeval-2020 task 11: Detection of propaganda techniques in news articles, p. 38
15. Mitrovic, J., O'Reilly, C., Mladenovic, M., Handschuh, S.: Ontological representations of rhetorical figures for argument mining. Argument Comput. **8**(3), 267–287 (2017). https://doi.org/10.3233/AAC-170027
16. Mladenović, M., Mitrović, J.: Ontology of rhetorical figures for Serbian. In: Habernal, I., Matoušek, V. (eds.) TSD 2013. LNCS (LNAI), vol. 8082, pp. 386–393. Springer, Heidelberg (2013). https://doi.org/10.1007/978-3-642-40585-3_49
17. Moens, M.F.: Argumentation mining: how can a machine acquire common sense and world knowledge? Argument Comput. **9**(1), 1–14 (2018). https://doi.org/10.3233/AAC-170025
18. O'Donnell, G.S.J.V.J.: Propaganda and Persuasion, p. 217. SAGE Publications (2018)
19. O'Reilly, C., Paurobally, S.: Lassoing Rhetoric with OWL and SWRL (2010)
20. Pan, J.Z., Pavlova, S., Li, C., Li, N., Li, Y., Liu, J.: Content based fake news detection using knowledge graphs. In: Vrandečić, D., et al. (eds.) ISWC 2018. LNCS, vol. 11136, pp. 669–683. Springer, Cham (2018). https://doi.org/10.1007/978-3-030-00671-6_39
21. Pennycook, G., Rand, D.G.: Fighting misinformation on social media using crowd-sourced judgments of news source quality. Proc. Nat. Acad. Sci. **116**(7), 2521–2526 (2019). https://doi.org/10.1073/pnas.1806781116
22. Ruchansky, N., Seo, S., Liu, Y.: Csi: a hybrid deep model for fake news detection. In: Proceedings of the 2017 ACM on Conference on Information and Knowledge Management, pp. 797–806. ACM (Nov 2017). https://doi.org/10.1145/3132847.3132877
23. Ruder, S.: Tracking progress in natural language processing — nlp-progress. https://nlpprogress.com/
24. Sabou, M., Fernandez, M.: Ontology (Network) evaluation. In: Suárez-Figueroa, M.C., Gómez-Pérez, A., Motta, E., Gangemi, A. (eds.) Ontology Engineering in a Networked World, pp. 193–212. Springer, Heidelberg (2012). https://doi.org/10.1007/978-3-642-24794-1_9
25. Shabani, S., Sokhn, M.: Hybrid machine-crowd approach for fake news detection. In: 2018 IEEE 4th International Conference on Collaboration and Internet Computing (CIC), pp. 299–306 (2018). https://doi.org/10.1109/CIC.2018.00048
26. Shu, K., Wang, S., Liu, H.: Beyond news contents: the role of social context for fake news detection. In: Proceedings of the Twelfth ACM International Conference on Web Search and Data Mining. p. 312–320. ACM (2019). https://doi.org/10.1145/3289600.3290994
27. Stirewalt, C.: Op-ed: I called arizona for biden on fox news. here's what i learned (2021). https://www.latimes.com/opinion/story/2021-01-28/fox-news-chris-stirewalt-firing-arizona
28. Tschiatschek, S., Singla, A., Gomez Rodriguez, M., Merchant, A., Krause, A.: Fake news detection in social networks via crowd signals. In: Companion of the The Web Conference 2018 on The Web Conference 2018 - WWW 2018, pp. 517–524. ACM Press (2018). https://doi.org/10.1145/3184558.3188722, http://dl.acm.org/citation.cfm?doid=3184558.3188722

29. Vo, N., Lee, K.: The rise of guardians: fact-checking URL recommendation to combat fake news. In: The 41st International ACM SIGIR Conference on Research and Development in Information Retrieval, pp. 275–284. ACM (2018). https://doi.org/10.1145/3209978.3210037
30. Walton, D.: Argument Evaluation and Evidence. LGTS, vol. 23. Springer, Cham (2016). https://doi.org/10.1007/978-3-319-19626-8
31. Wardle, C., Derakhshan, H.: INFORMATION DISORDER: Toward an interdisciplinary framework for research and policy making, p. 6, no. 27 (2017). https://tverezo.info/wp-content/uploads/2017/11/PREMS-162317-GBR-2018-Report-desinformation-A4-BAT.pdf
32. Woolley, S.: The reality game: how the next wave of technology will break the truth, 1st edn. PublicAffairs (2020)
33. Zhiwei, J., Cao, J., Zhang, Y., Luo, J.: News verification by exploiting conflicting social viewpoints in microblogs. In: Thirtieth AAAI Conference on Artificial Intelligence. AAAI Press (2016). https://www.aaai.org/ocs/index.php/AAAI/AAAI16/paper/view/12128/12049. technical Papers: NLP and Text Mining
34. Zhou, X., Jain, A., Phoha, V.V., Zafarani, R.: Fake news early detection: a theory-driven model. Digital Threats Res. Pract. 1(2), 1–25 (2020). https://doi.org/10.1145/3377478

Industry Track Papers

A Virtual Knowledge Graph for Enabling Defect Traceability and Customer Service Analytics

Nico Wilhelm[1]([✉]), Diego Collarana[2][iD], and Jens Lehmann[2]

[1] ZF Friedrichshafen AG, Friedrichshafen, Germany
nico.wilhelm@zf.com
[2] Fraunhofer IAIS and University of Bonn, Bonn, Germany
{diego.collarana.vargas,jens.lehmann}@iais.fraunhofer.de

Abstract. In this paper, we showcase the implementation of a semantic information model and a virtual knowledge graph at ZF Friedrichshafen AG company, with two main goals in mind: 1) integration of heterogeneous data sources following a pay-as-you-go approach; and the 2) combination core domain concepts from ZF's production line with meta-data of its internal data sources. We employ the developed semantic information model in two use cases, defect traceability and customer service, demonstrating and discussing the benefits and opportunities provided by following an agile semantic virtual integration approach.

1 Introduction

ZF Friedrichshafen AG, with a 105 years history, is a world-leading supplier of mobility systems for passenger cars, commercial vehicles, and industrial technology. The division Electrified Powertrain Technology (E-division) provides various electrified and conventional mobility applications within the passenger cars segment for decades. Therefore, diverse and complex data ecosystems have emerged. However, meta and context data is rarely formally documented. Moreover, if expressed at all, the meaning of business entities is not commonly shared within all domains (e.g., Production, Quality, among others). The E-division partly achieves data integration through platforms and data lakes, yet business entities' interlinking is missing. Hence, ZF requires new methods for holistic data enablement, defining common data and semantic standards, describing metadata to virtually explore all corresponding business data.

The fundamental challenge is to keep as much data "as it is" in the sources without expensive migration projects. A core requirement is creating an enterprise-wide model that defines the main business entities, e.g., "Product," "Machine," from a syntactic, but more importantly, from a semantic perspective creating a shared division-wide conceptualization of the domain. Furthermore, this semantic model must uniquely identify business concepts across all sources in the same way. A virtual semantic knowledge graph provides all elements to address those challenges. ZF and Fraunhofer IAIS partnered to implement such

© Springer Nature Switzerland AG 2021
R. Verborgh et al. (Eds.): ESWC 2021 Satellite Events, LNCS 12739, pp. 245–248, 2021.
https://doi.org/10.1007/978-3-030-80418-3_36

a semantic model to integrate ZF's data sources virtually. We prove the semantic model's value with two use cases following a "T-Shape" query principle. First, defect tractability for identifying domain-specific details. Second a warranty return case connecting several sources to support a broad information picture.

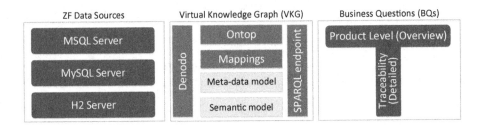

Fig. 1. Architecture

2 Virtual Knowledge Graph Integration Approach

Over the years, ZF has developed several data sources mainly composed of relational databases. Thus, different DBMS store heterogeneous but complementary knowledge about ZF's business entities and processes. Although useful for data analytics, these data sources generate different challenges related to knowledge integration and querying. By providing a Virtual Knowledge Graph (VKG) [5], we pursuit two goals. First, minimize the time required to answer new business queries (agile integration approach). Second, analyze the quality of data with a global approach (semantic data quality index). Following a pay-as-you-go integration approach [3], we have defined an innovative semantic layer for accessing ZF's existing data sources.

Figure 1 depicts the main elements of the semantic layer. The integration process starts by defining a set of **Business Questions (BQs)** that the VKG needs to answer. Following a T-Shape query principle, we firstly define overview questions. For example, in the defect traceability scenario, we start with a BQ like: "Show me quality, field, and plant data about my product." This BQ is the essential question starting quality-related product root cause analysis. Then, we add more triple patterns to answer detailed questions. For example, issue effects are evaluated through traceability BQs, e.g., "Show me all materials, tools, machines related to faulty products," thus, supporting domain production-specific drill-down questions. Once the BQs are defined, we extend the **Virtual Knowledge Graph** by updating entities and relationships in the semantic model required to answer those BQs. We use VoCol [1] to extend the semantic data model collaboratively. An innovation here is the combination of two data contexts to facility provenance of the data, i.e., two models encode both the domain and metadata of the sources linked together at mapping time. Then, we transform BQs into

SPARQL queries validating whether all required entities are mapped from ZF's data sources. When necessary, we create new mappings using the R2RML [4] standard. Ontop [6] and Denodo [2] are our engines to transform the SPARQL queries into SQL queries that the original data sources understand. **ZF Data Sources** layer is composed of different DBMS, including Microsoft SQL Server, MYSQL, and H2, and they remain intact.

3   Lessons Learned and Benefits

During the development of the project, ZF gained valuable *lessons*. ZF applied a new way to integrate data vertically and horizontally across different data sources semantically. We validated the approach of modeling the domain of discourse based on Business Questions. ZF got an innovative methodology to rethink the structure of current data sources regarding their ability and connectivity. We develop basics design guidelines to disseminate this new methodology company-wide. The most evident *benefits* are the following. ZF enhances data exploration, i.e., domains can be easily explained and discovered. The designed ontology serves as a data and role model for future applications across different ZF's units. ZF can now provide domain language standardization, and the definitions can be experienced. So far, standards were just part of a document on a random share drive. ZF can apply data quality methods over the semantic layer where data from different sources is connected.

4   Conclusion and Future Lines of Work

The virtual knowledge graph data integration and access approach are under evaluation by different units at ZF. So far, the project has revealed business potentials by providing an intuitive data retrieval process based on semantics and metadata guidance. Modeling business entities semantically, linking them to their metadata, and defining fundamental properties provide a closed-loop view on data that was not possible before. ZF is now extending this approach to make it company-wide applicable.

Acknowledgements. We acknowledge the support of the EU H2020 Projects Opertus Mundi (GA 870228) and LAMBDA (GA 809965), and the Federal Ministry for Economic Affairs and Energy (BMWi) project SPEAKER (FKZ 01MK20011A).

References

1. Halilaj, L., et al.: VoCol: an integrated environment to support version-controlled vocabulary development. In: Blomqvist, E., Ciancarini, P., Poggi, F., Vitali, F. (eds.) EKAW 2016. LNCS (LNAI), vol. 10024, pp. 303–319. Springer, Cham (2016). https://doi.org/10.1007/978-3-319-49004-5_20
2. Pan, A., et al.: The Denodo data integration platform. In: VLDB 2002, pp. 986–989. Morgan Kaufmann (2002)

3. Sequeda, J.F., Briggs, W.J., Miranker, D.P., Heideman, W.P.: A pay-as-you-go methodology to design and build enterprise knowledge graphs from relational databases. In: Ghidini, C., et al. (eds.) ISWC 2019. LNCS, vol. 11779, pp. 526–545. Springer, Cham (2019). https://doi.org/10.1007/978-3-030-30796-7_32
4. W3C: R2RML: RDB to RDF mapping language (2013). https://www.w3.org/TR/r2rml/
5. Xiao, G., et al.: The virtual knowledge graph system Ontop. In: Pan, J., et al. (eds.) ISWC 2020. LNCS, vol. 12507, pp. 259–277. Springer, Cham (2020). https://doi.org/10.1007/978-3-030-62466-8_17
6. Xiao, G., et al.: The virtual knowledge graph system Ontop (extended abstract). In: (DL 2020) Co-located with (KR 2020). CEUR Workshop Proceedings, vol. 2663 (2020). CEUR-WS.org

Constructing Micro Knowledge Graphs from Technical Support Documents

Atul Kumar[✉], Nisha Gupta, and Saswati Dana

IBM Research - India, G2 Block, Manyata Embassy, Outer Ring Road,
Nagavara, Bengaluru 560045, India
{kumar.atul,nisgup97,sdana027}@in.ibm.com

Abstract. Short technical support pages such as IBM Technotes are quite common in technical support domain. These pages can be very useful as the knowledge sources for technical support applications such as chatbots, search engines and question-answering (QA) systems. Information extracted from documents to drive technical support applications is often stored in the form of Knowledge Graph (KG). Building KGs from a large corpus of documents poses a challenge of granularity because a large number of entities and actions are present in each page. The KG becomes virtually unusable if all entities and actions from these pages are stored in the KG. Therefore, only key entities and actions from each page are extracted and stored in the KG. This approach however leads to loss of knowledge represented by entities and actions left out of the KG as they are no longer available to graph search and reasoning functions.

We propose a set of techniques to create micro knowledge graph (micrograph) for each of such web pages. The micrograph stores all the entities and actions in a page and also takes advantage of the structure of the page to represent exactly in which part of that page these entities and actions appeared, and also how they relate to each other. These micrographs can be used as additional knowledge sources by technical support applications. We define schemas for representing semi-structured and plain text knowledge present in the technical support web pages. Solutions in technical support domain include procedures made of steps. We also propose a technique to extract procedures from these webpages and the schemas to represent them in the micrographs. We also discuss how technical support applications can take advantage of the micrographs.

1 Introduction

Using Knowledge Graphs for storing domain specific knowledge extracted from unstructured and semi-structured documents is common in several domains including technical support [6,8,11,12]. KG stores knowledge in structured form where entities are linked with each other by certain edges representing relationship among them [1,4,7,10]. Knowledge graphs not only make it easy to lookup the desired information, the relations represented in form of direct edges and hierarchies also support reasoning and therefore answering complex questions. In technical support domains - both hardware and software - knowledge graphs are used

© Springer Nature Switzerland AG 2021
R. Verborgh et al. (Eds.): ESWC 2021 Satellite Events, LNCS 12739, pp. 249–253, 2021.
https://doi.org/10.1007/978-3-030-80418-3_37

extensively [6,11,12]. When data is available in semi-unstructured and/or plain text forms, developing a knowledge graphs which provides high performance on querying is a challenging task [8]. Architectural design of schema depends on the purpose and has significant impact on query performance [5,9]. We propose to augment knowledge bases that are developed using a popular category of technical support documents. These documents are relatively short web pages providing solutions to one or more problems or contain information to perform some task such as downloading and installing a software extension. Examples of such documents are IBM Technotes for DB2 and other IBM hardware and software products (Some example technotes can be browsed at [3]). We have also worked with similar technical support web pages for other non IBM hardware and software products. These technical documents are intended to be used by human end-users as self help guides. They are referred to by technical support human agents to answer customer queries and to resolve or troubleshoot their problems. Each of these documents contains rich information such as problem description with symptoms, diagnostic steps, solutions, and also the applicable constraints such as relevant hardware platforms and operating systems. Complexity of the information and it's hierarchy depends on the type of technical document, issue, solution steps and other details present in the page. Other than the usual challenges such as entity extraction and linking, it is also important to design a schema that can represent all the entities and their relations in a domain in a reasonable manner and can efficiently support knowledge graph tasks such as population, search, lookup, deletion etc. Every technical support page contains several dozen entities if not hundreds. Not all entities are equally important in the context of the primary topic of that page. Therefore, a typical choice of schema for building a knowledge graph from such pages is to identify key entities and actions/symptoms from these pages and store the URLs/identities of the pages as the solution nodes in the graph. A technical support application can present the URL(s) of the relevant page(s) containing solution/answer. User can then read and use the information present in the page without any additional help as these pages are short. This approach serves reasonably well for question-answer (QA) and search applications. But if there are multiple similar looking pages providing the solution for a problem related to similar entities (but differing on one or more situations) or if the page itself contains different solutions based on some condition (eg, OS version or hardware platform), then it is desirable to return most relevant page (or part of the page) to the user for a query. Understanding the solution presented in these pages at a fine grained level including various constraints, conditions and steps involved in the solutions (if any) is necessary for not only presenting the most specific page/part but also to support applications that require reasoning. For example, a chatbot that can ask a followup question to user in order to disambiguate between several possible answers. Or, an application that provides step by step guidance including conditional steps. Identifying individual steps from a solution procedure present in a support page is also useful for automating the support function where steps can be executed on user's behalf by the system. In the next section, we present algorithms and techniques to extract knowledge (including entities, actions and procedures) from short technical support web pages to construct the individual micrographs for these pages. We also show an example micrograph for a real technical support document (an IBM DB2 Technote web page).

2 Micrograph Construction

Technical support web pages use different structures across products and manufacturers/vendors. But a closer examination reveals many similarities among these pages. For example, they all have a title that contains important entities and actions. There are fixed number of document types such as troubleshooting, FAQ, Howto etc. These pages have sections that include symptoms, diagnostic steps, solution, constraints, links to related information and references. Before using the automatic micrograph generation system to process a document corpus, a manual step of examining a representative subset of that corpus is required. We create some meta-information in a predefined format for the given document corpus. The meta-information contains items such as the number and names of different document types present in the corpus, section headings expected in each type and their mappings to the generic types found in technical support documents, list of entities that are used to denote constraints (e.g., operating system, hardware platform), and dictionaries of product specific entities and action verbs. We have defined a generic set of schema to represent commonly seen types of documents in the technical support domain. If we come across a new document type in a document corpus then we create a new schema to represent that type. The high level architecture of the micrograph construction system is shown in Fig. 1.

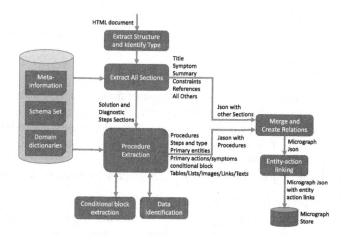

Fig. 1. Architecture of the micrograph construction system

We use the meta-information and HTML structure to identify sections in a page. All plain-text, structured elements and non text elements in a section are extracted for all sections. Contents of solution and diagnostic step sections, if any, are passed to the procedure extraction module that is described in details in Subsect. 2.1. Output of the procedure extraction modudle is then merged and linked with the contents of other sections. We use a custom entity extraction and linking algorithm to extract and link entities and actions from all text elements. This step is optional. Finally the constructed micrograph json is ingested in a graph store.

An example micrograph for a DB2 Technote page [2] is shown in Fig. 2

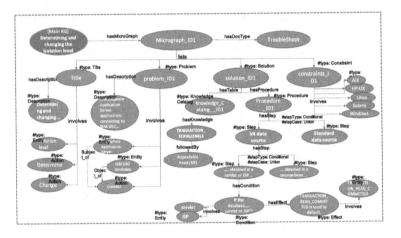

Fig. 2. An example micrograph constructed from a DB2 technote page

2.1 Procedure Extraction

This module takes as input the contents of Solution and Diagnostic Step sections in HTML format. Output of this module is the array of all procedures as a json. A procedure consists of a sequence of steps where each step is described by: (i) Type of step (i.e. Sequential or conditional), (ii) Conditional block if any, (iii) Nested steps/procedures, and (iv) Step's content.

At a high level, procedure extraction algorithm is described as follows:

- Find the different sets of steps within the solution section using information such as HTML Tags, patterns across the contents of the tags, relationship between the tags and documents and document meta-information along with predefined set of word vectors.
- Find the first set of steps among all sets such that the steps from this set covers the entire solution section as the parent stepsets. This is done based on the position of the steps in the document.

– Extract each step of the parent stepsets from the document along with its title and content using HTML navigation.
– Process the title of the steps using entity extraction and linking to find the type of the steps. Steps could be sequential or conditional.
– Repeat the above methods to similarly find the nested steps and step type within each step content. This recursive approach extracts every possible nested steps to the finest granular level of the solution section.
– Identify the type of the textual/pictorial content of the steps.
– Extract the conditional block from the textual content of the steps. Every conditional block has a conditional statement along with the effect statement of the condition. Identify such blocks using PoS tag and DEP tag from the parse tree of the textual content.

References

1. Bollacker, K., Evans, C., Paritosh, P., Sturge, T., Taylor, J.: Freebase: a collaboratively created graph database for structuring human knowledge. In: Proceedings of ACM SIGMOD, pp. 1247–1250 (2008)
2. IBM: Determining and changing the isolation level. https://www.ibm.com/support/pages/determining-and-changing-isolation-level
3. IBM: Technotes (faqs and troubleshooting tips) for ibm db2 data management console. https://www.ibm.com/support/pages/technotes-faqs-and-troubleshooting-tips-ibm-db2-data-management-console
4. Lehmann, J., et al.: DBpedia - a large-scale, multilingual knowledge base extracted from wikipedia. Sem. Web 6, 167–195 (2015)
5. Lei, C., Alotaibi, R., Quamar, A., Efthymiou, V., Özcan, F.: Property graph schema optimization for domain-specific knowledge graphs (2020)
6. Lin, Z.Q., et al.: Intelligent development environment and software knowledge graph. J. Comput. Sci. Technol. 32(2), 242–249 (2017)
7. Mitchell, T., et al.: Never-ending learning. In: Proceedings of AAAI (2015)
8. Noy, N., Gao, Y., Jain, A., Narayanan, A., Patterson, A., Taylor, J.: Industry-scale knowledge graphs: lessons and challenges. Queue 17(2), 48–75 (2019)
9. Oliveira, D., Sahay, R., d'Aquin, M.: Leveraging ontologies for knowledge graph schemas (2019)
10. Pellissier Tanon, T., Weikum, G., Suchanek, F.: Yago 4: A reason-able knowledge base. In: Proceedings of ESWC, pp. 583–596 (2020)
11. Sabou, M., et al.: Exploring enterprise knowledge graphs: a use case in software engineering. In: Gangemi, A., et al. (eds.) ESWC 2018. LNCS, vol. 10843, pp. 560–575. Springer, Cham (2018). https://doi.org/10.1007/978-3-319-93417-4_36
12. Wang, M., Zou, Y., Cao, Y., Xie, B.: Searching software knowledge graph with question. In: Peng, X., Ampatzoglou, A., Bhowmik, T. (eds.) ICSR 2019. LNCS, vol. 11602, pp. 115–131. Springer, Cham (2019). https://doi.org/10.1007/978-3-030-22888-0_9

Use Case: Ontologies and RDF-Star for Knowledge Management

Bob Kasenchak[✉] ⓘ, Ahren Lehnert ⓘ, and Gene Loh ⓘ

Synaptica, LLC, 11384 Pine Valley Drive, Franktown, CO 80116, USA
bob.kasenchak@synaptica.com

Abstract. Our client in this case study is a software company which develops, publishes, and distributes video games for consoles, PCs, smartphones, and tablets in both physical and digital formats. They also create educational and cultural software, cartoons, and literary, cinematographic, and television works. It owns several brands and a diversified portfolio of franchises.

The client required a centralized vocabulary management software platform to provide standardized concepts across a decentralized, global organization to find, browse, and discover enterprise content. They needed the ability to push vocabularies out to consuming systems and users while also allowing users to suggest new concepts without requiring them to log in to the taxonomy and ontology management software.

In addition to the out-of-the-box Graphite ontology management software functionality, the client required bespoke work in the system and dedicated API connectors which became part of the common code base for all versions going forward. Their requirements presented the opportunity for Synaptica to explore uses for the new specification, RDF-star (Arndt et al. 2021), in our implementation. As a new and developing specification in RDF graph databases, the use of RDF-star is groundbreaking work for commercial enterprise ontology management systems.

Keywords: Ontologies · RDF-star · Knowledge management

1 Background

1.1 Synaptica, LLC

Synaptica, LLC provides award-winning, enterprise-class enterprise taxonomy and ontology management software tools and professional services. Our company mission is to help people organize, categorize, and discover the knowledge in their enterprise.

Synaptica's Graphite is a powerful enterprise collaboration tool for quickly designing, building, managing, and sharing taxonomies and ontologies, also known as Knowledge Organization Systems (KOS), using an intuitive graphical user interface.

© Springer Nature Switzerland AG 2021
R. Verborgh et al. (Eds.): ESWC 2021 Satellite Events, LNCS 12739, pp. 254–260, 2021.
https://doi.org/10.1007/978-3-030-80418-3_38

This paper describes a client case study requiring custom features and integrations to use ontologies and taxonomies throughout their enterprise knowledge management (KM) information ecosystem.

2   The Business Challenge

The client faced challenges with outdated content which was difficult to find through browse or search due to inconsistent or missing metadata. In addition, there was no way to discover new content and users would re-create existing content because it could not be found. Taxonomy management was inefficient and included many concepts which were simply not valuable to the business.

The client wanted to be able to manage the vocabularies centrally while integrating with numerous home-grown and commercially available systems and content repositories, including the content management systems, Atlassian Confluence and Microsoft SharePoint. These vocabularies would in turn support internal knowledge management practices including the creation, tagging, and retrieval of product-specific content and user-specific suggested content to personalized home pages.

Finally, because the ontology management system would be integrated with other business applications and required users in various business roles from across the organization to access the vocabularies, more robust, group-based permissions were required.

3   The Business Solution

3.1   Ontology Management, Workflow, and Systems Integration

The client's guiding principles for controlled vocabularies include using ontologies to drive user experience such as search, browse, and discovery. Taxonomies and ontologies are used as metadata schemes by content creators to tag by topic and language. Vocabulary editors manage the taxonomies, ontologies, and the governance process.

Our client uses Graphite for ontology management including the dedicated Confluence and SharePoint connectors. Terms from specified taxonomies (knowledge models or schemes) from Graphite are available for tagging wiki pages in Confluence. Content creators working in Confluence tag pages with the appropriate scheme concepts and are allowed to suggest concepts in the same user interface. In our client's workflow, they allow users to choose the target scheme for the suggested concept.

Within Graphite, these concepts are stored in the target scheme in the "candidate" status to be reviewed by a dedicated team of ontologists. Ontologists develop the suggested concepts by adding metadata, properties, and relationships and move them to other, appropriate schemes as necessary. The ontologists use built-in workflow tools as part of their governance process to change the concept status from "candidate" to "accepted" and eventually "published" through the concept lifecycle to make them available for tagging (Fig. 1).

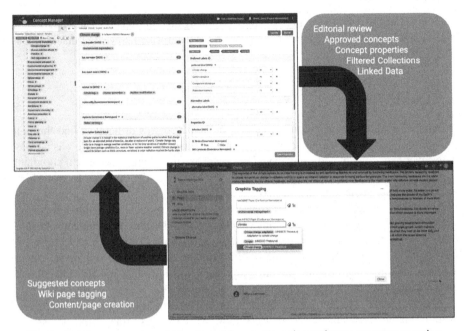

Fig. 1. Ontology concept workflow for wiki content tagging and new concept suggestion.

The client also required advanced concept, scheme, and project visualization, additional batch editing features, additional concept filters, and flexibility to transfer concepts across schemes. In Confluence, the ability to tag pages with existing and suggested concepts, filter available concepts by status and collections, copy and move pages and tags, and see all pages tagged with the same concepts were customized improvements to help the client realize their workflow and governance goals. Finally, specific additions to the SharePoint Connector to align schemes between Graphite and SharePoint Term Sets ensured client vocabularies could be reused across systems.

3.2 Permissions and RDF-Star

In addition to customizations supporting knowledge management, the client required new administrative features allowing for the creation of user groups and quick assignment of users to groups with pre-selected permissions settings. Making use of new features in the back-end graph database, Ontotext's GraphDB, Synaptica was able to deliver user and group permissions functionality on a revamped architecture utilizing RDF-star, making the creation and management of users and groups faster and with fewer triples than previously required.

4 The Technical Solution

4.1 RDF-Star

RDF-star (formerly known as RDF*) helps in cases in which the user needs to express a complex relationship with metadata associated for a triple. For example (Fig. 2),

```
1. <<:man :hasSpouse :woman>>
2.    :source :TheNationalEnquirer;
3.    :webpage <http://nationalenquirer.com/news/2020-02-12>;
4.    :retrieved "2020-02-13"^^xsd:dateTime.
```

Fig. 2. Complex relationship with metadata expressed in RDF.

Technically speaking, RDF-star makes it easier to attach metadata to edges in the graph. Or, in other words, to make a statement about another statement. This was already possible in the very first RDF 1.0 specification (W3C 1999) using the mechanism called *reification*. Unfortunately, reification introduces processing overhead due to the increased number of additional statements needed to identify the reference triple and appears too verbose when represented in RDF and SPARQL (Fig. 3).

```
1. :man :hasSpouse :woman .
2. :id1 rdf:type rdf:Statement ;
3.      rdf:subject :man ;
4.      rdf:predicate :hasSpouse ;
5.      rdf:object :woman ;
6.    :webpage <http://nationalenquirer.com/news/2020-02-12>;
7.    :retrieved "2020-02-13"^^xsd:dateTime.
```

Fig. 3. Complex relationship expression in RDF using reification.

The authors of RDF-star proposed a new compact syntax. Because of its elegance, GraphDB optimized its persistence to nearly double the loading speed for datasets with a large amount of statement-level metadata. The feature immediately received interest from ontology modelers who struggled to express complex relationships in a short and concise way.

4.2 The Significance of RDF-Star

The practical significance of RDF-star is that it increases the modeling expressivity with a new RDF resource type – an embedded triple – which works as a pointer to an RDF statement. This also fully matches the theoretical expressivity of the property graph (PG) model without the need to use reification, i.e., an abstract construct with the existing specific methods supported by the language.

Now every PG can be efficiently represented as an RDF model. The opposite direction is not true, because RDF is more expressive in various ways. In particular, with RDF-star method can attach arbitrarily complex descriptions to an edge in the graph, while in PG one can attach only key-value pairs.

The results for a given Wikidata dataset illustrate why RDF-star is a better approach to modeling RDF statements associated with complex metadata (Fig. 4).

Modeling approach	Total statements	Loading time (min)	Repository image size (MB)
Standard reification	391,652,270	52.4	36,768
N-ary relations	334,571,877	50.6	34,519
Named graphs	277,478,521	56	35,146
RDF-star	220,375,702	34	22,465

Fig. 4. RDF statements required to express relationships using various methods.

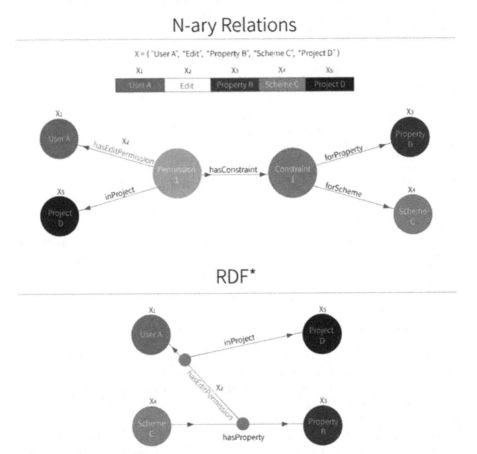

Fig. 5. Standard RDF relationships versus RDF-star to create permissions.

4.3 RDF-Star and Complex Access Control Lists (ACLs)

The ACL case fits scenarios in which metadata needs to be associated with a given statement. Graphite provides users the ability to define access permissions at the property level. One of the challenges faced by our design team when attempting to extend the Graphite permissions data model pertained to the limitations of native RDF triple constructs so that extending beyond three tuples became a cumbersome exercise.

For example, "User A has edit permissions to Property B for the concepts in Scheme C in Project D", requires a tuple with a minimum of five elements for semantic expression of relationships in the dataset (Fig. 5).

4.4 RDF-Star and Property-Level Permissions

In the context of the Graphite permissions data model, the workaround of adding RDF triples in a conventional setting was inefficient and greatly reduced human readability of the data structures and SPARQL queries.

After consolidating the new user and group access control and permissions model in Graphite, there were no issues remapping functionalities from the old model to the new. It is a testament to the design of RDF-star and SPARQL-star that migrating existing data from the previous RDF model to RDF-star can be performed in a straightforward series of SPARQL-star statements.

In addition, the syntax of embedded triples is intuitive, which shortened the learning curve for the Graphite developers. Beyond its use in the Graphite model, RDF-star would invariably simplify the representation of ontology structures like SKOS-XL. While the schematic representation in the data model is relatively straightforward, there are unique challenges in designing a user interface sufficiently intuitive for data entry and editing.

5 The Results

The use of centralized ontologies for tagging creates a unified language for the client and a foundational driving architecture for semantic applications throughout the organization. The application of controlled vocabulary concepts as metadata to content allows the client to improve browse, search, and discovery experiences on the front end within the organization. Users can browse internal content based on the metadata, see content grouped by key topics, and contribute to the ontology without accessing the ontology management software directly.

The changes to the back-end architecture and administrative functionality allow for more scalable adoption and onboarding throughout the organization as new teams begin utilizing the ontology management platform to drive semantic applications. In addition, the changes to the underlying architecture to use RDF-star makes the application faster and paves a path forward for additional functionality built on the standard.

The client's functionality requests served their immediate needs for enterprise requirements while also enhancing the semantic capabilities of the main application and connectors for all current and potential users of the product. This project reinforced Synaptica's commitment to maintaining a single software code-base and the development of specific connectors when necessary in conjunction with the use of general REST-based APIs.

Acknowledgments. Synaptica wishes to thank Vassil Momtchev, Ontotext CTO, for his contributions to this paper defining RDF-star and information detailing the Ontotext GraphDB implementation.

Reference

1. Arndt, D., et al.: RDF-star and SPARQL-star. W3C Community Group Draft Report. https:// w3c.github.io/rdf-star/cg-spec/2021-04-13.html. Accessed 11 May 2021

Correction to: The Semantic Web: ESWC 2021 Satellite Events

Ruben Verborgh⬡, Anastasia Dimou⬡, Aidan Hogan⬡,
Claudia d'Amato⬡, Ilaria Tiddi⬡, Arne Bröring⬡, Simon Mayer⬡,
Femke Ongenae⬡, Riccardo Tommasini⬡, and Mehwish Alam⬡

Correction to:
R. Verborgh et al. (Eds.): *The Semantic Web: ESWC 2021 Satellite Events*, LNCS 12739, https://doi.org/10.1007/978-3-030-80418-3

The name of one of the volume editors, Simon Mayer, was erroneously misspelt in an earlier version of the cover and inside cover of this volume. This has now been corrected.

The updated version of the book can be found at
https://doi.org/10.1007/978-3-030-80418-3

Author Index

Printed in the United States
by Baker & Taylor Publisher Services